Economic Literacy and Money Illusion an Experimental Perspective

The concept of money illusion, a recently resurrected phenomenon of behavioral economics, is a real fact of economic life, the potential role of which should no longer be dismissed. Despite money illusion being utterly suppressed by mainstream economists, small deviations from rationality, together with trends in behavioral economics, alleviate the denial of money illusion induced by the rational expectations revolution. This book argues that money illusion seems to be a ubiquitous phenomenon, affecting various areas such as financial markets, housing markets, labor markets, consumption-saving decisions, and even development at the aggregate level induced by coordination issues. Furthermore, in light of the educational efforts of central banks and other institutions, it is worth considering whether solid economic training would provide guidance for the public regarding their decision-making and thereby alleviate the effects of money illusion. The emerging field of experimental economics provides a unique opportunity for us to verify the presence of money illusion. Specifically, attention is devoted to the experimental investigation of reduction in the direct and indirect effects of money illusion with respect to the level of economic literacy acquired through economic education.

Economic Literacy and Money Illusion will be of interest to the general audience and to those who are interested in behavioral economics, economics education, and experimental economics, as well as to policy makers and institutions. Last but not least, it will help develop students' interest in alternative economic theories.

Helena Chytilova is Assistant Professor at the University of Economics, Faculty of Economics and Charles University, Faculty of Law, Prague, Czech Republic.

Routledge Advances in Experimental and Computable Economics

Edited by K. Vela Velupillai and Stefano Zambelli
University of Trento, Italy

1. **The Economics of Search**
   Brian and John McCall

2. **Classical Econophysics**
   Paul Cockshott et al.

3. **The Social Epistemology of Experimental Economics**
   Ana Cordeiro dos Santos

4. **Computable Foundations for Economics**
   K. Vela Velupillai

5. **Neuroscience and the Economics of Decision Making**
   Edited by Alessandro Innocenti and Angela Sirigu

6. **Computational Intelligence Techniques for Trading and Investment**
   Edited by Christian Dunis, Spiros Likothanassis, Andreas Karathanasopoulos, Georgios Sermpinis and Konstantinos Theofilatos

7. **A Computational Model of Industry Dynamics**
   Myong-Hun Chang

8. **Agent-Based Computational Economics: How the idea originated and where it is going**
   Shu-Heng Chen

9. **Economic Literacy and Money Illusion**
   An Experimental Perspective
   Helena Chytilova

Other books in the Series include:

Economics Lab: An intensive course in experimental economics
Alessandra Cassar and Dan Friedman

Economic Literacy and Money Illusion

An Experimental Perspective

Helena Chytilova

Routledge
Taylor & Francis Group
LONDON AND NEW YORK

First published 2018
by Routledge
2 Park Square, Milton Park, Abingdon, Oxon OX14 4RN

and by Routledge
711 Third Avenue, New York, NY 10017

Routledge is an imprint of the Taylor & Francis Group, an informa business

British Library Cataloguing in Publication Data
A catalogue record for this book is available from the British Library

Library of Congress Cataloging in Publication Data
A catalog record for this book has been requested

ISBN: 978-1-138-23557-1 (hbk)
ISBN: 978-1-315-30447-2 (ebk)

Typeset in Times New Roman
by Deanta Global Publishing Services, Chennai, India

FSC
www.fsc.org
MIX
Paper from responsible sources
FSC® C013604

Printed and bound by CPI Group (UK) Ltd, Croydon, CR0 4YY

Contents

Figures

Tables

Introduction

Since the term "money illusion" was first coined by Irving Fisher in 1928, it has regularly been invoked as a plausible phenomenon and a major influence on the real effects of money on the economy by many economists, including monetarist theories led by Milton Friedman. However, the impact of money illusion was utterly suppressed by the "rational expectations" revolution in 1970s and the consequent development of the neoclassical stream in modern macroeconomics.

Money illusion recaptured its significance again with the arrival of behavioral economics, which allows for psychological biases present in the behavior of individuals. Although it seems that these individual money illusion effects are largely irrelevant at the aggregate level, New Keynesian theories, characterized by strategic complementarity, show that the near-rational behavior of subjects is a second order effect, but the effect on the economy is of the first order, thereby creating space for money illusion at the aggregate level as demonstrated by recent experimental research.

This book suggests that money illusion might be a ubiquitous phenomenon, affecting various areas of economic life. Furthermore, with continuity related to money illusion occurrence, which is generally assumed by economists to be easily wiped out through learning, the question is addressed as to whether a certain level of economic literacy, induced through economic education, might not eventually suppress the aggregate-level effects of money illusion. In this sense, it appears that the experimental method represents a unique tool for investigation of whether a particular level of economic literacy, acquired through economic education, may account for improved decision-making and an alleviation of money illusion effects. We believe that selected phenomena of economic literacy, narrowed to the investigation of money illusion effects, seems to be highly topical considering the recent growing tendency of central banks and other institutions to promote economic and financial literacy by running a variety of education programs.

The book proceeds as follows:

Chapter 1 outlines the term "money illusion," which was first coined by Irving Fisher in 1928. Despite, as it might seem, there being no space in economics for this phenomenon since the revolution of rational expectations, it has been receiving considerable attention in contemporary research. Early theorizing about money illusion from Fisher's point of view shows that this phenomenon is still highly topical in contemporary real-world situations. Money illusion, as it is contained in the works of John Maynard Keynes, will be put under scrutiny due to its rather implicit presence in Keynes' work, which in and of itself suggests that the money illusion concept should not be neglected.

Chapter 2 presents a critical assessment of money illusion from the point of view of the rational expectations hypothesis, which left no space for money illusion. Friedman's theory of the natural rate of unemployment, which coincides with money illusion in the short run, is linked to Keynes' and Fisher's theories in order to identify common ties within this concept. Alternative theories developed in response to Lucas' rejection of money illusion aimed to account for the non-neutrality of money, including the near-rationality concept. These small deviations from rationality, together with the trend of behavioral economics, might alleviate the denial of money illusion induced by the rational expectations revolution.

Chapter 3 discusses the renewal of interest in money illusion, which emerged with the arrival of behavioral economics. Behavioral concepts are outlined, such as the framing effect, anchoring, loss aversion, mental accounting, fairness, and morale, with regards to the formation of money illusion and its effects. Individual effects of money illusion induced by psychological accounts are regarded as negligible, since they cancel out on average at the aggregate level. However, it proved to be the case that even a small amount of individual money illusion, multiplied in conditions of strategic complementarity by the behavior of sophisticated agents, might have important aggregate-level effects. As a result, the potential role of money illusion in economics may no longer be dismissed.

Chapter 4 represents an extension of Chapter 3 and shows that money illusion is a ubiquitous phenomenon, affecting various economic areas. Particular attention is paid to the Modigliani–Cohn hypothesis in financial markets, the effects of money illusion on housing markets, money illusion in labor markets with respect to nominal loss aversion and fairness issues, and connection with downward nominal wage rigidity, the incorporation of money illusion in the Phillips curve, the strategic environment and its role in dissemination of money illusion, consumption-saving decisions distorted by money-illusioned individuals, and the introduction of the euro as an illustrative natural experiment or money illusion from the point of view of neuroeconomics. Outlined research shows that experimental economics represent a unique opportunity for the investigation of money illusion effects.

Chapter 5 provides a synthesis of the money illusion concept and economic literacy related to the investigation of the potential effects of economic education. There is a growing tendency among central banks and other institutions across the world to promote economic and financial literacy by running various educational programs. Several factors responsible for this increased attention will be outlined. Measurement issues and the endogeneity problems of economic and financial literacy will be discussed, followed by an evaluation of international evidence and a disaggregated assessment by age, gender, and so on. Empirical findings suggest that there is scope for education programs, the efficacy of which is subject to criticism. The potential effects of economic education are questioned when our interest is restricted to the narrow field of money illusion, the direct and indirect effects of which might be significantly alleviated.

Chapter 6 presents the experimental method as a unique tool for investigation of whether a particular level of economic literacy, acquired through economic education, may account for improved decision-making and the alleviation of money illusion effects. Methodological considerations of a laboratory experiment and its implications at the aggregate level are discussed, followed by a brief description of experimental design. An hypothesis is outlined in which the distinction related to economic education will allow for two treatments, where the well-educated group is the experimental group, whereas the less-educated one is the control group. Through this mechanism, the effect of economic education under the nominal frame might be verified. In particular, the question is posed whether economic education might not eventually suppress the indirect effects of money illusion, proved in a designed experimental economy, and therefore weaken nominal inertia. In other words, solid economic training should provide sufficient support for individuals to coordinate successfully in a strategic environment and ensure proper adjustment to the equilibrium at the aggregate level through the elimination of money illusion.

The results in Chapter 7 reveal whether the indirect effects of money illusion in conditions of strategic complementarity are still present after the implemented nominal shock, even in the case of a solid economic education. This might have substantial implications for monetary policy in terms of nominal inertia and in the related short-run non-neutrality of money. If the educational effect can't be proven, it is possible that money illusion is a pervasive phenomenon, integrated in one of the New Keynesian models, built on a coordination problem. Notwithstanding, the results suggest that continuing the investigation of the effects of economic education with respect to money illusion is highly desirable.

1 Early theorizing about money illusion

Money is as money does, the dollar is what the dollar buys.
General F. A. Walker, economist (Fisher 1928, p. 18)

"Money illusion" as a concept is frequently referred to and, also, frequently rejected, where a ubiquitous belief in rationality dictates the trend of money illusion as being distant from standard economic thinking. In addition, many economists reacted with hesitation to explanations based on the simplistic concepts of money illusion, since it was in contradiction to the maximizing behavior of individuals and the equilibrium states of economies. In addition, irrational behavior inside a general equilibrium framework might appear to be rational outside that framework, considering the systemic coordination problems that subjects have to cope with.

The position of money illusion in economics is documented by Howitt (1987, pp. 518–519), who considers it as a more equivocal concept. Not only is the absence of money illusion the main presumption in the long run for neutrality of money, but, in contrast, money illusion was considered to be responsible in the short run for the non-neutrality of money such as in the case of Fisher's explanation of business cycles.

The money illusion refers to the tendency of individuals to think more in nominal monetary values than in real ones. There are many definitions, differing slightly, used by authors. Leontief (1936) defines money illusion as a violation of the "homogeneity postulate." According to him, demand and supply functions are homogeneous of degree zero in all nominal prices, where they depend on relative and not absolute prices. Patinkin (1965, p. 22), states that "An individual will be said to be suffering from such an illusion if his excess-demand functions for commodities do not depend solely on relative prices and real wealth." Shafir, Diamond, and Tversky (1997, p. 348) interpret money illusion as "a bias in the assessment of the real value of economic transactions, induced by a nominal evaluation." However, as Fehr and Tyran (2001) emphasize, the basic problem is how people perceive the veil of money, that is, whether they are able to recognize purely nominal changes that should not affect their decision.

There are many other recent studies, such as Brunnermeier and Julliard (2008), Vaona (2013), Cannon and Cipriani (2006), Agell and Lundborg (2003), and so on, showing that money illusion is still a topical issue that is receiving increased interest in contemporary research.

This chapter describes the early theorizing of economists about money illusion, its roots and origins. Attention will be devoted to Irving Fisher, who first coined the term "money illusion" and devoted his whole book to it. The second part deals with money illusion as contained in the works of John Maynard Keynes, which is scrutinized due to its rather implicit presence in Keynes' work.

Irving Fisher's *Money Illusion*

In 1928, Irving Fisher wrote a whole book entitled *The Money Illusion*, which was based on lectures given in the summer of 1927 at the Geneva School of International Studies. This book introduced the term "money illusion" to economic science, however, the term had already been coined in his article "Stabilizing the Dollar" in 1919. Fisher (1928, p. 4) defined money illusion in his book as a "failure to perceive that the dollar, or any other unit of money, expands or shrinks in value." *The Money Illusion* was written in the 1920s, prior to the 1929 Crash, and the main point was primarily to highlight the existence of a money illusion linked to the human fallacy of thinking about the dollar as something fixed. The instability of buying power of all monetary units, including the dollar, is demonstrated on various illustrative examples based on the author's empirical observation. This is followed by the identification of hidden causes, for example, inflation and deflation, generating this instability, with resulting harm, which is often attributed to other causes. Consequently, the author proposes various remedies, emphasizing specifically the role of the government and monetary authorities in weakening negative consequences of harm.

Fisher is widely believed to have coined the term money illusion, but the concept had already been mentioned in the theories of classical economists, although not explicitly. Ricardo (1811), cited by Hahn (1947), states that when new money is introduced, prosperity spreads like magic, since the judgment of market participants is overly optimistic. Prices rise faster than costs, creating illusory high profits and making a stimulus for the creation of new enterprises. This boosts prices even further. The illusion is discovered only later once prices rise and the boom spiral goes in the opposite direction.[1]

As Fisher suggests, people simply take it for granted that a dollar is a dollar and that all money is stable, emphasizing that almost everyone is subject to money illusion with respect to his own currency. This topic attracted his attention because of the trend of increasing prices caused by World War I and the related value of the dollar, which was unstable in its buying power. On the contrary, followers of Fisher, such as Shafir et al. (1997), Modigliani and Cohn (1979), and Akerlof and Shiller (2009), do not assume complete deception by money illusion, but rather a consciousness of nominal values, as will be mentioned later.

Together with another economist (Professor Frederick W. Roman), Fisher studied price changes in Europe and talked with various individuals they met by chance during their travels in Germany in 1922, as well as with Americans—including his own dentist. He concluded that "all people assumed that their own respective moneys had not fallen in value, but that goods had risen" (Fisher 1928, p. 8), believing various other reasons, such as the blockade or the destruction wrought by the war, were the cause of the high cost of living, but denying that the change in the value of the dollar could be responsible.

A particularly famous example is Fisher's discussion with a very intelligent German shopkeeper in Berlin, when the German mark had depreciated by more than 98 percent (the price level had risen by about fifty-fold, leaving the currency to be a fiftieth of its original value). She sold him a shirt, explaining further that she bought the shirt initially for less and thereby made a profit. Unfortunately, she was deceived by money illusion: she made no profit, since the dollar was not the same value as she had thought, but had fallen. She instead assumed that the marks paid by her for the shirt a year ago were the same marks that she received from Professor Fisher. She has not recognized the hidden cause, "inflation," which had led to the rise in the volume of marks, instead finding many trivial reasons for the high prices. Since her accounts were in a fluctuating currency (instead of translating her accounts into dollars or units of commodities), it looked like a profit, which was only a nominal one and she instead suffered a loss in real terms.

This example may be well generalized by the statement of Lord D'Abernon, British Ambassador to Germany, who said: "Professor Fisher, you will find that very few Germans think of the mark as having fallen" (Fisher 1928, p. 5). Additionally, Fisher (1928) claims that after World War I, people in America were aware of the fall of the German mark, as opposed to very few Germans who knew about it. However, Americans were not different in terms of their inability to perceive the value of their own currency. They generally thought of the dollar as fixed, despite the fact its buying power was changing. Based on these empirical observations, Fisher concluded that people tend to perceive the value of other currencies as better than the value of their own currency.

The gold standard present that time in the United States intensified this notion even further. Actually, the dollar was fixed in terms of grains of gold, but it was not fixed in terms of goods and benefits it could buy. In the United States, pure gold was sold at about $20.67 an ounce, and had remained unchanged since 1837 when the dollar was fixed at 23.22 grains of pure gold. These two figures "mutually imply each other" (Fisher 1928, p. 15), with no evidence that gold is constant in its buying power. An ounce of gold would always buy $20.67, given by the fixation of the dollar at 23.22 grains of pure gold. As a result, it means that gold is constant in terms of gold but not in its buying power over other commodities. As gold fluctuated, the dollar fluctuated as well, keeping the ratio between those two unchanged and leading to the false notion that the dollar is stable in terms of its buying power.

In other words, Fisher (1928) claims that the dollar could be used accurately for measuring the weight of sugar, but not for measuring the value. This may be further illustrated with the help of an example that he provides:

> Our fixed-weight dollar is a poor substitute for a really stable dollar as would be a fixed weight of copper, a fixed yardage of carpet, or a fixed number of

> eggs. If we were to define a dollar as a dozen eggs, thenceforth the price of eggs would necessarily and always be a dollar a dozen. Nevertheless, the supply and demand of eggs would keep on working. For instance, if the hens failed to lay, the price of eggs would not rise [in dollars] but the price of almost everything else would fall. One egg would buy more than before [because they are more rare]. Yet, because of the Money Illusion, we would not even suspect the hens of causing low prices and hard times.
>
> (Fisher 1928, p. 17)

In other words, people affected by money illusion tend to confuse the fixed weight of the dollar with a fixed value. The dollar is a unit of weight, which is "masquerading as a stable unit of value, or buying power" (Fisher 1928, p. 16).

Perception of inflation and deflation from viewpoint of money illusion

Based on this fact, Fisher (1928) aims to answer why the currency fluctuates in its buying power and links it, consequently, to the concept of money illusion, responsible for the false perception of the public about the fixed value of the currency.

The concept of relative inflation and deflation is applied, that is, inflation and deflation relative to the volume of trade in a given period. Fisher (1928) argues that if the circulation of money and the circulation of goods, each of the same number of dollars in value, should keep going at the same rate year after year, there is no reason for deflation or inflation. In other words, the flow of money is adjusting the pace with respect to the growth or shrinkage of the business. However, if these two circulations do not develop at the same pace, then the situation is different. If for instance the circulation of money rises, despite the constant rate of circulation of goods, the price level has to rise necessarily. Inversely, if the circulation of goods rises, keeping the flow of money fixed, the price level will decline. To sum up, if the flow of money is rising relatively to the flow of goods, the price level will rise. If the flow of money is falling with respect to the flow of goods and services, the contrary will happen with the price level. The former case is named "relative inflation," the latter "relative deflation."

Fisher emphasizes that the real income is of crucial importance for every economy. Man's real income is given by its buying power multiplied by the nominal number of dollars he gets. This real income per capita expands or contracts in proportion to the circulations, the flow of goods and services per capita, and the flow of money per capita. As a result, possible causes of general price level changes are expressed in per capita terms:

- Per capita increase of money circulated.
- Per capita decrease of money circulated.
- Per capita increase of goods circulated.
- Per capita decrease of goods circulated.

If we assume the flow of goods per capita to be unaltered, any change in the price level may be solely attributed to a change in the money flow. If, however, the flow of money per capita is the same, any change in the price level may be attributed only to a change in the flow of goods per capita. Change in the flow of money per capita is called absolute inflation and absolute deflation respectively, whereas the change in goods per capita is known as relative inflation and relative deflation.

The most important outcome of these considerations is that money illusion hides the money side of the market, as people consider wholly or chiefly the goods market. The thinking is that the change in price level is due to a scarcity or a superabundance of the individual goods in the market. As a result, they consider the relative inflation/deflation to play a role. However, according to the empirical observation of various economists (Professor Cassel of Sweden, Professor Keynes of England, and Professor Holbrook working in California) named by Fisher, including his own findings, the money stream is varying greatly, in contrast with the goods stream which is varying little. Based on that, it can be derived that people should instead put greater emphasis on absolute inflation; however, they suffer from money illusion.

This implies the necessity to distinguish between the individual movements of prices (caused by individual supply and demand) and the general movements of prices (caused by money demand and supply). Most people ascribe an important role to the supply and demand of a commodity, which will equalize the price of everything, and neglect the forces of money demand and supply in changing the price level. The result of this money illusion is direct and indirect harm to the economy.

The direct harm caused by the money illusion

It seems at first sight that if price movements are solely governed by the movements in the value of money (and not determined by the scarcity of goods), the harm is dubious. For instance, if prices double because people use twice as many dollars to buy things, the monetary yardstick changes, but the thing measured does not change. However, as Fisher (1928) argues, everybody's income is not adjusted to the price changes and therefore the change in the monetary yardstick is serious. The monetary yardstick not only affects all sales as the universal monetary unit in exchange, but it is also applied in the case of long-term contracts.

Standard contracts to pay present dollars for future dollars and their outcome are affected by inflation and deflation, which either expands or shrinks the dollar value. As a result, the effects of the monetary yardstick are tremendous in terms of the redistribution of buying power and consequently affecting bond markets, insurance policies, saving bank deposits, pensions, leases or wage contracts, and so on. On the contrary, the effect of a change in the physical yardstick is not considered that serious, since it merely affects the sale of goods measured in yards (e.g., ribbon market), but its changes do not affect the sale of most goods (e.g., the wheat, sugar, cola, or steal markets), measured in units like bushels, ponds, tons, or days' work. Additionally, a change in the physical yardstick is discovered at once. On the contrary, the change in the monetary yardstick is more harmful, since money illusion comes into play and the source remains unrecognized (Fisher 1928).

Based on the disastrous effects of a change in the monetary yardstick, it is worth stressing the illusory nature of nominal wage gains.

Laborers are, according to Fisher (1928), victims of deflation resulting in unemployment, but also victims of the high cost of living in the case of inflation. In the case of rising prices, the laborer is able to get and keep a job easily, but his wage is considerably lagging behind the rising cost of living. Although wage contracts and salaries run for shorter periods with a possibility of readjustment, they are rarely adjusted promptly. This is well documented in the period of the great inflation in Germany, which began in 1922. In January 1923, the wages of skilled labor had risen to more than 500 times the level of 1913, however the cost of living had increased more than 1,100 times. As a result, the workman's weekly wage of 18,000 marks in 1923 was less than half of the purchasing power of his weekly wage of 35 marks in 1913. At that time, the wages for both skilled and unskilled labor were lagging behind prices. A striking absurdity might be mentioned in the case of a German metal worker, whose average weekly wage in December 1923 was about 850 billion times the 1913 wage. Notwithstanding, the cost of living was 1,250 billion times as high. As a result, his buying power was only about 70 percent as much as it had been in 1913.

The trend of rising prices with money wages lagging behind them, such as the German example, might be illustrated well by "counterfeit wages," a term first coined by Filene (1923). These wages refer to any wages, however large in nominal value, that have too little value. They are unable to serve their purposes—to purchase the basic necessities of life, provide motivation to make working more desirable, or ensure appropriate provision for sickness or retirement. Filene (1923) agrees with Fisher (1928) that it is a question of what people can buy with what they earn. As a result, the concept of counterfeit wages has important ties with the concept of money illusion.

In Fisher's sense, money illusion again plays a crucial role during the period when counterfeit wages were passing for real wages. The workman was the victim of this illusion, not realizing that his real buying power had decreased. Even when he is able to see through the veil of nominal values and make a distinction between nominal and real wages, he is still not aware of the fact that the dollar or mark is responsible for his situation. Instead he puts the fault on his employer. In the case of falling price levels, those who keep their jobs benefit from a reduced cost of living. However, high unemployment causes the laborer to lose on average in the long run due to falling prices.

The laborer loses in either case. The real wage of the laborer is either reduced due to nominal wages lagging behind prices, or during deflation, when workers are unemployed and have no wage at all. It appears again that stabilization of the monetary unit is crucial for workers in the case of inflation or deflation as emphasized by Fisher (1928), since it affects their buying power. This is documented by the appearance of a working man in front of the Dawes

Commission,[2] who emphasized that labor needs "a more stable currency" to avoid counterfeit wages.

Also, the illusory nature of a nominal interest rate deserves attention. Fisher (1928) comments on the works of Smith (1928) and Van Strum (1925). These authors independently showed that bondholders are not safe in terms of investment as measured in buying power, as long as the inflationary environment affects the value of the dollar. Actually, bondholders occasionally experience a loss in terms of purchasing power instead of getting interest rate. Nevertheless, they thought that the interest rate was merely a return of the principal; instead, they were actually losing part of their principal.

Fisher (1928) specifically points out that the evil of an unstable currency is not primarily general impoverishment, but social injustice itself. Giving the example of the disturbance of loan contracts, he shows the inflation to benefit the debtors and harm the creditors. On the first sight, it looks like no harm is done to society, since the debtor gains what the creditor loses. But in the same way it might be argued that the robbery of a bank vault in a person's house keeps the society just as well off since what the person lost, the burglar has gained. This provoking example just shows that the dollar is defrauding people in the same way as a burglary. However, in both cases, the cause of harm is social injustice rather than general impoverishment. Unlike burglary, there is no violation of law in the case of an unstable currency.

As Fisher demonstrates on many other examples, including the Central European hyperinflation, money illusion has hidden the truth from people and has harmed them seriously.

Fisher (1928) illustrates the case of millions of European savings bank depositors (subject to money illusion), who had lost all their life savings because they didn't withdraw their money in the early stages of inflation and reinvest them to profit by the price increases. An example of an American depositor illustrates the case of nominally confused depositors even further. In 1920, our depositor could buy only about three-quarters as much with \$300 as he could buy with \$100 in 1896. Fisher argues that the depositor should have turned his \$100 deposit into some representative commodity and simply keep this commodity until 1920. What's more, this commodity would have appreciated four-fold compared to the deposited money. In the current state, money illusion has hidden the truth from him and instead of having interest, our depositor was punished and lost also part of his principal. He deposited \$100 in 1896, but in 1920 each dollar was worth 26⅔ cents of the 1896 buying power. When he withdrew \$300 in 1920, it was worth $300 \times 26\frac{2}{3} =$ \$80 of the 1896 buying power. As a result, he lost 20 percent of his original principal and received no such thing as interest. The nominal interest rate again appeared to be illusory.

Similarly, millions of middle-class bondholders were ruined after World War I by the fall of the German mark, the Polish mark, the Russian ruble and the Austrian crown. Fisher's example about a lady who was left a legacy of \$50,000 by her father in 1892 is worth attention. During that time the dollar was worth the most. The money inherited was put in trust and invested into so-called "safe" bonds. In 1920, when the dollar was worth the least, the lady visited the trustee together with Professor Fisher. The trustee claimed that there was only a loss of $2,000 out of $50,000, due to an unwise investment made by the lady's father. He argued therefore that the principal had been left intact, apart from this minor loss, reaching a value $48,000. Fisher, however, argued that the $50,000 dollars invested in bonds was the equivalent of about $190,000 in 1920. The final amount was not $48,000 dollars in real terms, because of depreciation of the dollar. The total loss was almost 75 percent, since $48,000 does not reflect the buying power of $190,000 in 1920. The lady was paid a life annuity of $2,500 or $3,000 a year, which was, however, consumption of the principal rather than income. Fisher recommended that the trustee should have adopted a different investment strategy to fight against the depreciation of the principal. We may apply again the concept of social injustice, since the debtors/stockholders won what the lady in this example lost.

In other words: "Inflation has picked the pockets of bondholders and put the value into the stockholder's pockets, simply through unstable value of the dollar" (Fisher 1928, pp. 79–80).

Fisher (1928) asserts that due to uncertainty in the purchasing power of the dollar, the public and businessmen act like unconscious gamblers. They are running the risk and they will either benefit or lose. Those losers, who were subject to money illusion, blame the lucky winners of the lottery, who won the money from their neighbors' pockets without any intent to defraud. The fault is not the winners, who are unconscious gamblers just like the rest of general public. They only played the game, which should be stopped.

Fisher claimed that the effects of price levels on the economy result from changes in the real interest rates, which are given by an incomplete perception of changing price levels, and by the wrong price expectations held during the time the loan or nominal contract was signed. He mentions the so-called "peculiar behavior of the real interest rate," which is largely responsible for the crises and depressions through price movements (Fisher 1913, p. 56, cited in Dimand 1993). Money illusion is again the factor that is responsible for this peculiar behavior, since the nominal interest rate is of illusory nature for confused individuals.

Fisher gives an example of the borrower and debtor, whose relationship should be kept the same during rising prices as before and after. Not only will lenders require higher interest rates, but borrowers are capable of paying higher interest rates. This, however, requires higher nominal interest rates than the stationary prices require. Unfortunately, individuals tend to consider the dollar as a stable thing, regardless of the time and the fact that the process of adjustment is slow and imperfect. This is yet strengthened by law and custom, keeping the interest rate down (Fisher 1913, pp. 57–58).

According to Fisher (1913, pp.60, 69), when prices are rising, "the rate of interest rises, but not sufficiently," when prices are falling, "the rate of interest falls, but not sufficiently." The insufficient adjustment of a nominal interest rate was attributed to confusion between nominal and real variables: "If there were a better appreciation of the meaning of changes in the price level and an endeavor to balance these changes by adjustment in the rate of interest, the oscillations might be very greatly mitigated. It is the lagging behind of the rate of interest, which allows the oscillations to reach so great proportions" (Fisher 1913, pp. 71–72). Marshall (1907, p. 594) says on this point: "The cause of alternating periods of inflation and depression of commercial activity … is intimately connected with those variations in the real rate of interest which are caused by changes in purchasing power of money."

If the public would correctly perceive and anticipate price changes, it would not affect real interest rate and consequently economic activity. According to Dimand (1993), Fisher did not suppose that borrowers dispose more precise information, only that they perceive an increase in money receipts, inducing them to borrow even more, before they find out that the purchasing power had changed. The same holds for lenders who observe a rise in demand for loans and only later realize that the price level has changed. These arguments markedly resemble the theory of imperfect information developed by Lucas, as we shall see in Chapter 2, and some economists like Dimand (1993) emphasize this similarity.

As a result, the famous Fisher equation relating the nominal interest rate to the real interest rate was then a rather imperfect description of the real world. It could only work in a world with "foresight," which is very close to rational expectations, as emphasized by Thaler (1997). Fisher's extensive empirical research (1930) proved a very slow adjustment of the nominal interest rate to changes in inflation and with very long lags.[3] He analyzed interest rates in five markets (London, New York, Berlin, Calcutta, and Tokyo) and concluded that the real interest rate in terms of commodities is from seven to thirteen times as variable as the nominal interest rate in terms of money. This suggested the inability of people to adjust promptly the nominal interest rate to changed price level.

This finding might be closed by a poignant statement: "Erratic behavior of real interest is evidently a trick played on the money market by the money illusion" (Fisher 1930, p. 415).

It is interesting to add that, for instance, Rutledge (1977) claimed that Fisher did not interpret the lag between inflation and the full adjustment of nominal interest rates in terms of inflation expectations. He neglected Fisher's book, *The Money Illusion* (1928), showing that Fisher believed real interest rates to depend on past inflation during the period of transition. But as Dimand (1993) points out, this view is consistent with changes in real interest rates due to the slow perception and adjustment of inflation expectations (the nominal interest rate lagging behind the inflation) in Fisher's sense.

Fisher formulates explicitly implications of the movement of real interest rates on the economy. He gives an example during the period of 1896 to 1920, when the real rate of interest was wiped out, whereas in 1921 in a period of deflation, the nominal interest rate adjusted incompletely and the real interest rate rose as high as 60 percent. A period of deflation followed by a resulting rise in real interest rate was formulated explicitly by Fisher to affect aggregate production and employment and thereby strengthen the severity of the Great Depression.

Indirect harm caused by the money illusion

Fisher's major contribution apart from direct effects of inflation and deflation was the business fluctuations and its indirect effects. Unstable money is not only responsible for pick-pocketing, but it also partially explains the nature of business cycles. Monetary depreciation/appreciation caused by rising/falling price level stimulates/depresses the economy.

In the case of rising prices, at first producers don't experience higher cost due to rising wages or salaries, which are fixed by contract. This implies that wages and salaries don't rise too fast and only a higher rent or interest rate is paid. However, the lagging of such important expenses is causing a lagging of total expenses behind total revenues. It seems at first that profits have increased. Thereby when the price level has increased and profits have increased, the industry expands and business booms. Profit-takers, who follow the profit motive, are likely to suffer from money illusion. For instance, the cost of raw materials and other costs seem to be lower during inflation. But the dollar was worth more when the costs were incurred, whereas it was worth less later when the product was sold. The dollar was not the same dollar as before. The producer is simply lured by money illusion, as was the German shopkeeper. The false notion of high profits motivates him or her to expand his output and extend his debt. Only later does the producer start to see through the veil of nominal values and finds him- or herself to be ruined by overexpansion.

On the contrary, a fall in prices leads exactly to the opposite trend of diminishing profits, a contraction of the industry and depression of business, which is deceived by money illusion. Therefore, an unstable dollar is responsible for excessive expansion of the business during inflation and excessive contraction during deflation. Additionally, unstable money is also connected with unstable unemployment documented by Fuss, the chief of the Unemployment Service of the International Labor Office at Geneva. His findings suggest that during the deflation period 1919–1925, the depression of trade was followed by increased unemployment in nineteen out of twenty-two countries (Fisher 1928).

Fisher (1926) observed that the postwar deflation of 1920–1921 in the United States, England, Czechoslovakia and Norway was followed by substantial unemployment of million workers. However, inflation caused a stimulation to trade and increase in employment. He points out that these references to inflation or deflation have been almost neglected when applied to the so-called theory of "business cycle" and instead almost every other factor was considered. This passage refers implicitly to Wesley Mitchell's real theory of business cycles and contrasts it with Fisher's own monetary theory of business fluctuations.

Fisher (1926) pays attention to "Business Cycles and Unemployment," the report created for the President's Conference on Unemployment, which was written under the supervision of Mitchell (Mitchell 1923), the research director of the National Bureau of Economic Research. Fisher's criticism of this approach appears in his paper from 1923, "The Business Cycle Largely a Dance of Dollar," and calls for more use of economic theory in theory of business cycle. Additionally,

Fisher's reference to the "so-called business cycle" was a simple rejection of cyclical theories of fluctuations. Mitchell considered economic fluctuations to be cyclical, with real rather than monetary causes. Moore (1923) considered economic cycles to be similar to fluctuations of meteorological cycles. Schumpeter (1935, 1939) presented fluctuations as a forty-month Kitchin cycle superimposed on a nine or ten-year Juglar cycle and a fifty-five- or sixty-year Kondratieff cycle. Contemporary business cycle theories, real or monetary, reject the explanation of fluctuations based on constant periodicity and amplitude, siding on this phenomenon with Fisher against Jevons, Mitchel, Moore and Schumpeter or Kondratieff. The term "cycle" in the field is now used only for historical reasons, as suggested by Dimand (1993).

It is worth noting that Fisher's monetary theory of business cycles is an analysis of transition periods, during which output, employment, and real interest are affected due to fluctuations in the purchasing power of money and therefore money is not neutral. In this case, money illusion is believed to account for the short run non-neutrality of money. In the long run, money is neutral, since monetary changes affect only nominal variables (price level, nominal interest rate) and the real interest rate is determined by time preference and the productivity of capital. As a result, there is no space for money illusion.

Suggestions

Fisher was convinced that an unstable currency, which is causing economic fluctuations during transition, is intensified by the presence of money illusion and fixed long-term contracts (not adjusted for changes in price level). It seems that the behavior of people, subject to money illusion is unconscious, since they are not aware of inflation or deflation. As a result, suboptimal decisions are made. This results in direct harm in the form of the redistribution of wealth from creditors to debtors, or from bondholders to stockholders, or labor troubles due to illusory nature of nominal wage rate, and so on. It also means that suboptimal decisions are translated to the aggregate level through the behavior of businesspeople affected by money illusion. This indirect effect has even more serious consequences.

If we return to Fisher's example of bondholders, he claimed that social injustice is present because one party loses and another has gained. There was little space for the application of general impoverishment. However, if we consider now the indirect effects, it is not only the transferring of values from one party to the other, but it means primarily a loss to society as a whole. Clearly, losses exceed gains owing to uncertainty, depression, unemployment, strikes, riots, or violence. In the case of rising price levels, the prosperity of bondholders and wage earners is far from being "prosperous." At this time, ordinary gambling picks the lucky winners, who enjoy increased welfare through profits at the expense of the welfare of others, who suffered from money illusion. However, the gains of these profit-takers are mostly swept away due to the secondary effects of the rising price levels (i.e., strikes, riots, violence), which block the wheels of industry. On the contrary, bondholders are lucky winners of gambling during deflation, but are also as likely to lose their winnings over time. Being in the role of simple investors and silent partners, they only find out, once there is no profit left for them. The unconscious forces of money illusion are responsible, in the form of an inability of captains of industry to reckon the dollar value. Millions of unemployed men and idle machines are generated due to the fall of the industry. Their wages lost in depression are never regained by them or by any counterpart like employers. As a result, this situation represents a total loss to all society. Summing up, money illusion leads in Fisher's sense to a general loss of the society in form of social injustice, social discontent and social inefficiency. This motivated Fisher to suggest a number of remedies of this direct and indirect harm.

For Fisher, the biggest problem was that people do not observe "the dance of the dollar"[4] and therefore cannot adjust in advance. The monetary theory of business fluctuations associated with the unstable buying power of the currency led Fisher to work on a reliable price index. This index was needed to test the monetary theory of cycle and served as a basis for a monetary policy stabilizing the price level. It was also useful for informing the public about changes in the purchasing power of the currency. It is worth noting that already Fisher (1923) believed that money illusion was pervasive and that economics should somehow fulfill its role in educating the public to see through the nominal veil of values.

Fisher's major work *The Making of Index Numbers* in 1922, cited by Dimand (1993), addressed how money could be measured in terms of real value, that is, through index numbers. He wrote a highly specialized, 500-page work, which was not welcomed by commercial publishers and so was published by the Pollak Foundation for Economic Research and financed by Waddill Catchings. Based on his findings, Fisher founded the Index Number Institute housed in New Haven and its weekly index of wholesale prices was regularly published in the *Journal of the American Statistical Association* (1923–1930, expect 1929). In addition, the Institute published price indices of many kinds from 1923 to 1936 based on worldwide data (Tobin 1987).

Another utilization of price indices, as seen by Fisher (1928), was forecasting business conditions. Any pronounced change in price level might be a good indicator for a business and its plans. Many other indicators, not related to unstable money are equally useful. Fisher also put emphasis on the advice of professional agencies, which could provide warnings with respect to the probable fluctuations in business conditions. Statistical and forecasting services in this sense provided helpful protection against the harmful effects of inflation and deflation and the related money illusion. Fisher clearly states that the ability to predict the dollar's value might be an advantage for many people. Using again the German example of inflation after the World War I, he shows that speculating in real estate, stocks, and foreign exchange was a good strategy as opposed to investment in bonds (payable in marks) and saving deposits. Modern business information services may partially strengthen the ability to see signs of upcoming inflation or deflation and allow people to benefit from it instead of being harmed.

Based on his work with price indices, Fisher later suggested a policy rule called "compensated dollar." This plan aimed to stabilize the value of the currency—to preserve the same level of prices it is necessary to increase gradually the weight of the dollar. "The increasing number of grains of bullion to make a dollar would then compensate for the lessening purchasing power of each grain" (Fisher, 1913, p. 218). Thereby the name of the plan "a compensated dollar." Furthermore, gold would circulate solely in the form of gold bullion dollar certificates, where a $100 certificate would be exchangeable for $100 of gold bullion (at whatever the legal weight might be at the time of exchange). To put the plan into effect, Fisher (1913) suggested to institute an official price index, with some initial year given as a base year. The government was supposed to readjust the official weight of the virtual dollar or so called "redemption bullion" (the quantity of bullion in which it will redeem the gold dollar) regularly, according to the finding of the price index. As a result, the purchasing power of the dollar would always be the same. Later, he even extended his plan and proposed to apply this rule uniformly and synchronously in the currencies of all countries linked by fixed exchange rate parities, in proportional amounts linked to an international price index (Patinkin, 1987). This rule was similar to Keynes' (1923) less formal rule for the United Kingdom (Patinkin 1987). Fisher (1928) later claimed that as long as the stabilization of the dollar is attained, it makes little difference if the United States apply the scheme on their own.

Another of Fisher's suggestions (aimed to alleviate the effects of an unstable dollar and related money illusion), was investment in well-diversified common stocks with some preferred stocks and bonds too. Diversification is subject to constant care and advisory services by the so called "Investment Counsel" and therefore investment is safeguarded. Another suggestion was to invest into investment trusts, which do diversify by themselves (Fisher 1928).

Contracting out is another remedy, which aimed to avoid the negative effects of an unstable currency. By contracting out, individuals could escape wildly fluctuating currency by turning it into a better currency (either by buying foreign currency or by making domestic contracts payable in foreign currency, or by selling securities and investing them abroad [Fisher 1928]). Basically, an instrument "contract out" enabled people to use another unit of measure, in which contracts are expressed. However, contracts in single-commodity standards (monetary unit) are subject to the same fluctuations as the original currency. The widespread opinion was that gold was a poor standard by which to form wages or other contracts. Contracts required correction for variations in the buying power of gold. An advancement was a contract in a multiple-commodity standard, under which money was adjusted based on an index number. This so-called tabular standard, according to Tobin (1987), was nothing more than facilitation of price indexed contracts, which dates back to the eighteenth century.

After World War I, price changes stimulated development and the spreading of price indexation in a wider sense. The index of the cost of living was applied to a labor market to serve as an indicator for raising wages during inflation. Wages of millions of workers in America, and soon afterwards in Europe, started to be adjusted with respect to an index of the cost of living. Wage adjustments were popular during periods of inflation but the reverse was the case as soon as deflation appeared. Wage adjustment was largely abandoned in times of deflation. Fisher claims that money illusion was largely accountable for the reluctance of workers toward the downward adjustment of wages. The false notion of falling buying power led workers to object to any downward wage indexation.

In Fisher's view, money illusion could be significantly eliminated through negotiation of contracts avoiding nominal rigidities. Price indexing of various contracts partially corrects for nominal rigidities. Fisher (1928) mentions the so-called "stabilized bond" issued by Rand Kardex Company (later Remington Rand), of which Fisher was director. When the purchasing power of the dollar rose or fell (i.e., the price index of commodities rose or fell), the company was obliged to compensate the bondholders and guarantee a steadier income in terms of real purchasing power.

Ties of Fisher's money illusion to contemporary economic knowledge

Fisher's research on money illusion, although subject to criticism, might be linked to contemporary research, which incorporates many of his insights. This section will provide a brief overview of Fisher's money illusion insights in light of contemporary economic knowledge. More thorough attention to these issues will be devoted in subsequent chapters of the book.

Fisher's original definition of money illusion rests on the assumption that people might be fully unconscious about fluctuations in currency, the changing of its purchasing power, and resulting effects. This definition might be considered a bit narrow in today's world, as it is difficult to imagine that people are not aware of the effects of inflation. The availability of a consumer price index as a lever of the public and bond market awareness represents in some way a fulfillment of Fisher's intention to educate the public about the effects of an unstable currency.

This is supported by Fisher's idea that in a world with adequate price indexation of various contracts, money illusion is substantially eradicated. Additionally, with the economics of Friedman's natural rate theory and later rational expectation hypothesis in the 1960s, it seemed like there was no space left for money illusion.

Disregarding money illusion went particularly far with Tobin (1972), who wrote in his article "Inflation and Unemployment" that: "An economic theorist can, of course commit no greater crime than to assume money illusion" (Tobin 1972, p. 3). It is important to note that this statement was already mentioned at Tobin's presidential address to the American Economic Association, just four years after the introduction of Friedman's natural rate theory. However, as noted by Akerlof and Shiller (2009), money illusion was, just a few years earlier, explicitly or implicitly part of the views of well-reputed economists like John Maynard Keynes, Paul Samuelson, Robert Solow, Irwing Fisher, Franco Modigliani, and James Tobin. Later it became taboo.

Even Akerlof and Shiller (2009) claim that money illusion presented by Fisher or Keynes was a naïve belief. However, they called for serious *revision* of money illusion, thereby not neglecting it fully. Their attitude implies that there is scope for research, which is documented by the fact that a lot of insights from Fisher's work were elaborated more thoroughly in a modified form by other authors. They believed that money is not just a veil and losses might be experienced when translating nominal dollars to real dollars, due to money illusion. A rather imperfect form of the indexation of wages on a labor market as inflation actually occurs (a cost of living adjustment [COLA]) documents either an inability or an unwillingness to adjust contracts during wage bargaining. The unwillingness of workers to adjust contracts reflects a downward nominal wage rigidity, which might be considered as another indicator of money illusion. This is again in line with Fisher's statement.

Akerlof and Shiller (2009) also claim that the absence of a perfect indexation of bonds and only a partial indexation of mortgage contracts, makes an additional argument for a persistent money illusion. This opinion is also shared by Shafir et al. (1997). This argument is closely related to Fisher's initial suggestion of the "stabilized bonds," aimed to alleviate the effects of money illusion.

Fisher's insights into money illusion present in the case of bondholders and stockholders have been also utilized by Modigliani and Cohn (1979). Modigliani and Cohn's hypothesis of financial markets suggests that stock market investors don't see through the veil of nominal values and discount real cash flows at nominal discount rates. Consequently, other authors followed their investigation (Cohen, Polk, and Vuolteenaho 2005, Basu, Markov, and Shivakumar 2010, or Basak and Yan 2010 and others) and empirically proved the presence of money illusion in the stock market.

Brunnermeier and Julliard (2008) also utilized Fisher's examples in their investigation of the presence of money illusion in the housing market. They refer specifically to Fisher's opinion that nominal rates should move one-for-one with expected inflation, its puzzling nature, and interpretation with respect to money illusion in the stock market. Similarly, Thaler (1997) mentions that Fisher was aware of the fact that his famous equation was designed in the conditions of a perfect world. Instead, it was empirically proved that the nominal interest rate is rather lagging behind the inflation, which is documented by substantial variability of the real interest rate.

Money illusion also found a place in the field of behavioral economics, which witnessed a resurrection of money illusion in some aspect, as shown by Akerlof (2002) or Shafir et al. (1997), who don't presume that people are completely deceived by money illusion. Instead, money illusion might be elicited even in case of rational individuals due to the so called "framing effect" associated with psychological bias and consequent deviations from rationality.

Paradoxically, money illusion is present also in the early works of Lucas and Rapping (1969), who incorporated money illusion into the labor supply and tried to make it compatible with rationality assumption. Additionally, studies of near-rationality (Akerlof and Yellen 1985), strategic interactions (Haltiwanger and Waldman 1985), and behavioral economics issues (Kahneman and Tversky 2000) document deviations from full rationality, supporting a further potential role for money illusion effects. Furthermore, the implications of money illusion have been extended to the aggregate level (Fehr and Tyran 2001). As a result, Fisher's legacy is still topical, with money illusion being an important phenomenon, which will be subject to elaboration in subsequent chapters.

John Maynard Keynes and the presence of the money illusion in his work

Fisher's definition of money illusion, called by some economists "Fisher's effect" (Tyran 1999), was primarily based on the inability of people to perceive that the monetary yardstick (basically one dollar) is changing its value in real terms, based on the forces of inflation and deflation (Fisher 1928). This definition, however, underwent a substantial transformation over time, starting with Haberler (1941, p. 460), who outlined it as synonymous to a violation of what Leontief (1936) called the "homogeneity postulate" (Howitt 1989).

Under this postulate, demand and supply functions are homogenous of degree zero in all nominal prices, including the initial quantity of financial assets, since they depend upon relative prices but not upon the absolute price level. To put it more formally: "The quantity of any service or any commodity demanded or supplied by a firm or an individual remains unchanged if all the prices upon which it (directly) depends increase or decrease exactly in the same proportion" (Leontief 1936, p. 192).

In other words, this means that all supply and demand functions, with prices as independent variables and quantity as a dependent variable, are homogenous functions of the zero degree. The homogeneity postulate might be demonstrated with the help of Ricardo's well-known hypothetical experiment, as noted by Leontief (1936). If we suppose an overnight doubling of the cash holdings of all business enterprises and households, the prices of all commodities and services will change equally proportionally. Thereby the quantities produced, traded, and consumed by firms and households will remain unchanged. Although not explicitly stated, Ricardo's example is based upon the homogeneity postulate. This instantaneous adjustment of prices to any primary variation is conditioned on the economic system, absent of any kind of frictions and time-lag effects, which is unrealistic.

And Leontief (1936, p. 194) continues: "In a frictionless system with at least one or more non-homogenous elements, the quantity of money ceases to be a neutral factor."[5] In other words, the frictionless, lag-less and homogenous system is modified in a way that one demand or supply curve of any single household or enterprise violates the assumption of homogeneity. Consequently, this household or enterprise would demand (or supply) larger or smaller quantities (of one or more commodities) induced by rising or falling prices, while other subjects are still subject to homogeneity condition. However, this discrepancy is incompatible with the conditions of general equilibrium and implies that any equilibrium quantity of commodity or service, sold or bought, is now a function of the quantity of money. Consequently, the monetary maximum for the output or for the maximum employment of labor might be determined. It is highly unlikely that monetary quantity, which brings maximum output of a given commodity, will coincide with monetary optimum bringing maximum employment. Notwithstanding, the difference between the monetary maximum (for the output or labor) and the actual figure of production and employment might tell us the size of monetary underproduction or the size of monetary unemployment. Based on the non-homogeneity assumption, a conclusion may also be formulated for the interest rate, which also becomes a function of the quantity of money, like the employment and output of the economy.

Leontief neither mentions explicitly the term money illusion in Keynes' work, nor aims to define it. He merely discusses how Keynes advocates his own standpoint toward an orthodox classical scheme, putting forward the issue concerning non-homogeneity of labor supply function, amongst others. The most important implication is that monetary theory of unemployment, and thereby non-neutrality of money, stands and falls with the violation of homogeneity postulate.

This was sufficient to apply it in further studies such as Miao and Xie (2013), Fehr and Tyran (2001), Modigliani and Cohn (1979), Brunnermeier and Julliard (2008), and Basak and Yan (2010), which denote a violation of the homogeneity postulate in Leontief's view as a definition of money illusion. The definition of money illusion, based on the violation of the homogeneity postulate, differs from Fisher's view in two aspects as noted by Howitt (1989). It is built in operational terms as a property of potentially observable supply and demand functions, as opposed to Fisher's property of people's misperception. It has also been mentioned that these functions depend on the relative level of prices, rather than the absolute level of prices. The illusion-free character of demand functions is further explored in the works of Howitt and Patinkin (1980a, 1980b) and Dusansky (1980), who discuss the necessary conditions of utility function that would meet those requirements.

Patinkin (1949) objects to the latter definition of money illusion and modifies a homogeneity assumption to account for the real initial wealth. When all money prices double, people's demand functions necessarily fall, because the real value of their initial money holdings (the value of initial real wealth) falls. In this context, the real balance effect is a crucial item, which should not be omitted in the homogeneity postulate. The resulting absence of money illusion is defined then as the homogeneity of function of degree zero in all money prices and initial real wealth.

Does Keynes labor suffer from money illusion?

As stated by Leontief (1936, p. 195), Keynes assumed the supply function for labor to be non-homogenous. Nevertheless, the clear-cut statement of this basic postulate is absent. Despite that, Keynes points out that the classic homogeneity postulate is at variance with facts. Nevertheless, a series of empirical observations was needed to show that all the prices capable of affecting the labor supply would differ in absolute terms, although remain constant in their relative magnitude: "The non-homogeneity of the labor supply function would be proven if, under these conditions and in absence of friction and time lags, the amount of labor employed would change with the variation of the price level, instead remaining constant as expected by orthodox theorists" (Leontief 1936, p. 196).

Unfortunately, no such evidence is given by Keynes in his *General Theory of Unemployment*, as noted by Leontief (1936). Further critique is also provided by Tobin (1971), who claims that the non-homogenous nature of labor supply should also be reflected in other demand and supply functions.[6]

Nevertheless, it became common habit to claim that Keynes assumed workers to suffer from money illusion.[7]

According to Keynes' theory (1936), ordinary experience tells us that labor negotiates for a money wage rather than a real wage. While workers usually tend to resist a cut to money wages—and if the money wage is cut, they withdraw the labor—it is not the case for real wages. If they experience a cut in real wages, resulting from an increase in price levels, they neglect it and do not reduce their supply of labor. Although it appears illogical at first to resist the reduction of money wages and neglect the reduction of real wages, Keynes notes that it might not sound that illogical. Apparently, Leontief (1936) notes, Keynes comes to a formulation of the crucial issue that the supply of labor depends not only upon the real but also? upon the money wages. This claim will be elaborated further.

Observation about the presence of money illusion in Keynes' work has been interpreted in the following way, as suggested by Ferguson (2013) and many others. Workers measure their wages only in terms of the number of currency notes (nominal valuation) instead of measuring it in terms of buying power. They suffer from the false notion that a fall in the nominal wage reduces their standard of living and supply less labor. In contrast, if prices rise and nominal wage is fixed, they ignore the fall in real wage and supply the same quantity of labor. Keynes did not mention that workers suffer from money illusion. He argued instead that workers' reactions differ in the case of real wage cuts due to price increases and in the case of real wage cuts due to nominal wages. It is evident that workers neglect any fall in real wage due to price increases. But once prices rise to an extreme degree, affecting significantly the cost of living, workers will react. Anyway, there will be periods in which wages will be lagging behind the cost of living.

Keynes mentioned another feature of labor force, important for our discussion about money illusion. Workers in his sense are not said to totally neglect real wage cuts due to price increase; actually, they notice them in some way. It just appears that workers are more tolerant of real wage cuts due to price increases rather than to nominal wage cuts. In other words, this fact alleviates the widely believed notion that workers suffer from money illusion and don't notice any price changes in Fisher's sense. The fact that real wages fall as a result of an increase in the cost of living, leaving the quantity of labor supplied unchanged, is as such not theoretically fundamental for the concept of money illusion as stated by Ferguson (2013).

This behavior of workers might be summarized in the vein of Keynes (1936, p.14):

> Thus it is fortunate that the workers, though unconsciously, are instinctively more reasonable economists than the classical school, inasmuch as they resist reductions of money-wages, which are seldom or never of an all-round character, even though the existing real equivalent of these wages exceeds the

> marginal disutility of the existing employment, whereas they do not resist reductions of real wages, which are associated with increases in aggregate employment and leave relative money wages unchanged.

However, apart from money illusion, is there any rationale behind the fact that labor objects to money wage cuts and neglects real wage cuts through rising prices? It seems important to discuss this issue further, since it has been thought that Keynes presumed a presence of money wage illusion, based on the different response of labor toward the same change in relative prices.

Apparently, there is no difference between a cut in money wages and a fall in real wages due to an increase in price level. If we suppose that money wages were cut elsewhere and if workers knew it, they would not object against it and would keep their labor supplied fixed. In contrast, if they believed that wages were just cut in their job, they would choose unemployment. In a nutshell, if money wages are cut by one employer, this does not automatically mean that they are cut by other employers. As a result, workers rightly consider that wages are not cut elsewhere. On the other hand, if price levels rise, workers have less reason to believe that their real wage is lower than elsewhere. As a result, employees are unlikely to refuse immediately a lower real wage induced by higher price level, but they would object against an equal money wage cut in their present job. This implies that the distinction between the wage in present job versus wages in all other jobs should not be downplayed as suggested by Glasner (2012).

This statement is consistent with Keynes' explanation of the different response of labor toward nominal versus real wage cuts, which rests on a relative income explanation.

A good example is the situation in 1925–1926, when Britain returned to the Gold Standard set at the pre-World War I parity, overvaluing the pound and in the process overpricing British exports (Keynes 1925). The coal industry was the first industry to be hit by the overvaluation of the pound. This industry needed to cancel out the effect of the return to gold on British coal's foreign currency prices by reducing prices in domestic terms. This required a reduction in costs and particularly a cut in the wages of the coal miners, since labor was the most significant part of total costs. Other export industries would be required to apply similar price cuts. This implies that significant widespread reductions in nominal pay and cuts in prices of non-tradable goods were required to offset the effect of the overvaluation of the pound and restore competitiveness of British exports. As noted by Keynes (1925), this kind of general cut could not be imposed in a democratic society, but would have to be reached by an agreement between employers and labor. However, labor had no guarantee that once accepting the wage cut, owners would cut the prices in the same proportion, thereby keeping real wages unchanged, but stimulating exports. Rather, the coal miners in Keynes' example considered this pressure for nominal wage cut as attack on them and were resistant to nominal wage cuts. To summarize, a lack of trust was responsible for the fact that individual groups of labor perceived those nominal wage cuts as attacks on them and this required sacrifice in the form of rising unemployment. In contrast, an increase in the general cost of living, which is generally thought to affect everyone, would make labor less resistant.

Keynes (1936) also claimed that in the case of a change peculiar to a particular industry, the change in real wages will follow the same direction as the change in money wages. However, if applied to a change in the general level of wages, the change in real wages associated with a change in money wages will be in the opposite direction. When money wages rise, real wages are going to fall, and vice versa. Money wages in the short run tend to fall due to the willingness of labor to accept wage cuts when employment is falling off. On the other hand, real wages are rising under the same conditions due to the increasing return to a given capital equipment, when output is getting lower. Thus, falling money wages and rising real wages accompany falling employment.[8]

This relation of real and nominal wages is closely associated with the second postulate of the classical school, which was subjected to criticism by Keynes. This classical postulate states that the real wages of labor are based on the wage bargaining between entrepreneurs and workers. Clearly, real wages are not independent of the level of money wages. As a result, labor is in a position to decide about the real wage through change in its money wage, but is unable to affect the quantity of employment. This means that workers in a classical model can bring their wage into equality with marginal disutility of labor. So, as soon as the money wage is above the equilibrium wage, equilibrium will be restored at full employment through money wage negotiations accompanied by consequent fall of real wages.

However, Keynes argued that cuts in nominal wages will not lead to a reduction in real wages.

First, Keynes (1936) would have expected classicists to argue that if money wages fall, prices would have to change in the same proportion, to keep the real wage and the level of unemployment fixed. But because of the second postulate about real wages being based on wage bargaining, classical school diverts from this line of thought. Second, it is impossible to analyze the market in partial equilibrium terms.

An example in Britain might be used again, based on Keynes' argument directed to the Macmillan Committee (Keynes 1930a, 1930b). The case of disequilibrium was considered, in which gold flew out of Britain. In that case, the interest rate would have to rise, which would lead to capital inflow and therefore gold inflow. Domestic investment and investment would be discouraged, followed by unemployment. This would put downward pressure on nominal wages. As wages fell, prices would also fall, not changing labor's real income significantly. This suggests that the real standard of living would not be affected very much by devaluation.

To sum up, even if negotiations about money wages are successful, it cannot be assumed that it will lead to the reduction in real wages, which is necessary to restore equilibrium and restore full employment.

As Keynes (1936) suggests, the classical school has slept in an illicit assumption that the struggle over money wages determines the general level of real wages. Instead the struggle about money wages represents a struggle over the distribution of the aggregate real wage between different labor groups. In other words, the presence of imperfect mobility of labor (under which wages do not tend to an exact equality of net advantage in various occupations), leads in the case of a money wage cut to a reduction in real wage relatively to others. In this case, workers will have sufficient justification to resist the wage cut. However, a reduction in real wages due to price fluctuations affects everybody alike in their purchasing power and workers neglect it unless it reaches an extreme degree.

Since there exists no way by which labor can reduce its real wage to bring it equal to the marginal disutility of labor, the existence of so-called involuntary unemployment is inevitable. Resulting involuntary unemployment follows:

> Men are involuntarily unemployed if, in the event of a small rise in the price of wage-goods relatively to the money-wage, both the aggregate supply of labor willing to work for the current money-wage and the aggregate demand for it at that wage would be greater than the existing volume of employment.
>
> (Keynes 1936, p. 15)

The equality of real wages and marginal disutility of labor is called "full employment" by Keynes.

Still, some economists like Tobin (1971), whose contribution will be discussed later, identify implicit presence of money illusion in above-discussed behavior of workers. It was generally argued that reduction in real wages, resulting from the rise in prices, stimulated the so-called Keynes' effective demand. In other words, the success of public investment policies was ensured through a channel of deception of labor, which accepted a lower wage with consequent favorable effects on employment. This implicit form of money illusion enabled to achieve the same result as would be achieved by a more direct attack on real wages through the reduction of money wages, whilst leaving prices unchanged. As Keynes (1939) himself notes, this view was also shared by Professor Pigou and many other economists. However, Keynes also suggests that he developed his own argument over time in a more complete form, calling for the revision of Chapter 2 of the *General Theory of Unemployment, Interest Rate and Money*. Particularly, he suggests that the falling tendency of real wages in periods of rising demand might not necessarily be the case. In other words, real wages may exhibit rather pro-cyclical tendencies. If this argument holds, an explanation based on money illusion will be rendered invalid.

However, Keynes (1939) also claims that previous conclusions should not be discarded completely, since they have survived for many years the scrutiny of experience. Rather, further empirical investigation is recommended. This partially speaks in favor of the fact that money illusion should not be entirely dismissed.

The presence of money illusion might also be a subject of discussion in other works by Keynes apart from *General Theory of Unemployment*. As Akerlof and Shiller (2009) claim, Fisher is not alone among well-known economists in believing that people are subject to money illusion, and they refer to John Maynard

Keynes' 1940 book *How to Pay for the War* as an example. This book was a proposal for a macroeconomic strategy for financing the war effort by the United Kingdom, which would meet the demands of war together with the claims of private consumption. The policy of inflationary war finance as it occurred during World War I was discussed, followed by the development of a model of inflation, which would be more in line with his desire to pursue policy, relying upon inflation to a minimal extent. The problem of social inequity was emphasized as a possible consequence of the policy of so called "unbridled" inflation. One might ask whether there is any reason to presuppose the presence of money illusion in this context, as Akerlof and Shiller (2009) note.

The inflationary method of financing World War I through the system of voluntary savings is illustrated on the basis of numerical example in Keynes (1940, pp. 65–67). Supposing that the government could raise its war expenditures significantly, this would create excess of aggregate demand over aggregate supply. An inflationary gap is created, in which case actual real wage exceeds the full employment equilibrium real wage. A rise in prices of 20 percent would be needed to equilibrate the economy and close the inflation gap and depress real wage. With rising prices, profiteers would gain extra income. This would happen through converting the part of unsaved earnings of workers into voluntary savings of entrepreneurs. However, for this mechanism to work, two conditions are necessary according to Keynes: the high marginal propensity to save, especially of large businesses; and very high profit and income tax. Consequently, this group of businesspeople was considered as a source of government war financing, either in the form of voluntary savings or of higher taxes.

But the issue is solved only momentarily. Sooner or later workers, affected by a fall in living standards, would bid with partial success for higher nominal wages. The adjustment of the economy to equilibrium is jeopardized. But as Keynes notes, there is still "one more card to play" (Keynes 1940, p. 66). During war, lags in the adjustment of wages to price changes are undisputable lasting advantage for profiteers. The adjustment, accompanied by other impediments, takes time. Although wages and other costs would later raise prices, prices would be always 20 percent ahead of wages. The act of spending wages (increased by bidding) would always push prices well in advance.

At this stage, it is worth commenting on the possible presence of money illusion in this work, although not explicitly mentioned by Keynes. The restoration of equilibrium (through reduction in inflationary gap and adjustment of real wage to the full employment equilibrium wage) could be ensured by the money illusion, as widely believed by neo-Keynesians. Instead of supposing time lags, they claim that money illusion on the part of workers would restore the equilibrium. The inflationary gap would generate an increase in prices, which would not be matched by equiproportionate wage increases. Wages would only rise by a fractional proportion of the percentage change of prices, leaving workers in the illusion that a rise in their money incomes was sufficient to correct for the fall in their real incomes. This would produce similar outcome like under Keynes theory, redistribution of unsaved earnings of workers in favor of voluntary savings of entrepreneurs (Trevithick 1975).

Neo-Keynesians believe that certain passages in the *General Theory* and other of Keynes' writings, are indicative of the presence of money illusion. In particular, a modest increase in prices of 5 to 10 percent is sufficient to prevent retaliatory wage bidding and as such might be considered as a form of money illusion. However, once this threshold limit is exceeded, money illusion no longer operates, since labor will no longer neglect this change. Keynes (1941) claimed that during war, inflation, even a modest excess of aggregate demand could generate an unlimited rise in prices, which is not in accordance with the outlined concept of money illusion. The argument about the exclusive reliance on money illusion is questioned by Leijonhufvud (cited by Littleboy 2013), who refers to Keynes' concept of workers willing to receive lower real wages due to inflation, but resisting cuts in money wages. Although this is taken as an assumption about the presence of money illusion, Leijonhufvud considers it as inadequate. Specifically, he emphasizes that consumption expenditure is rather a function of real income, so an interpretation in terms of money illusion might not be plausible.[9] Still, Leijonhufvud admits that in disequilibrium the system might be confused and individuals might act under the illusion, but Keynes omitted to clarify this phenomenon. First, it might be possible that the inelasticity of expectations of ill-informed workers is responsible for their maintenance of high reservation prices, while they search for alternative employment. Second, workers, due to the impossibility of a general wage cut, resist a money wage cut because of the fear of lower remuneration relative to other workers. In either case, wages do not adjust to a new equilibrium. Leijonhufvud favors the first alternative, but his view is regarded as implicit in what Keynes said explicitly.

Nevertheless, the presence of money illusion, implicit or otherwise, is well documented by Duesenberry (1950), Smithies (1942), and Maital (1972).

Coming back to the inflationary method of financing the war, this method proved to be no longer feasible at the end of 1930s and Keynes (1940) therefore offered the method of compulsory savings by deferred pay.[10] The time lag between wages and prices proved to be insufficient to make inflationary financing of the war efficient. Particularly, the trade unions, among many others, became index-number conscious, with wage contracts tied to the cost of living. As a result, the lag between rising prices and wages shortened significantly, and inflationary financing became an expensive luxury.

Still, a central question remains which factor accounts for a decline in a real wage and the adjustment of the economy toward equilibrium. Is it money illusion, which is accountable or time lags in adjustment?

As already mentioned, Keynes rejected the policy of inflationary finance due to the negligible lag between wage and price changes. However, if money illusion was the case then there was no reason for the rejection of this method. Paradoxically, the shortening of the time lag would make inflation a much more efficient instrument due to the faster adjustment of the economy to equilibrium. Trevithick (1975) points out that either Keynes was inconsistent in his explanation or he had not proposed a model of money illusion. Particularly interesting were the reflections of Hamilton (1952), Hansen (1925), and Mitchell (1903), who related money illusion to the already discussed lags between wage and price changes. According to them, the existence of a lag in the adjustment of wages to prices determines the ability of workers to distinguish between price level increase and nominal wage cut. If there would be no lag in adjustment during inflation, the cut in real wage ensuing from a rise in price level and from nominal wage cuts, would not be a relevant basis for a different perception of workers. But since the wage-price lag is the case, workers might perceive price increases differently as opposed to a nominal wage cut, although both cases lead to reduction of real wage. Mitchell (1903) and Lerner (1956) argued in favor of the wage-lag hypothesis and concluded that monetary inflation caused the decline in real wages. However, Alchian (1969) and Alchian and Kessel (1959, 1960) were unable to find evidence of the wage-price lag. Although the assumption of wage lag is highly problematic and with little empirical support, according to Alchian and Kessel (1959), it still accounts for possible presence of money illusion.

Last, Keynes did not consider inflationary war finance as a convergent process, but as a process of an unlimited rise in prices. Money illusion in his sense was regarded as being present below some threshold limit. It seems, therefore, that money illusion is only of partial importance in an explanation behind the theory on "How to Pay for the War," as Akerlof and Shiller (2009) mention, although it is acknowledged to play a role in Keynes' other works.

Tobin's view of money illusion

However, even some well-known economists were not entirely persuaded about the absence of money illusion in Keynes' theory, changing their views over time. The most thorough elaboration was provided by James Tobin in his research.

Tobin's undergraduate honors thesis (published as Tobin, 1941), supervised by his final year tutor, Edward Chamberlin, and more active advisor, Wassily Leontief, considered the presence of money illusion in Keynes' labor supply (in line with Keynes' postulate of non-homogenous labor supply held by Leontief) rather than overlapping contracts or consideration of relative wages (cited by Dimand, 2014).

Later, Tobin (1972) claimed in his presidential address to the American Economic Association that for psychological reasons workers are reluctant to agree to nominal wage cuts, but accept real wage cuts induced by inflation, which alleviates their purchasing power. However, it is easier to achieve nominal wage cuts when there is moderate inflation than when inflation is low. As inflation declines toward lower values, the entire distribution of nominal wages moves down in a lockstep, reaching eventually the zero wall and ending up with wage freezes instead cuts. In particular, money illusion responsible for downward nominal wage rigidity would indicate a very flat version of the long-term Phillips curve for high unemployment (indicating a permanent trade-off between inflation and unemployment), and vertical shape at low levels of unemployment. This view sharply contrasts with Tobin's claim that: "An economic theorist can, of course commit no greater crime than to assume money illusion" (Tobin 1972, p. 3).

Consequently, Tobin stated at the 1983 Keynes Centenary Conference: "Why are labor markets not always cleared by wages? Keynes' … answer is usually interpreted to depend on an ad hoc nominal rigidity or stickiness in nominal wages and thus to attribute to worker's irrational money illusion. I now think, however, that Keynes provides a theory free of this taint" (reprinted in Tobin 1987, p. 45).

LeRoy (1985, pp. 671–72) cited by Dimand (2014, p. 6), on the occasion of the Keynes centenary conference in Cambridge, quoted Tobin above and added:

> It is this propensity to engage in such verbal argumentation divorced from disciplined economic theorizing that critics of Keynesian economics find so frustrating. Little wonder that recent generations of graduate students—tired of trying to remember for exam purposes that Keynesian unemployment is due to inertia in nominal wage and price paths but not to ad hoc nominal rigidity (or is it vice versa?)—have responded with enthusiasm when invited by Lucas and others to take economic theory completely seriously in thinking about macroeconomic issues.

Tobin (1971) in his *Essays in Economics* criticizes "Keynesian money wage doctrine" that money wage is not an independent determinant of employment. Tobin, in the beginning, mentioned money illusion to be present in Keynes' work, although Keynes has not referred to money illusion explicitly. Tobin referred, like Leontief (1936), to the non-homogeneity of labor supply function, which is considered to imply money illusion. According to him, the thesis about the existence of involuntary unemployment, based on money illusion within the non-homogenous labor supply, is critically flawed due to the removal of certain restrictive assumptions, which clash with other basic assumptions. Particularly, the following drawbacks are identified by Tobin (1971):

- the labor as the only variable factor of production;
- money illusion built in the labor supply;
- absence of non-homogeneity implying money illusion on other markets.

The labor as the only variable factor of production

If we suppose that all factors are variable and their prices fixed, a money wage cut would result in the substitution between other factors of production and labor. Preference for cheaper labor would affect employment, and Keynes' doctrine about the money wage as a non-independent determinant of employment fails. However, Keynes rules out the possibility of substitution resulting from money wage changes by an assumption of the labor as the only variable factor. Nevertheless, Tobin criticized this assumption and added that the model may be preserved only by introducing additional assumption. If all factors are allowed to be fully employed with perfectly flexible prices, their prices would always change in the same direction and proportion as money wage rate. In case of money wage rise, employers would substitute labor with other factors. But since all other factors (apart from labor) are fully employed, substitution results only in pushing their prices up. The incentive for substitution vanishes. A similar process occurs in the case of wage cuts, which induce employers to substitute labor and reduce employment of other factors. Substitution toward labor will be prevented by a fall in the prices of these other factors to keep them at full employment.

If the price of any other factors of production was rigid, money wage cuts would induce the substitution of labor with this factor, and consequently a rise in the employment of labor. The opposite effect occurs in the case of money wage rise, when the employment of labor falls.

Money illusion built into the labor supply

Normally consumers and business firms behave consistently and rationally. Consumers maintain the same amount of consumption when their income doubles if the prices of all other things they buy double. The firm won't change its output, if the price of a product and the price of all factors change in the same proportion. When applied to the labor market, a proportionate change in money wages and all other prices keeps the labor supply unchanged. In other words, labor will react in the same way toward real wage cuts whether this cut is accompanied by a money wage cut or by a rise in current prices. In this sense the homogeneity postulate enters on markets, with all demand and supply functions being homogenous, with prices as independent variables of the zero degree. This ensures consistent, rational behavior, free of money illusion.

However, a denial of the homogeneity postulate allows for the occurrence of money illusion on the labor market as already mentioned. From Keynes' point of view, money illusion is built into the labor supply. With rising money wages, more labor will be supplied at the same real wage.

Tobin (1971) questions the relevant reasons for such non-rational behavior of labor. First, wage bargaining is affected by trade union's resistance to a cut in money wages to avoid a relative fall in real wages. In particular, the aim is to preserve real wages relative to other groups in environment of imperfect labor mobility. However, changes in the costs of living, given by price level changes, are beyond the control of labor. Money wage bargaining should be made for periods in which the cost of living is changing frequently.

Second, labor has fixed obligations in terms of money, such as debts, taxes, contractual payments in form of insurance premiums, and so on. In the case of wage cuts, they represent a greater burden despite a proportional fall of all current prices.

Third, labor exhibits inelastic expectations. For some reason workers expect a certain normal price level in future. With the same real wage, they tend to maximize their current money income (even when price level rises) by supplying more labor. With higher money income, followed by greater money savings, their future expected consumption rises due to the return of the price level to its normal level. On the contrary, workers are unwilling to accept a money wage cut (even when price level falls) due to two reasons. The first is the lack of trust that wages will rise again when prices rise, and the second is the fear of the reduction of the real value of current money savings.

Fourth, the ignorance of labor of price development or deception by money illusion might be an adequate reason. Tobin partially dismisses this explanation due to labor's conscious awareness of the cost of living in United States in 1946.

Notwithstanding, from an overall point of view, Tobin considered Keynes' assumption about non-homogenous labor supply as convincing and compatible with real-world situations.

Absence of money illusion on other markets

According to Tobin (1941), it appears surprising that Keynes' workers in the labor market are concerned with their money wages and are unconscious of price levels, whereas consumers keep an eagle eye on the price level and their real incomes. Since workers are at the same time consumers, it seems inconsistent to have both non-rational wage demand and rational consumption decisions.[11]

There seems to be partial inconsistency, since the homogeneity postulate is assumed to be present for all other demand and supply functions, but is denied for the labor supply function. The Keynesian money wage doctrine requires revision in terms of the consumption function and in terms of the supply functions of other factors. It is therefore necessary to discuss two phenomena outlined by Tobin (1941).

First, if we consider the supply of other factors, they are admitted to be fully employed with flexible prices in line with homogeneity postulate. However, Keynes puts away the existence of other factors, and thereby a distinction between labor and other factors is not present. However, owners of other factors[12] have the same reasons, like labor, to have non-rational money price demand. Frequent rigidities are present due to obligations fixed in terms of money, through contracts and inelastic price expectations. The behavior of owners of factors of production, which is subject to rigidities, implies money price demand, analogous to the non-rational money wage demand of labor. It appears that money illusion (i.e., non-homogeneity) should have been considered not only for the labor market, but for all other markets.

Second, Keynes assumes consumption to be a function of real income alone, neglecting nominal income. In other words, the same amount of goods will be consumed and saved at any level of money income, out of a given real income, in line with homogeneity postulate (Tobin 1941). This implies the rational behavior of consumers not affected by money illusion.

Once denial of the homogeneity postulate allows for money illusion in money and saving decisions, real consumption expenditure would be not only the function of money income, but also real income. In that case, nominal wage changing the level of money income and prices would affect the real demand for the consumption of goods, followed by increased output and employment. We already tackled the fact that the behavior of wage earners subject to money illusion is not consistent with an assumption of their rational behavior to the market as consumers.

If labor is subject to money illusion on the labor market, it should also be influenced by it in consumption terms to ensure consistency of Keynesian doctrine.

If we allow for money illusion on the market for consumption, there will be an inverse relationship between money income and real consumption with real income remaining constant. In the case of a money wage cut, workers are assumed to feel worse off and prefer to consume more and save less.

Inelastic expectations of labor, as one of the reasons for non-homogenous labor supply, is one effect responsible for this causality, since they also influence present consumption expenditure. If the current price level is below the level expected to prevail in the future, consumers will substitute present consumption for future consumption and thereby will save less now and more in future. If the current price level is above the expected price level, consumers will reduce present consumption in favor of a future one, and therefore will save more now and less in future. This implies that the real consumption (from the same real income) will be lower, the higher the current level of money incomes and prices.

The second effect, which implies inverse causality between money income and real consumption expenditure, is as follows. The propensity to consume is affected by the volume of accumulated savings. The greater the volume of accumulated savings, the higher the satisfaction of consumers, and the greater part of income will be devoted to consumption. These assets are assumed to be fixed in their money value, apart from equities. Now, if we suppose a higher money income and prices in general, the real value of savings will fall, thereby decreasing the marginal propensity to consume. Conversely, a general fall in incomes and prices implies a higher real value of accumulated savings and a higher marginal propensity to consume.

These two effects are thereby responsible for the fact that real consumption is an inverse function of money income and a direct function of real income.

If we apply it to a wage cut, which causes a general decline in money income and prices, an increased marginal propensity to consume will stimulate the real demand for consumption goods, and real output, income, and employment would rise. This implies that a wage would regain its independent power. Prices will be lower in the new equilibrium.

Prices will fall more than the money wage if decreasing marginal costs prevail and vice versa. In the former case, the expansion of output and employment will be greater either due to higher substitution of present for future consumption, or because of a larger increase in the real value of accumulated savings.

The case for dismissal of money illusion within Keynes' theory

As it appears, there is an inconsistency in Keynes' money wage doctrine, which failed to generalize a denial of the homogeneity postulate. Keynes introduced involuntary unemployment, which cannot be remedied by a money wage cut, implying that the wage rate does not affect employment. This doctrine succeeds due to an assumption of homogeneity on all other markets apart from labor market as Tobin (1941) states. In other words, it appears that if the denial of the homogeneity postulate (money illusion respectively), is applied on other markets, then the money wage is not a powerless instrument and affects employment. Specifically, we drop two assumptions on which this Keynesian doctrine rests. First, factors of production other than labor behave as perfectly flexible in prices and are always at full employment. Second, the effects of money illusion on real consumption expenditure, together with inelastic price expectations of accumulated savings on the propensity to consume. By dropping the former assumption, wage cuts can increase employment due to substitution, even if the level of real income is unchanged. By dropping the latter assumption, a wage cut will increase employment and real income. As a result, the withdrawal of these two assumptions makes the money wage rate an independent determinant of employment.

Therefore, the introduction of money illusion on other markets apart from the labor market implies that labor is not powerless to reduce unemployment by reducing its money wage demands.

Since Keynes' money wage theory, based on money illusion, is critically flawed due to inconsistency of assumptions, which would account for non-homogeneity on all markets, alternative explanations emerged for positive relationships between money wages and employment and the related non-neutrality of money.

One of those solutions is the "Pigou effect," proposed by Tobin (1971) as an alternative, unintended explanation. In the case of higher price levels, the higher money wage at the same real wage makes households poorer in wealth. As a result, they can afford less leisure and labor supply increases. Another reason was offered: if other determining variables denominated in the monetary unit do not rise proportionally with current prices, real consequences occur. Basically, it takes some time for these variables (such as assets, debts, and expected prices) to adjust and there is nothing irrational in the changes of labor supply or consumption, which would necessarily account for money illusion.

Although the Keynesian money wage theory exhibits inconsistency and money illusion has not been explicitly mentioned, we may not dismiss it entirely. Naturally, people are aware of the distinction between nominal and real wages. Thereby, full deception of people by money illusion in Fisher's sense is not the case. However, how do we explain the short-term horizon of behavior when people neglect changes in real wage? If an individual's wage rises by less than inflation, it indicates nothing about the development of other money wages with respect to inflation. It seems that the difference in behavioral response to a cut in a real wage based on a money wage cut or price level change, unless considered symmetrical by individuals, might account for some form of money illusion.

Additionally, it is worth emphasizing that the definition of Keynes' involuntary unemployment rests on the different response of workers to a real wage cut ensuing from a rise in price level and from a money wage cut. The difference in perception of a price level increase and nominal wage cut is allowed through the existence of a wage lag, in which output prices rise ahead of wages. This implies some form of money illusion as confirmed by Hamilton (1952), Hansen (1925), and Mitchell (1903). If, however, prices and wages should rise simultaneously, there would be no space for a different perception of workers, and thereby for money illusion.

Second, as Leontief points out, non-homogeneity of labor was not proven, but was not said to be non-existent. The assumption of labor supply to be a function of not solely real wages but also nominal ones appears to be the critical element of his critique of neoclassical theory of unemployment. In this sense, money illusion cannot be completely dismissed. Also, Tobin (1971) states that Keynes' denial of the homogeneity postulate for the labor supply is convincing and constitutes a theoretical fundament of the facts of real economic life.

Even Wood et al. (2000) confirm Leontief's hypothesis that money illusion is present in the case of non-homogenous labor supply function of degree zero. He calls for a more precise definition of money illusion in line with Patinkin (1949), which would take into account that people affected by money illusion are not concerned with the real value of any of their assets.

Furthermore, as Trevithick (1975) claims, there is some indication of money illusion being operational in the case of a modest increase in prices in the order 5 to 10 percent. Workers do not respond to price increase by raising their labor supplied within these modest limits. The reason is that the increase in prices is sufficiently small to prevent retaliatory wage demands. Therefore, it might be regarded as some form of money illusion. However, once this threshold is exceeded, money illusion ceases to be operational.

The findings of Leontief and Trevithick suggest two conjectures about the presence of money illusion. Either Keynes was inconsistent in his theory or has not primarily focused his attention on the money illusion phenomena.

Notes

1 Ricardo's theory resembles in many aspects Fisher's monetary theory of fluctuations based on money illusion, which will be elaborated more thoroughly later.

2 The Dawes Commission proposed the Dawes Plan as an attempt in 1924 to solve the World War reparation problem and fight the hyperinflation, (Boyden, 1924).

3 As emphasized by Thaler (1997) or Dimand (1993), Fisher was a pioneer in inventing "distributed lag econometrics."

4 The term used by Fisher in the title of his article from 1923 "The Business Cycle Largely a Dance of Dollar."

5 The possibility of monetary influence on the economy might be achieved according to Leontief (1936) either by introduction of time lags and frictions of various kinds as modern orthodox monetary theory does or by violating homogeneity postulate. Although J. M. Keynes does not neglect time-lag phenomena, introduction of non-homogeneity assumption itself is sufficient to make behavior of money non-neutral.

6 Tobin's view will be subject to further elaboration later.

7 The money illusion argument (implicitly present in Keynes' work), was utilized in the Phillips Curve debates of 1970s, which will be subject to discussion in Chapter 2.

8 It is worth to note that this claim has been amended later by Keynes (1939) in his article "Relative Movements of Real Wages and Output," in which real wages could be even procyclical, (develop in the same direction with nominal wages). This argument will be subject to elaboration later.

9 Relevance of this issue will be discussed in consequent section in works of Tobin.

10 A method of compulsory saving was based on the obligatory saving of a part of income, whose consumption was deferred until the end of the war (45Keynes 1940).
11 Here we may refer to earlier considerations of Leijonhufvud, which were mentioned previously.
12 Other factors include not only the services of land, other natural agents, or existing items of capital equipment, but also services and unfinished goods that serve as inputs for other firms.

References

Agell, J. and Lundborg, P., 2003. Survey Evidence on Wage Rigidity and Unemployment: Sweden in the 1990s. *Scandinavian Journal of Economics*, 105 (1), pp. 15–30.

Akerlof, G. A., 2002. Behavioral Macroeconomics and Macroeconomic Behavior. *American Economic Review*, 92 (3), pp. 411–433.

Akerlof, G. A. and Shiller, R., J., 2009. *Animal Spirits, How Human Psychology Drives the Economy and why it Matters for Global Capitalism*, Princeton, NJ: Princeton University Press.

Akerlof, G. A. and Yellen, J. L., 1985. A Near-Rational Model of the Business Cycle, with Wage and Price Intertia. *Quarterly Journal of Economics*, 100 (5), pp. 823–838.

Alchian, A. A., 1969. Information Costs, Pricing and Resource Unemployment. *Economic Inquiry*, 7 (2), pp. 109–128, June.

Alchian, A. A. and Kessel, R. A., 1959. Real Wages in the North during the Civil War: Mitchell's Data Reconsidered. *Journal of Law and Economics*, 2, pp. 95–114.

Alchian, A. A. and Kessel, R. A., 1960. The Meaning and Validity of the Inflation-Induced Lag of Wages Behind Prices. *American Economic Review*, 50 (1), pp. 43–66.

Basak, S. and Yan, H., 2010. Equilibrium Asset Prices and Investor Behavior in the Presence of Money Illusion. *Review of Economic Studies*, 77 (3), pp. 914–936.

Basu, S., Markov, S., and Shivakumar, L., 2010. Inflation, Earnings Forecasts, and Post-Earnings Announcement Drift. *Review of Accounting Studies*, 15 (2), pp. 403–440.

Boyden, R. W., 1924. The Dawes Report. *Foreign Affairs*, 2 (4), pp. 583–597.

Brunnermeier, K. M. and Julliard, C., 2008. The Causes and Consequences of Recent Financial Market Bubbles. *The Review of Financial Studies*, 21 (1), pp. 135–180.

Cannon, E. and Cipriani, G., 2006. Euro-Illusion: A Natural Experiment. *Journal of Money, Credit and Banking*, 38 (5), pp. 1391–1403.

Cohen, R. B., Polk, C., and Vuolteenaho, T., 2005. Money Illusion in the Stock Market: The Modigliani-Cohn Hypothesis. *Quarterly Journal of Economics*, 120 (2), pp. 639–668.

Dimand, R. W., 1993. The Dance of the Dollar, Irving Fisher's Monetary Theory of Economic Fluctuations. *History of Economics Review*, 20 (1), pp. 161–172.

Dimand, R. W., 2014. James Tobin and Modern Monetary Theory. *Chope* WP No. 2014–05, Center for the History of Political Economy at Duke University.

Duesenberry, J., 1950. The Mechanism of Inflation. *Review of Economics and Statistics*, 32 (2), pp. 144–149.

Dusansky, R., 1980. Utility Function Transformations and Money Illusion: Reply and Further Results. *American Economic Review*, 70 (4), pp. 823–825.

Fehr, E. and Tyran, J., 2001. Does Money Illusion Matter? *American Economic Review*, 91 (5), pp. 1239–1262.

Ferguson, B. S., 2013. Lectures on John Maynard Keynes' General Theory of Employment, Interest and Money (2): Chapter 2, The Postulates of the Classical Economics. *University of Guelph Department of Economics and Finance Working Paper* No. 2013–07.

Filene, E. A., 1923. Minimum Wage. *Monthly Labor Review*, 17 (1), pp. 116–119.

Fisher, I., 1913. A Compensated Dollar. *Quarterly Journal of Economics*, 27 (2), pp. 213–235.

Fisher, I., 1919. Stabilizing the Dollar. *American Economic Review*, 9 (1), Supplement, Papers and Proceedings of the Thirty-First Annual Meeting of the American Economic Association (Mar., 1919), pp. 156–160.

Fisher, I., 1922. *The Making of Index Numbers. Pollak Foundation for Economic Research*, Publication No.1, Cambridge, MA: Houghton Mifflin.

Fisher, I., 1923. Business Cycle Largely a Dance of the Dollar. *Quarterly Publications of the American Statistical Association*, 18 (144), pp. 1024–1028.

Fisher, I., 1926. A Statistical Relation between Unemployment and Price Changes. International Labor Review 13 (6), Reprinted as: I discovered Phillips Curve. *Journal of Political Economy*, 81 (2), pp. 496–502.

Fisher, I., 1928. *The Money Illusion*. New York: Adelphi Publishers.

Fisher, I., 1930. *The Theory of Interest*. London: Macmillan.

Glasner, D., 2012. Money Wages and Money Illusion, Discussion of Alchian, A., Thompson, E., *blog uneasymoney.com*. Available at: www.uneasymoney.com [Accessed 19 September 2016].

Haberler, G., 1941. *Prosperity and Depression*. 3rd edition, Geneva: League of Nations.

Hahn, L. A., 1947. The Economics of Illusion. A Lecture at the Studiengessellschaft fur Wirtschaftspolitik, Zuirch, Switzerland, 12 September 1947. Available at: https://mises.org/library/economics-illusion [Accessed 19 September 2016].

Haltiwanger, J. and Waldman, M., 1985. Rational Expectations and the Limits of Rationality: An Analysis of Heterogeneity. *American Economic Review*, 75 (3), pp. 326–340.

Hamilton, E. J., 1952. Prices and Progress. *Journal of Economic History*, 12 (4), pp. 325–349.

Hansen, A. H., 1925. Factors Affecting the Trend of Real Wages. *American Economic Review*, 15 (1), pp. 27–42.

Howitt, P., 1987. Money Illusion. In J. Eatwell, M. Milgate and P. Newman (1987), *The New Palgrave: A Dictionary of Economics*, New York: W. W. Norton, pp. 519–519.

Howitt, P., 1989. Money Illusion. In J. Eatwell, M. Milgate and P. Newman (eds.), *The New Palgrave: Money*. New York: Norton.

Howitt, P. and Patinkin, D., 1980a. Utility Function Transformations and Money Illusion: Comment. *American Economic Review*, 70 (4), pp. 819–822.

Howitt, P. and Patinkin, D., 1980b. Utility Function Transformations and Money Illusion: A Further Comment. *American Economic Review*, 70 (4), pp. 826–828.

Kahneman, D. and Tversky, A. (eds.), 2000. *Choices, Values, and Frames*. New York: Cambridge University Press.

Keynes, J. M., 1923. *A Tract on Monetary Reform*. London: Macmillan.

Keynes, J. M., 1925. The Economic Position in England, 14 September 1925. Available at: http://la.utexas.edu/users/hcleaver/368/368keynespositiontable.pdf [Accessed 19 September 2016].

Keynes, J. M., 1930a. The Question of High Wages. In *The Collected Writings of John Maynard Keynes*, Vol. 10, London: Macmillan, pp. 3–16.

Keynes, J. M., 1930b. Economic Possibilities for our Grandchildren. In *The Collected Writings of John Maynard Keynes*, Vol. 9, London: Macmillan, pp. 321–332.

Keynes, J. M., 1936. *The General Theory of Interest Employment and Money*. London: Macmillan. Available at: http://cas.umkc.edu/economics/people/facultypages/kregel/courses/econ645/winter2011/generaltheory.pdf [Accessed 19 September 2016].

Keynes, J. M., 1939. Relative Movements of Real Wages and Output. *Economic Journal*, 49 (193), pp. 34–51.
Keynes, J. M., 1940. *How to Pay for the War: A Radical Plan for the Chancellor of the Exchequer*. London: Macmillan.
Keynes, J. M., 1941. P.R.O.T. 171, *The Theory of the Gap*, 26 December 1940.
Leontief, W., 1936. The Fundamental Assumptions of Mr Keynes' Monetary Theory of Unemployment. *Quarterly Journal of Economics*, 5 (4), pp. 192–197.
LeRoy, S. F., 1985. Book Review: Worswick and Trevithick (eds.), Keynes and the Modern World: Proceedings of the Keynes Centenary Conference. *History of Political Economy* 17 (4), pp. 671–674.
Lerner, E. M., 1956. Inflation in the Confederacy, 1961–65. In M. Friedman (ed.) *Studies in the Quantity Theory of Money*, Chicago, IL: University of Chicago Press.
Littleboy, B., 2013. *On Interpreting Keynes: A Study in Reconciliation*. London Routledge.
Lucas, R. E. Jr and Rapping, L. A., 1969. Real Wages, Employment, and Inflation. *Journal of Political Economy*, 77 (5), pp. 721–754.
Maital, S., 1972. Inflation, Taxation and Equity: How to Pay for the War Revisited. *Economic Journal*, 82 (325), pp. 158–169.
Marshall, A., 1907. *Principles of Economics*. 5th edition. London: MacMillan.
Miao, J. and Xie, D., 2013. Economic Growth under Money Illusion. *Journal of Economic Dynamics and Control*, 37 (2013), pp. 84–103.
Mitchell, W. C., 1903. *A History of the Greenbacks*. Chicago, IL: University of Chicago Press.
Mitchell, W. C., 1923. *Business Cycles*. Chapter 1 of Business Cycles and Unemployment, New York: McGraw Hill for the NBER. Reprint 1944 in Gottfried Haberler (ed.), *Readings in Business Cycle Theory*, Philadelphia: Blakiston for the American Economic Association.
Modigliani, F. and Cohn, A. F., 1979. Inflation, Rational Evaluation and the Market. *Financial Analyst Journal*, 35 (2), pp. 24–44.
Moore, H. L., 1923. *Generating Economic Cycles*. New York: Macmillan.
Patinkin, D., 1949. The Indeterminacy of Absolute Prices in Classical Economic Theory. *Econometrica*, 17 (1), pp. 1–27.
Patinkin, D., 1965. *Money, Interest and Prices*. 2nd edition. New York: Harper and Row.
Patinkin, D., 1987. Walras's Law. In J. Eatwell, M. Milgate, and P. Newman (eds.), *The New Palgrave: A Dictionary of Economics*. London, Macmillan.
Ricardo, D., 1811. *The High Price of Bullion*. 4th edition, London, pp. 35–37.
Rutledge, J., 1977. Irving Fisher and Autoregressive Expectations. *American Economic Review*, 67 (1), pp. 200–205.
Schumpeter, J. A., 1935. The Analysis of Economic Change. *Review of Economic Statistics* 17. As reprinted in Gottfried Haberler, (ed.), *Readings in Business Cycles Theory*. Philadelphia: Blakiston for the American Economic Association, 1944.
Schumpeter, J. A., 1939. *Business Cycles*. New York: McGraw-Hill.
Shafir, E., Diamond, P., and Tversky, A., 1997. Money Illusion. *Quarterly Journal of Economics*, 112 (2), pp. 341–374.
Smith, E. L., 1928. *Common Stocks as Long Term Investments*. Reprint 2012, Eastford, CT: Martino Fine Books.
Smithies, A., 1942. The Behavior of Money National Income Under Inflationary Conditions. *Quarterly Journal of Economics*, 57 (1), pp. 113–128.
Thaler, R., 1997. Irving Fisher: Modern Behavioral Economist. *American Economic Review*, 87 (2), Papers and Proceedings of the Hundred and Fourth Annual Meeting of the American Economic Association, pp. 439–441.

Tobin, J., 1941. A Note on the Money Wage Problem. *Quarterly Journal of Economics*, 55 (3), pp. 508–516.

Tobin, J., 1971. *Essays in Economics*. Vol. 1. Amsterdam: North Holland.

Tobin, J., 1972. Inflation and Unemployment. *American Economic Review*, 62 (1), pp. 1–18.

Tobin, J., 1987. Irving Fisher. In John Eatwell, Murray Milgate and Peter Newman (eds.), *The New Palgrave: A Dictionary of Economics*, Vol. 2, London and New York: Stockton Press.

Trevithick, J. A., 1975. Inflation and Money Illusion. *Economic Journal*, 85 (337), pp. 101–113.

Tyran, J. R., 1999. *Money Illusion and Strategic Complementarity as Causes of Monetary Non-Neutrality*. Berlin: Springer.

Van Strum, K. S., 1925. Investing in Purchasing Power. Reprint 2010, Whitefish, MT: Kessinger Publishing, LLC.

Vaona, A., 2013. Money Illusion and the Long-Run Phillips Curve in Staggered Wage-Setting models. *Research in Economics*, 67 (1), pp. 88–99.

Wood, C. and Kates, S., 2000. *John Baptiste Say: Critical Assessments of Leading Economists*. London: Routledge.

2 Rejection of money illusion

An economic theorist can, of course commit no greater crime than to assume money illusion.

(Tobin 1972, p. 3)

The process of the erosion of money illusion in Fisher's sense, followed by the critique of non-homogenous labor supply within Keynesian theory called for further elaboration of the existence of the money illusion concept. This has been reflected in the theory of the natural rate of unemployment, crowned later by the rational expectations hypothesis with no space left for money illusion. In response to the rational expectations revolution, economics schools like New Classics or New Keynesian resting on the assumption of "as if" full rationality, aimed to account for alternative explanation for the non-neutrality of money, the former based on informational frictions, the latter on price adjustment costs. Later, small deviations from rationality have been admitted in the form of near-rationality by some economists. This chapter will evaluate the position of money illusion at the time of Phillips' curve utilization, during the rational expectations revolution and afterwards with the appearance of alternative theories accounting for the non-neutrality of money. Finally, it will be shown, that consideration about small deviations from rationality connected with behavioral economics, might alleviate the denial of the money illusion phenomenon induced by the rational expectations revolution.

Money illusion utilization in Phillips curve debates

Money illusion received considerable attention in the Phillips curve debates of the 1970s.

New Zealand-born economist A.W. Phillips (1958) put this theory forward in his article "The Relation between Unemployment and the Rate of Change of Money Wage Rates in the United Kingdom, 1861–1957," in which he estimated empirically the negative relation between wage inflation and the rate of unemployment. Fall in unemployment was associated with higher wage inflation and vice versa. This relationship was quickly transformed from wage inflation to price inflation by Samuelson and Solow (1960) through an assumption of prices being a constant percentage mark up over wages. Although the Phillips curve was considered by its inventor as some interesting oddity, Phillips had never expected such a powerful response. The Phillips curve was utilized by Keynesian economists to serve as an appealing instrument for policy makers. The stable trade-off between inflation and unemployment looked like a simple choice to keep unemployment at low level at some constant rate of inflation. Furthermore, it was not unusual to hear that this policy device rested on Keynes' assumption of workers suffering from money illusion.

As Tobin (1987, p. 6) pointed out:

> The Phillips curve idea is in a sense a reincarnation in dynamic guise of the original Keynesian idea off money illusion in the supply of labor. The Phillips curve says that increase in money wages-and more general, other money incomes-are in some significant degree prized for themselves, even if they do not result in equivalent gains in real incomes.

As already mentioned in Chapter 1, Keynes described the behavior of workers tolerating real wage cuts due to an increase in the cost of living, but not tolerating real wage cuts due to money wage cuts. Workers subject to money illusion are not aware of the fact that rising inflation will reduce their purchasing power. This money illusion concept was a piece of knowledge on which the Phillips curve as a policy device was based. However, workers will tolerate a wage lag behind the cost of living only to a certain degree. Once price changes proceed to an extreme degree and affect substantially the standard of living, labor will eventually react. This was the argument opposing the utilization of Phillips curve as a policy device. Soon, workers' response to the inflation of the 1970s was bargaining for real wages by having contracts that incorporate cost of living adjustments. As a result, the trade-off between unemployment and inflation is not as stable as it appears and soon vanishes. However, as Ferguson (2013) states, it was not uncommon to hear at that time that Keynes assumed workers to suffer from money illusion.

Natural theory of unemployment coincides with money illusion

Phillips wrote his article for a world in which everyone anticipated stable nominal prices. People therefore bid only for a nominal wage increase depending on the level of unemployment. Basically, it contained the failure to distinguish between nominal and real wages. Friedman suggested that it is impossible to fool all of the people all of the time and refuted the notion of a stable Phillips curve.

The natural rate hypothesis

Milton Friedman's presidential Address to the American Economic Association in Washington, DC on December 29, 1967, published as "The role of monetary policy" in 1968, introduced a natural rate of unemployment[1] inferred from the general principle of adding inflationary expectations one for one in the wage and price setting, where no trade-off between inflation and unemployment existed in the long run.[2] Contrary to the previous belief that people bid for nominal wages, Friedman considered such behavior irrational. The labor supply curve does not depend on a nominal wage, but instead workers bargain for real wages where inflationary expectations are added apart from a wage increase at a given level of unemployment. The absence of money illusion was a critical assumption for emphasizing the natural rate of unemployment. This theory was in line with the scientific conception of the behavior based on principles of maximization with no space for money illusion.

Disregarding money illusion went particularly far with the statement from Tobin (1972), who wrote in his article "Inflation and Unemployment" (1972, p. 3): "An economic theorist can, of course commit no greater crime than to assume money illusion." It is important to note that this statement was already mentioned at Tobin's presidential address to the American Economic Association, just four years after the introduction of Friedman's natural rate theory.

The mechanism suggested by Friedman was as follows: if the monetary authority tries to target a rate of unemployment below the natural rate, the authority will increase the monetary growth, which will lower the interest rate, followed by a rise in spending and income. A rise in income will be followed by an increase in output and employment. This is possible, because prices are expected to be stable and wages and prices are set for some time in the future. Producers will respond by increasing output and workers will be willing to work for longer, which is in line with standard doctrine.

Friedman (1968) put emphasis on the fact that prices of factors of production lag behind the selling prices of products. This is responsible for a simultaneous fall *ex post* in real wages to employers and rise *ex ante* in real wages to employees.[3] This fact leads to rise in employment.

A high demand for labor and a high demand for goods under low unemployment conditions will stimulate firms to increase their prices relative to others. These price increases will exceed inflationary expectations. Additionally, the decline *ex post* in real wages will affect anticipation of employees who will realize a fall in their standard of living. As a result, they revise their inflation expectations and bid for higher nominal wages. However, since unemployment is below the natural level, there is still an excess of demand for labor. Firms will continue to set their prices in advance of inflation expectations. This will provoke employees again to revise their inflation expectations and to bid for higher nominal wages to compensate for their fall in standard of living. This process will tend to raise real wages, which in turn will ensure return of unemployment to its natural rate. If inflationary expectations are added one-for-one in both wage and price settings, then there is only one level of unemployment called "natural" one. As a result, a long run trade-off between inflation and unemployment may be dismissed. This suggests that if the monetary authority wants to keep unemployment below its natural level, it has to raise monetary growth even further, which leads to an acceleration of inflation. Conversely, if the monetary authority chooses to target unemployment above the natural rate, it will decrease monetary growth and produce deflation and an accelerating deflation at that (Friedman 1968, 1976).

It is important to note that Friedman has not denied a temporary trade-off between inflation and unemployment. He just suggested that there is no permanent trade-off. The temporary trade-off comes from unanticipated inflation (from rising inflation), but any attempt to use it will only result in accelerating inflation.

Based on that, recommendations for monetary policy have been formulated by Friedman (1968). The monetary authority can control nominal quantities to peg a nominal quantity (such as an exchange rate, the price level, the nominal level of national income, the quantity of money), but is unable to peg real quantities (such as the real interest rate, the rate of unemployment, the level of real national income, etc.) through this channel. As a result, monetary authorities were recommended to stabilize unemployment around natural level and avoid an inflationary or deflationary spiral.

Implications for money illusion

Money illusion is believed to be instrumental in Friedman's theory, although the term was not mentioned explicitly in his work, similarly to Keynes.

Friedman admits that money illusion is present only under the assumption that wage and price setters fail to update inflationary expectations within wage bargaining and price setting. Apparently, it is clear from a previous description that workers based their decision on real wage. However, as already mentioned, the lag of prices of factors of production behind the selling prices of products causes workers to rely on *ex ante* (higher) real wage. A false perception of workers affected by money illusion leads to the fact that nominal wages don't rise proportionally with inflation. Workers are not able to identify a fall in their purchasing power and their expectations are lower than current price level. This induces them to supply more labor, despite their real wage having *ex post* fallen. Thus, money illusion is responsible in the short run for the trade-off between inflation and unemployment, implying thereby non-neutrality of money.

However, once inflationary expectations are added one-for-one in wage and price setting, there is no space for money illusion at all. Workers will break though the money illusion and start to target *ex post* real wage, bidding for higher nominal wages. The supply of labor will slide back down after updating their inflation expectations, followed by a reduction of employers' demand for labor. Real wage will soon rise to its initial level and unemployment will converge to its natural rate, at which a rise in nominal wages is proportional to a rise in prices. As a result, there is no space for money illusion in the long run.

On the contrary, workers in Keynes' view stipulate for relative real wage and not for real wage like in Friedman's sense. It is worth emphasizing Keynes' statement that workers are in his view unconsciously more reasonable economists than classical school. Whereas Friedman's theory of expectation rests on its adaptive nature based on past experience, workers in Keynes' view are not deceived as might be the case at the first sight. They notice that real wage falls due to rise in price level, but tolerate it within certain limits. Anyway, they tend to measure their wages in nominal terms instead of measuring its real buying power. Once the price level is higher, workers neglect the fall in their standard of living, fail to negotiate, and supply the same quantity of labor at a lower real wage. As a result, labor supply is rather a function of nominal wage than real wage due to money illusion. As already argued before, time lags also play a substantial role in Keynes' work, but his explanation is not based on *ex ante* and *ex post* real wage. Time lags in wage adjustment toward inflationary disturbance imply that workers convey in a different way, information about reduction in real wages caused by rising prices and information about reduction in real wages caused by a cut in money wages.

We may find few common links in the description of Friedman's and Keynes' mechanism, which generates money illusion.

First, as Wood et al. (1990) indicate, the countercyclical real wage theory of Keynes proved to be essential for Friedman's employment theory. A fall in the real wage was necessary to generate an initial increase in employment of workers, affected by money illusion. It also played a role in the automatic reversal of the employment, since the ensuing rise in the real wage caused employers to reduce their demand for labor and employees to turn back down their supply curve. Although the countercyclical real wage concept was a cornerstone in Friedman's explanation, it is striking that Friedman assigns such importance to the lack of empirical evidence of a countercyclical real wage in criticizing Keynes. Actually, it is difficult to reconcile Friedman's interpretation in 1970 with his later interpretation in 1972 and 1976. The interpretation of Friedman in 1970 suggests that nominal wages and prices are said to be rigid and the real wage may be unaffected by a change in demand. However, Friedman in 1972 and 1976 interprets Keynes in such a way that an increase in prices produces a fall in the actual real wage and this causes a rise in employment due to the willingness of workers to accept lower wages.

Second, it might be said that Friedman's short-run Phillips curve based on expectations, explains the non-homogenous nature of labor supply of degree zero. Expectations of workers lagging behind the current price level are responsible for the fact that nominal wages don't rise proportionally with inflation. Whereas workers always satisfy the homogeneity postulate in terms of perceived real wages, it is not satisfied in the short run due to errors in expectations. Once expectations are updated, the homogeneity postulate is satisfied since inflationary expectations would be added one-for-one in wage and price setting. As a result, money illusion ceases in the long run. Thus, we may find important ties with Leontief's definition of money illusion based on denial of homogeneity postulate. Since Keynes' implicit concept of money illusion rests on Leontief's formulation, non-homogeneity postulate is another common feature.

Another common link between Keynes and Friedman theory in terms of money illusion is its relevance in case of higher price variability.

In Friedman's sense, money illusion is not operational in the short run, when prices are not stable. A reasonably stable relationship between inflation and unemployment is ensured for any period for which the average rate of change of prices (the anticipated rate), has been relatively stable. Thus, Phillips curve is stable in the case of simultaneous co-movement of nominal and real wages. However, higher variability of the average rate of price change of some countries represents a problem since the Phillips curve won't be well defined. As a result, a stable relationship between inflation and unemployment does not hold already in the short run and money illusion is not operating. Instead, the Phillips analysis should be restated in terms of the rate of change of real wages (more specifically anticipated real wages) to account for the stable Phillips' curve relationship.

We may find this reminiscent of Keynes' theory of money illusion. Workers exhibit money illusion only under a modest increase in prices of negligible order. However, money illusion ceases to be operational once it exceeds a particular threshold limit. Workers will be no longer be tolerant of a decrease in their purchasing power.

Money illusion and rational expectations revolution

Since the success of the rational expectations revolution (Muth 1961; Lucas 1972), economists have regarded money illusion as a concept which implies a lack of rationality, that is, something which is in contradiction with economists' assumptions of rational, profit-maximizing agents. Since these models in general focus solely on the equilibrium state of economies without consideration of how economic agents move from the one equilibrium to the other, the presumption of the absence of money illusion is in line with the equilibrium assumption. In other words, it is highly improbable for money illusion to persist in the equilibrium. Instead, a dichotomy takes place where agents successfully set apart real and nominal values. To account for the short-run non-neutrality of money, two economic streams emerged after the rational expectations revolution. New Classical economists in the vein of Lucas (1972) work up informational frictions, whereas New Keynesian economists focus on price adjustment costs (Mankiw 1985), sticky information (Mankiw and Reis 2002) and staggered contracts (Fischer 1977; Taylor 1979; Mankiw and Romer 1991). This section will outline the evolution of the rational expectation revolution and identify its ties to money illusion concept.

Reconciliation of rational behavior with money illusion

Before the formalization and introduction of the theory of rational expectations into economics, Lucas had not abandoned adaptive expectations altogether and instead incorporated money illusion within labor supply and tried to make it consistent with the rationality assumption. In his study, co-authored with Rapping (1969), they explore the workings of the American labor market with a secondary purpose of rationalizing supply and demand terms of the observed relationship between inflation and the unemployment rate, or Phillips curve. The model is quite extensive, but it is worth addressing a few features with respect to money illusion. The model itself builds a form of the money illusion defined as a non-homogenous labor supply function of degree zero in current prices and money wages, in line with the Leontiefian and Keynesian view.[4] It is emphasized that money illusion is present in the supply of labor. However, money illusion is not caused by a myopic concentration of money values, but rather ensues from an assumption of the adaptive behavior of the suppliers of labor, who expect a return to normal price level regardless of current prices, and from the empirical observation that the nominal interest rate does not change proportionally to the actual inflation rate. With a rising price level, workers affected by money illusion increase their current supply of labor and current savings.

The mechanism for money illusion is induced by the labor supply choice depending on a multi-period decision problem, in which the non-homogenous labor supply function of zero degree in current money wages and prices is put in line with the rational behavior of households. Particularly, a model of the aggregate supply function rests on the Fisherian two-period model of a representative household. Suppliers of labor react to an anticipated normal (permanent) real wage, to the deviation of the current real wage from normal wage rate, and to the deviation of the price level from its normal trend. The first having negligible effect on labor supply, the last two having a strong positive effect. The demand side of the market is derived from marginal productivity. However, the asymmetrical treatment of demand and supply of labor with respect to homogeneity mentioned by Lucas and Rapping (1969) persists. Thus, critical thought, mentioned by Tobin (1971) in Chapter 1, with respect to the inconsistency of the homogeneity postulate, is neglected and unexplained.

Lucas and Raping (1969) based their money illusion assertion on the thoughts of Hicks (1946), who thoroughly describes the reluctant attitude of concerned parties to bargain for money wages due to their inability to distinguish between permanent and temporary changes. Agents have some sense of normal prices, but it takes time for them to find out that price changes are not temporary, but permanent, which explains the rigidity of wages and slow adjustment. The rigidity of money wages ceases once parties become convinced that price changes are permanent and update their expectations.

Second, the money illusion assertion is based on the thoughts of Tobin (1952) and his concept of inelastic price expectations of labor. Wage earners expect a certain normal price level to prevail in the future, regardless of the current price level. As a result, with rising prices, they tend to achieve the highest possible money income with the same real income and increase their supply of labor. With higher money income, their money savings increase, implying higher expected consumption opportunities in future.

The article was aiming at the reconciliation of rational behavior with money illusion in the sense of non-homogenous labor supply of zero degree in current money wages and prices. Dealing with the inconsistency of the homogeneity postulate was not subject to attention as it was not the aim of the paper. The main message of importance to us is that only the short-run trade-off between inflation and unemployment is the case in line with Friedman (1968). The long-run trade-off is dismissed, since the empirical performance of the Phillips curve is highly unstable across countries with different inflation rates or rates of productivity change. Also, the trade-off is impossible for countries tolerating high rates of inflation, which is consistent with the claims of Friedman and Keynes that money illusion (and thereby trade-off) is no longer relevant once inflation exceeds particular threshold.

Rational expectations revolution and denial of money illusion

An article by Lucas (1972) was the turning point that triggered the rational expectations revolution. Money illusion as such was rigorously excluded from the analysis with the arrival of the concept of so-called "rational expectations." Agents, free of money illusion, behave optimally and form expectations optimally based on the available information and in an environment where all prices are clearing.

Lucas created an environment in which information has imperfect character due to a crucial assumption about traders randomly allocated over two physically separated markets. This also enabled the introduction of the first source of disturbance, that is, fluctuations in relative prices between the two markets. The second source of disturbance was random fluctuations in the quantity of money. Information about the development of real and monetary disturbances is transmitted to agents in the form of prices. However, prices provide imperfect information about the kind of disturbance, since each agent knows information from his own market. As a result, "agents hedge on whether a particular price movement results from a relative demand shift or a nominal (monetary) one" (Lucas 1972, p. 103). This hedging behavior is of crucial importance since agents, due to imperfect information, have difficulties in distinguishing between those two disturbances.

In line with the Lucas–Phelps model (Lucas 1972; Phelps 1970), the producer is uncertain whether a change in the price of the product reflects a change in its relative price or a change in the aggregate price level. Since the producer suffers from a signal extraction problem, he or she considers that there is some probability that a rise in the price of his or her product reflects partially a rise in the relative price, apart from some rise in the price level. This induces the producer to increase their production. As a result, an erroneous estimation of price development on the side of producers motivates producers to rise the product. This concept therefore allows for a short-run non-neutrality of money and the nature of the Phillips curve observed which, however, breaks in the long run. In other words, the long run neutrality of money is present in line with the classical view and there is no exploitable trade-off between inflation and unemployment. Within the scope of these considerations, Lucas formulated implications for a monetary policy inspired by Friedman, by introducing a so-called "k-percent rule." The k-percent rule, by fixing the rate of growth at a constant percentage rate k, represents a policy leading to a competitive Pareto-optimal allocation. Furthermore, he suggested that only unanticipated changes in the quantity of money will lead to real effects, whereas an anticipated change will be expected to affect all prices proportionately (Lucas 1973, 1975).

The theory of rational expectations, based on the nature of imperfect information, became much more representative than the conventional adaptive expectations approach. As such, the nature of imperfect information leaves no scope for the presence of money illusion. The rational expectations hypothesis has become the fundamental assumption of mainstream economics because of its simple and elegant manner.

Ironically, some economists argue about the nature of imperfect information model of New Classical economics presented by Lucas (1981), among them Manski (2004), Mises (1998), Rutherford (1984), and Miller et al. (1975).[5] To mention one with respect to money illusion, the Lucas model is considered to incorporate, by its nature, features similar to a formalization of money illusion, as suggested by Dimand (2014). A suggested interpretation is as follows: workers, who find themselves on imperfectly communicating islands, tend to be deceived by money illusion, since they regard changes in money wages as changes in real wages. As a result, employment fluctuates. An example is provided of the lasting unemployment of the 1930s, which could be clarified within the model by assuming that workers in the United States learned for several years about the Great Depression and the price level decline.

However, since no better alternative was developed, rational expectations represent the most suitable mechanism frequently incorporated in mainstream economic models. As Rutherford (1984) claims, neither Keynes nor the post-Keynesians provided satisfactory alternatives and instead remained caught within similar presumptions, like neoclassicists. Also, Manski (2004) claims that rational expectations have one big advantage over adaptive ones. To assume that expectations of agents just depend on past observations implies the assumption that agents are stupid. Furthermore, it is more comfortable to follow rational expectations convention in the model, than to infer the character of expectations possessed by agents. Also rational expectations can't be challenged on data grounds. If expectations are measured with surveys, it may happen that the theoretical model, econometric method, and the expectations data are exposed to distortion. If, instead, rational expectations are assumed, the behavior of people may distort only the model itself. Substituting theoretical assumptions for empirical results makes the model subject to less distortion. As a result, further discussion on the critique of rational expectations is irrelevant and beyond the scope of this book.

Money illusion and other theories explaining non-neutrality of money

After the rational expectations revolution, it appeared that the concept of money illusion was too simple and ad-hoc to account for the non-neutrality of money. There was suddenly a challenge for economists to identify various factors other than money illusion, which may account for nominal rigidities and the non-neutrality of money.[6] As argued by Akerlof and Yellen (1987), it is not sufficient to explain nominal rigidity by assuming that markets do not clear based on trade union policy or implicit contracts. Even economy characterized by real rigidities like in efficiency wage models, is not sufficient to account for nominal rigidities and the consequent neutrality of money. However, it appears, according to Tyran (1999), that the combination of real rigidities with exogenous nominal frictions (like menu costs), or with boundedly rational agents, is a sufficient combination to explain non-neutrality of money. In other words, the assumption of boundedly rational agents accounts for the endogenous nature of nominal rigidities. As money illusion was dismissed, economists aimed to find another explanation, sticking to the "as if assumption" of full rationality, like New Keynesians (price adjustment costs) or New Classical Economists (informational frictions). However, some theories admit that the small exactly defined deviation of a few actors from rationality may generate substantial economic fluctuations, such as Akerlof, Yellen (1985), Haltiwanger and Waldman, (1985, 1989).

This section will focus on a short overview of otherwise extensive literature, with attention to selected models, which explain non-neutrality of money by other means than money illusion, or money illusion is mentioned implicitly, or its presence is derived later based on behavioral features. The debate will also partially focus (where it is possible) on the identification of common or similar ties with respect to money illusion and possible implications of some of them for consequent occurrence of money illusion.

Menu costs

As already mentioned, various theories emerged to explain nominal rigidities with Mankiw (1985) among those to account for exogenous nominal frictions. An assumption of costless price adjustment is relaxed by introducing an assumption of small menu costs within the model of monopolistic competition. It is shown that in case of a nominal shock, individual losses to firms (which are in equilibrium), from not adjusting their nominal prices may be of the second order. On the contrary, the welfare effects of this non-adjustment at the aggregate level may be of the first order. The fact that the second order effect of changing prices may lead to large first order changes in output and welfare is documented also by Blanchard and Kiyotaki (1987). Effects are also analyzed under menu costs combined with monopolistic competition. Additionally, authors refer to so-called "aggregate demand externality," in which case a decrease in producer's individual price increases the demand for his goods and at the same time it increases real money balances, leading to a higher demand for other goods. In conditions of this aggregate demand externality, small menu costs can make prices sticky. When the firm decides whether to cut its price, it compares the benefit of the price cut with costs of the cut, but it ignores the aggregate demand externality. As a result, it may decide not to cut the price, despite the fact that the price cut would lead to an increase in welfare due to the aggregate demand externality.

Mankiw's concept of the first order effects of this non-adjustment were utilized in the subsequent works of Akerlof and Yellen (1985), and later also incorporated in the near-rational wage and price setting model of Akerlof, Dickens and Perry

(2000). Additionally, it has been utilized by Akerlof (2002) in his article about behavioral macroeconomics with respective ties to money illusion. Later on, theoretical fundamentals were partially utilized by Fehr and Tyran (2001) in their experimental analysis of the aggregate-level effects of money illusion, which will be subject to detailed elaboration in Chapter 3.

The concept of near-rationality

The studies of Akerlof and Yellen (1985), and later Akerlof, Dickens, and Perry (1996; 2000) represent a contribution, which abstracts from the assumption of full rationality, introducing so-called "near-rationality." It might be argued that a later study of Akerlof et al. (2000) addresses some features of behavioral economics, which are also associated with the implicit presence of money illusion. First, Akerlof and Yellen (1985), in their study, offer an explanation as to why changes in the nominal supply might not be neutral in the short run after a fully anticipated monetary shock is implemented.[7] The concept of near rationality is introduced to provide an alternative, where in fact inertial wage-price behavior may not be very costly. Firms, in the context of a monopolistically competitive economy, which adjust their wages and prices rather slowly, suffer losses from failure to optimize correctly, though such losses might be very small in terms of near-rational behavior. This is because near-rationality is suboptimal, but imposes very small individual losses on subjects compared with the consequences of their first-best policy. However, whereas near-rational inertial wage and price behavior is considered to be a second order loss to its practitioners, it might be of the first order with respect to changes in real activity. As a result, only a small amount of non-maximization behavior (inertial behavior) might yield a short-run non-neutrality of money in response to money supply shock.

Akerlof et al. (2000) introduce the model of near-rational wage and price setting based on behavioral assumptions, which translates this setting into the long-run Phillips curve and represents an alternative to the natural rate hypothesis. An important implication is rejection of a unique natural rate and the existence of the long-run Phillips curve relationship for steady and low rates of inflation.

A crucial role in their explanation is attributed to the behavior of individuals, who have the available information but treat it in a way which exhibits features of psychological bias. Near-rational individuals are aware of the costs associated with full rationality and of small losses in case of near-rationality. As a result, they tend to ignore much that could be potentially relevant and focus on the few issues that matter the most.

There are several features of this decision-making worth attention.

Simple rules are responsible for sticky wage/price behavior. According to Nisbett and Ross (1980), individuals as intuitive scientists summarize information and make choices based on simple mental frames, with reliance on the rules of thumb. As already argued, Akerlof and Yellen (1985) show that the rule of thumb of keeping prices constant following a monetary shock are a second order effect to practitioners, whereas the impact on the economy is of the first order. It is argued by Akerlof (2002) that even rules of thumb involving money illusion are sensible, since losses of this reliance are very small.

When inflation is low, near-rationality of subjects induces them not to perceive it, as consequent losses are rather small. Only once inflation tends to exceed a particular salient threshold do subjects start to perceive it. This resembles closely Keynes' implicit view of money illusion, which is present only below some particular threshold. In contrast to Keynes, the non-homogeneity of labor supply is built on behavioral features.

The behavioral features of near-rationality are well confirmed in case of employees who systematically misperceive inflation with respect to their nominal wages. Shafir, Diamond, and Tversky (1997), in their study about money illusion argue that employees are pleased with the increase in their nominal wages, although simultaneous rises in prices keep the real wage unchanged. Basically, employees fail to perceive the income in terms of buying power.

An additional feature is related to the reluctance of workers to nominal wage cuts. Akerlof et al. (2000) refers to Keynes' intuitive understanding of the psychological resistance of workers: "It is sometimes said that it would be illogical for labor to resist a reduction of money-wage, but not to resist a reduction of real wages … But whether logical or illogical, experience shows that this is how labor in fact behaves" (Keynes 1936, p. 9).

However, Akerlof (2002) emphasizes the crucial role of prospect theory. The prospect theory of Kahneman and Tversky (1979) is based on the evaluation of the gains and losses relative to some reference point. Basically, individuals suffer from loss aversion and tend to evaluate losses at much greater weight than gains. If applied to the behavior of the individual on the labor market, money wage represents the reference point in evaluating gains and losses. Naturally, if greater weight is attributed to losses, employees tend to avoid those losses, and consequently avoid wage cuts. This is empirically confirmed by Shafir et al. (1997), who posit that individuals, by voting for money wage as a reference point, exhibit some form of money illusion in terms of downward money wage rigidity. McDonald (2008) points out that certain features of the loss aversion in the case of resistance toward money wage cuts, might be identified even in Keynes theory (1936).

Furthermore, wage setting of employers is not oriented toward a real wage target, but is affected by a variety of other information. Fortin (1996) points out that the distribution of nominal wage changes is asymmetric around zero in Canadian data. Between 1992 and 1994, at 1.2 percent inflation and 11 percent unemployment, only 5.7 percent of non-COLA[8] union agreements adopted first-year wage cuts, whereas 47 percent of wages were fixed. Bewley (1999) empirically proves that managers in Connecticut were willing to cut wages as a last resort and mostly considered money wage cuts as unfair or almost insulting. Fehr and Goette (2005) find that even a long period of low inflation and low productivity growth in Switzerland has not affected the frequency of nominal wage cuts. Also, Shafir et al. (1997) note the concept of fairness makes employers reluctant to impose money wage cuts. So, although with falling inflation together with low productivity growth, the need for frequent nominal wage cuts rises rapidly, employers are quite averse to nominal wage cuts.

To sum up, the long-run trade-off between inflation and unemployment exists, according to Akerlof (2002), due to:

- An aversion on the part of employers to nominal wage cuts, which results in higher rates of unemployment. Especially the real wage is higher at every level of employment and at low inflation. Unemployment thereby rises as inflation falls to low levels.
- Non-saliency of inflation below some threshold, at which anticipated future changes in inflation are ignored in wage bargaining.

To conclude this discussion, behavioral economics contributes significantly to the thesis that under certain assumptions, monetary policy is able to affect real outcomes. In other words, very low inflation is associated with costly high unemployment and low output.

When these behavioral aspects are applied to the model of Akerlof et al. (2000), the crucial aspect is the variance of wage-setting behavior with the inflation rate. One group of firms is expected to fully incorporate wage adjustments in accordance with expected inflation; another group of firms exhibits a near-rational manner of behavior, with wage adjustment reflecting current conditions but only partially expected inflation. As already argued, near-rationality at low rates of inflation is associated with negligible losses. As a result, with little or no inflation, large fractions of the firms will exhibit near-rational behavior with incomplete wage and price adjustment. Since the behavior of near-rational and full-rational firms at low inflation coincides, equilibrium unemployment lies at its natural rate. At a higher rate of inflation, the fraction of firms being near-rational declines, because losses of near-rationality are no longer negligible. In this case, higher inflation is associated with lower unemployment, because near-rational firms increase employment and their effect prevails over the effect of fully rational firms, who cut their employment. At high inflation rates, most of the firms will be fully rational, with sufficient adjustment for expected inflation. In this case, higher inflation is associated with higher unemployment, since firms with fully rational behavior cut their employment.[9]

The concept of strategic complementarity

Haltiwanger and Waldman (1985, 1989) also relax the assumption of full rationality to demonstrate that in the economy, composed of heterogeneous agents, the nature of strategic environment determines the presence of nominal rigidities and non-neutrality of money. The economy consists not only of rational sophisticated agents, but also of naïve agents with limited ability to form expectations. In conditions of strategic complementarity, a negligible number of naïve agents appears to be disproportionately important for the adjustment at the aggregate level. On the contrary, in conditions of strategic substitutability, the few naïve agents in the economy have a disproportionally small impact on aggregate-level behavior. Ball and Romer (1991) also confirm the theoretical relevance of strategic complementarity in an explanation of rigidities in nominal wages and prices. Theoretical fundamentals of strategic complementarity have been empirically proved to hold in real economies, with important implications, as suggested by Oh and Waldman (1994).

Strategic complementarity, which will be subjected to more thorough attention later, appears to be a crucial element in the research of Fehr and Tyran (2001). In particular, it serves as an explanation of the indirect effects of money illusion with important implications at the aggregate level in terms of the non-neutrality of money.

Fischer's theory of long-term contracts

Although Fischer's model is based on an assumption of the full rationality of individuals, it is worth commenting on the possible presence/absence of behavioral features associated with money illusion. Fischer (1977) constructs a rational expectations model with overlapping labor contracts being made for two periods. The presence of these overlapping models, which are updated rather infrequently, induces an element of wage stickiness in the short run, since it provides the time for reaction of monetary authority. This has substantial implications for monetary policy in terms of the short-run non-neutrality of money. As a result, despite fully anticipated monetary policy in the economy with fully rational individuals, this element of stickiness in labor contracts affects output in the short run.

Two assumption are outlined. First, the nominal wage is assumed to be set in wage bargaining to maintain constant real wage. The potential role of a stabilizing monetary policy is induced by assuming that the economy is exposed to real supply and nominal demand disturbances. Two models are constructed, the first one with wage contracts for one period, in which the monetary policy proves to be irrelevant in terms of accommodating the current shocks. The second model is constructed with two-period non-indexed labor contracts, in which case the monetary authority has the time to react to disturbances and affects thereby the real wage for the second contractual period and thus output.

The monetary authority could lose its effectiveness in the case of more frequent indexation. Fischer argues that possible absence of these contracts in reality is due to transaction costs associated with calculation of their terms. Another reason might be that in the face of real disturbances, the real wage in the non-indexed two-period contract model proves highly unstable relative to the one-period contract. As a result, it appears that an indexed contract appears for a labor to be less attractive than a non-indexed contract.

Based on Fischer's assertion that people bargain for nominal and not real wages, a connection might be made with respect to the possible occurrence of money illusion. Shafir et al. (1997) empirically prove that a risk-averse decision-maker, who is anchoring nominal income, may perceive indexed contracting as riskier, since the resulting indexed amount might be greater or smaller in nominal terms than a fixed dollar amount. As a result, the tendency to favor an unindexed contract is strong, which is also confirmed by Akerlof and Shiller (2009) in their discussion about COLA indexation, which according to them suggests the possible presence of money illusion. This implies that particular signs of money illusion are present in Fischer's work.

There are many staggered price (wage) models in which price-wage setting is affected by keeping nominal prices fixed for a period of time. Taylor (1979) deals with a staggered contract model, in which half of firms during each period sets a nominal price that is valid for the subsequent two periods. Calvo (1983) works with a model in which fixed nominal prices are reset at randomly changing intervals. Although New Classical economists argue that such price setting is not maximizing and firms would do better by setting prices frequently in accordance with inflation expectations, Akerlof (2002) argues that behavior of firms reflects near-rational price/wage setting strategies. These are related to the already discussed behavioral concept of rule of thumb, whose effect is a second order to its practitioners, but of a first order to the economy. Mankiw and Reis (2002) argue in a similar manner in favor of near-rationality within their model based on sticky information. The difference compared to Calvo (1983) and Taylor (1979) is that prices respond slowly due to considerable costs of gathering, processing, and sharing information. An experimental evidence of near-rationality based on New Keynesian features of monopolistic competition and near-rationality was utilized by Fehr and Tyran (2001) as a basis for incorporation of money illusion phenomena. They prove (in conditions of strategic complementarity) the reluctance of firms to cut prices in response to fully anticipated negative nominal shock. Price setters may fully maximize, but in their view follow rule of thumb pricing behavior, biased by money illusion, in which they expect other firms to follow also similar biased behavior. As a result, non-neutrality of money is reinforced.

Concluding remarks

As we have seen, in studies devoted to near-rationality, strategic interactions, and others, substantial evidence about deviations from full rationality exists, supporting a further potential role for money illusion effects. These might be summarized below in line with Fehr and Tyran (2005a, 2005b), Haltiwanger and Waldman (1985), Akerlof and Yellen (1985), Kahneman and Tversky (2000), Caplan (2001), and others.

First, opponents often claim that if deviations from rationality exhibit random character, they will cancel out at the aggregate level. However, it appears that some anomalies might be characterized as having a systematic pattern rather than random, see for instance, Kahneman, Slovic and Tversky (1982), Kahneman and Tversky (1974), and Camerer (2003). Since these deviations are not random but systematic, they will not cancel out at the aggregate level, and may have substantial effects.

Second, it is argued that individuals will learn from their mistakes, even if they are sometimes irrational. However, there is a substantial number of anomalies, which are resistant to individual learning in markets, like updating of expectations in Bayesian manner (Camerer 1987; Kluger and Wyatt 2003). Thus, there is no reason to believe in the correction mechanism of markets, which will enhance rationality over time.

Third, experimental results based on competitive double auctions reveal that individual anomalies are irrelevant at the aggregate level, since markets converge to the competitive equilibrium allocation under certain conditions (Smith 1962, 1982). At the same time, however, experimental evidence suggests the presence of systematic mispricing in competitive double auctions (Smith, Suchanek and Williams 1988; Fehr and Falk 1999). Gneezy, Kapteyn, and Potters (2003) also confirm that individual deviations from full rationality may significantly affect competitive market outcomes. As a result, all individual anomalies are by no way eliminated at the aggregate level.

Additionally, opponents claim that rational agents will drive the irrational from the market over time, because they make higher profits. Their impact at the aggregate level is said to increase over time. Still this is not the case with many markets, for instance the financial market, labor market, or consumer goods market. The consumer with intransitive preferences is not driven out of the market (Laibson and Yariv 2007); the same holds for irrational traders on financial markets, who take higher risks and may experience higher returns on average, which may ensure their long-term survival (de Long et al. 1991). Professional traders might be more prone to loss aversion than ordinary individuals (Haigh and List 2005).

Furthermore, the robustness of many individual market anomalies is substantial, which refutes the commonly held view that rational participants will dominate the aggregate outcome. It has been shown that in conditions of strategic complementarity and heterogeneous agents in the economy, the behavior of rational agents is overplayed by naïve ones, leading to suboptimal adjustment and consequent effects at the aggregate level (Haltiwanger and Waldman 1985; Cooper and Haltiwanger 1996; Fehr and Tyran 2005a, 2005b, 2007, 2008). Russel and Thaler (1985) show in their study that a small fraction of rationally bounded agents might have important aggregate effects. Also, it has been demonstrated that small deviations from rationality might cause losses, which are of the second order to its participants but are of the first order to the economy (Akerlof and Yellen 1985).

The arguments reflecting departure from full rationality are a step toward the resurrection of money illusion effects. Chapter 3 will present a theoretical framework in the vein of behavioral economics, which may account for the microeconomic effects of money illusion. Subsequently, potential macroeconomic effects of money illusion will be addressed.

Notes

1 The natural rate of unemployment is an unemployment rate consistent with the labor market equilibrated by real force, that is, real wage. However, it is not immutable or unchangeable.

2 In Friedman's view, the short-run trade-off between inflation and unemployment applies only if wage and price setters suffer from money illusion.

3 In other words, employees evaluated the wages offered at previous price level, so implicitly anticipating that they have risen.

4 However, in the long run the stability of wages and prices is resolved by a long-run labor supply depending on the real wage.

5 The theory of rational expectations is subject to critical evaluation by several economists. Manski (2004), with his article in *Econometrica*, subjects the rational expectations to criticism. Supposing that the true state of nature is the realization of a random variable distributed P, an agent faces the problem of identification and induction from finite samples. The ability to draw inferences depends on the availability of the data and on the assumptions one brings to bear. Since it is difficult to learn objective probability distributions of interest, it is impossible to learn that much. Additionally, the economic model includes stochastic process, in which agents have to make guesses. Furthermore, economic agents are making the same guesses as the economist who is writing the model down. Also economic agents are unable to learn about all of the possible outcomes in the economy that never occur. At macroeconomic level, it is sometimes possible to make only one decision at a time and this kind of limited knowledge makes rational expectations especially difficult in a macroeconomic context. There are other important elements worth mentioning. One of them is the distinction between rational expectations and rational behavior, which is often dismissed. Individuals may be equally rational when forming adaptive expectations, because they may consider it as a less costly alternative to forming rational expectations. As a result, human action is necessarily always rational when not depending on the character of expectations, as suggested by Mises (1998). An additional element which polemicizes with theory of rational expectations is the nature and availability of information itself. Not only is the gathering of information costly, as Stigler (1961) suggests, but dispersion of knowledge might disable the collection of available information despite its costless nature (Hayek 1945), not leaving out the problematics of rational expectation creation with respect to different degrees of uncertainty regarding the future (Robbins 1932).

6 Causes of inertia in the adjustment of wages and prices are questioned by many economists, including Blinder et al. (1998), who conducted a survey where managers have been asked why and how they change prices.

7 Of course, Akerlof and Yellen (1985) note that anticipated monetary shock in the neoclassical model with market clearing causes no fluctuations in the rational framework. New Classical macroeconomists offer the explanation that money is non-neutral in the case of imperfectly informed rational agents fooled by unanticipated shock. However, this has been subject to considerable debate regarding its applicability. In the Keynesian model, the phenomenon of wage and price inertia causes fluctuations in real output. However, inertial behavior is irrational and costly, and substantial gains are made in the case of quick adjustment. Thus, an alternative explanation is provided as to how anticipated changes might affect real output.

8 Cola refers to the cost of living adjustment, generally equal to the percentage increase in the consumer price index.

9 Results of Akerlof et al. (2000) are consistent with research of Wyplosz (2001) in a way that unemployment tends to decline at rates of inflation above 2 percent, thereby supporting the relevance of near-rationality.

References

Akerlof, G. A., 2002. Behavioral Macroeconomics and Macroeconomic Behavior. *American Economic Review*, 92 (3), pp. 411–433.

Akerlof, G. A. and Shiller, R. J., 2009. *Animal Spirits, How Human Psychology Drives the Economy and Why It Matters for Global Capitalism*. Princeton, NJ: Princeton University Press.

Akerlof, G. A. and Yellen, J. L., 1985. A Near-Rational Model of the Business Cycle, with Wage and Price Intertia. *Quarterly Journal of Economics*, 100 (5), pp. 823–838.

Akerlof, G. A. and Yellen, J. L., 1987. Rational Models of Irrational Behavior. *American Economic Review*, 77 (2), pp. 137–142.

Akerlof, G. A., Dickens, W. T., and Perry, G. L., 1996. The Macroeconomics of Low Inflation [including comments by Gordon and Mankiw]. *Brookings Papers on Economic Activity*, 27 (1), pp. 1–59.

Akerlof, G. A., Dickens, W. T. and Perry, G. L., 2000. Near-Rational Wage and Price Setting and the Long-Run Phillips Curve. *Brookings Papers on Economic Activity*, 31 (1), pp. 1–60.

Ball, L. and Romer, D., 1991. Sticky Prices as Coordination Failure. *American Economic Review*, 81 (3), pp. 539–552.

Bewley, T. F., 1999. *Why Wages Don't Fall During a Recession*. Cambridge, MA: Harvard University Press.

Blanchard, O. J. and Kiyotaki, N., 1987. Monopolistic Competition and the Effects of Aggregate Demand. *American Economic Review*, 77 (4), pp. 647–666.

Blinder, A. S., Canetti, E. R. D., Lebow, E. D., and Rudd, J. B., 1998. *Asking About Prices: A New Approach to Understanding Price Stickiness*. New York: Russell Sage Foundation.

Calvo, G., 1983. Staggered Prices in a Utility-Maximizing Framework. *Journal of Monetary Economics*, 12 (3), pp. 383–398.

Camerer, C. F., 1987. Do Biases in Probability Judgment Matter in Markets? Experimental Evidence. *American Economic Review*, 77 (5), pp. 981–997.

Camerer, C. F., 2003. *Behavioral Game Theory: Experiments in Strategic Interaction*. Princeton, NJ: Princeton University Press.

Caplan, B., 2001. Rational Ignorance versus Rational Irrationality. *Kyklos International Review for Social Sciences*, 54 (1), pp. 3–26.

Cooper, R. W. and Haltiwanger, J., 1996. Evidence on Macroeconomic Complementarities. *Review of Economics and Statistics*, 78 (1), pp. 78–93.

De Long, J. B. and Summers, L. H., 1991. Equipment Investment and Economic Growth. *Quarterly Journal of Economics*, 106 (3), pp. 445–502.

Dimand, R. W., 2014. James Tobin and Modern Monetary Theory. *Chope* WP No. 2014-05, Center for the History of Political Economy at Duke University.

Fehr, E. and Falk, A., 1999. Wage Rigidities in a Competitive Incomplete Contract Market. *Journal of Political Economy*, 107 (1), pp. 106–134.

Fehr, E. and Goette, L., 2005. Robustness and Real Consequences of Nominal Wage Rigidity. *Journal of Monetary Economics*, 52 (4), pp. 779–804.

Fehr, E. and Tyran, J., 2001. Does Money Illusion Matter? *American Economic Review*, 91 (5), pp. 1239–1262.

Fehr, E. and Tyran, J., 2005a. Expectations and the Effects of Money Illusion. In B. Agarwal and A. Vercelli (eds.), *Psychology, Rationality and Economic Behavior: Challenging Standard Assumptions*. New York: Palgrave Macmillan/International Economic Association.

Fehr, E. and Tyran, J., 2005b. Individual Irrationality and Aggregate Outcomes. *Journal of Economic Perspectives*, (19) 4, pp. 43–66.

Fehr, E. and Tyran, J., 2007. Money Illusion and Coordination Failure. *Games and Economic Behavior*, 58 (2), pp. 246–268.

Fehr, E. and Tyran, J., 2008. Limited Rationality and Strategic Interaction: The Impact of the Strategic Environment on Nominal Inertia. *Econometrica*, Econometric Society, 76 (2), pp. 353–394.

Ferguson, B. S., 2013. Lectures on John Maynard Keynes' General Theory of Employment, Interest and Money (2): Chapter 2, The Postulates of the Classical Economics. *University of Guelph Department of Economics and Finance Working Paper* No. 2013–07.

Fischer, S., 1977. Long-Term Contracts, Rational Expectations, and the Optimal Money Supply Rule. *Journal of Political Economy*, 85 (1), pp. 191–205.

Fortin, P., 1996. The Great Canadian Slump. *Canadian Journal of Economics*, 29 (4), pp. 761–787.

Friedman, M., 1968. The Role of Monetary Policy. *American Economic Review*, 58 (1), pp. 1–17.

Friedman, M., 1970. A Theoretical Framework for Monetary Analysis. *Journal of Political Economy*, 78 (2), pp. 193–238.

Friedman, M., 1972. Comments on the Critics. *Journal of Political Economy*, 80 (5), pp. 906–950.

Friedman, M., 1976. *Price Theory*. Chicago, IL: Aldine.

Gneezy, U., Kapteyn, A., and Potters, J. J. M., 2003. Evaluation Periods and Asset Prices in a Market Experiment. *Journal of Finance*, 58 (2), pp. 821–838.

Haigh, M. S. and List, J., 2005. Do Professional Traders Exhibit Myopic Loss Aversion? An Experimental Analysis, *Journal of Finance*, 60 (1), pp. 523–534.

Haltiwanger, J. and Waldman, M., 1985. Rational Expectations and the Limits of Rationality: An Analysis of Heterogeneity. *American Economic Review*, 75 (3), pp. 326–40.

Haltiwanger, J. and Waldman, M., 1989. Limited Rationality and Strategic Complements: Implications for Macroeconomics, *Quarterly Journal of Economics*, 104 (3), pp. 463–483.

Hayek, F. A., 1945. Use of Knowledge in Society. *American Economic Review*, 35 (4), pp. 519–530.

Hicks, J., 1946. *Value and Capital*. Oxford, UK: Clarendon Press.

Kahneman, D. and Tversky, A., 1974. Judgment under Uncertainty. Heuristics and Biases. *Science*, 185 (4157), pp. 1124–1131.

Kahneman, D. and Tversky, A., 1979. Prospect Theory: An Analysis of Decision under Risk. *Econometrica*, 47 (2), pp. 263–291.

Kahneman, D. and Tversky, A. (eds.), 2000. *Choices, Values, and Frames*. New York: Cambridge University Press.

Kahneman, D., Slovic, P., and Tversky, A. (eds.), 1982. *Judgment Under Uncertainty: Heuristics and Biases*. New York: Cambridge University Press.

Keynes, J. M., 1936. *The General Theory of Interest Employment and Money*. London: Macmillan.

Kluger, B. D. and Wyatt. S. B., 2003. Are Judgment Errors Reflected in Market Prices and Allocations? Experimental Evidence Based on the Monty Hall Problem. *Journal of Finance*, 59 (3), pp. 969–97.

Laibson, D. and Yariv, L., 2007. Safety in Markets: An Impossibility Theorem for Dutch Books. Available at: www.scholar.harvard.edu/files/laibson/files/safety_in_markets_an_impossibility_theorem_for_dutch_books.pdf [Accessed 19 September 2016].

Lucas, R. E. Jr., 1972. Expectations and the Neutrality of Money. *Journal of Economic Theory*, 4 (2), April, pp. 103–124.

Lucas, R. E. Jr., 1973. Some International Evidence on Output-Inflation Tradeoffs. *American Economic Review*, 63 (3), pp. 326–334.

Lucas, R. E. Jr., 1975. An Equilibrium Model of the Business Cycle. *Journal of Political Economy*, 83 (6), pp. 1113–1144.

Lucas, R. E. Jr., 1981. *Studies in Business Cycle Theory*. Oxford, UK: Basil Blackwell, and Cambridge, MA: MIT Press.

Lucas, R. E. Jr. and Rapping, L. A, 1969. Real Wages, Employment, and Inflation. *Journal of Political Economy*, 77 (5), pp. 72–54.

Mankiw, N. G., 1985. Small Menu Costs and Large Business Cycles: A Macroeconomic Model of Monopoly. *Quarterly Journal of Economics*, 100 (2), pp. 529–537.

Mankiw, N. G. and Romer, D. H., 1991. *New Keynesian Economics*, vol. 1 and vol. 2, Cambridge, MA: MIT Press.

Mankiw, N. G. and Reis, R., 2002. Sticky Information versus Sticky Prices: A Proposal to Replace the New Keynesian Phillips Curve. *Quarterly Journal of Economics*, 117 (4), pp. 1295–1328.

Manski, Ch., 2004. Measuring Expectations. *Econometrica*, 72 (5), pp. 1329–1376.

McDonald, I., 2008. Behavioral Macroeconomics and Wage and Price Setting: Developing Some Early Insights of John Maynard Keynes and Joan Robinson. *CAMA Working Papers 2009–11*, Centre for Applied Macroeconomic Analysis, Crawford School of Public Policy, The Australian National University.

Miller, P., Nelson, C., and Supel, T., 1975. Categories of Criticism of the Rational Expectations Theory. *Working Paper 49*, Federal Reserve Bank of Minneapolis.

Mises, L., 1998. *Human Action*. Reprint of 1949, Auburn, AL: Ludwig von Mises Institute.

Muth, J. F., 1961. Rational Expectations and the Theory of Price Movements. *Econometrica*, 29 (3), pp. 315–335.

Nisbett, R. and Ross, L., 1980. *Human Inference: Strategies and Shortcomings of Social Judgement*. Englewood Cliffs, NJ: Prentice Hall.

Oh, S. and Waldman, M., 1994. Strategic Complementarity Slows Macroeconomic Adjustment to Temporary Shocks. *Economic Inquiry*, 32, pp. 318–329.

Phelps, E. S. (ed.), 1970. *Microeconomic Foundations of Employment and Inflation Theory*. New York: Norton.

Phillips, A. W., 1958. The Relation between Unemployment and the Rate of Change of Money Wage Rates in the United Kingdom, 1861–1957. *Economica*, 25 (100), pp. 283–299.

Robbins, L., 1932. *An Essay on the Nature and Significance of Economic Science*. London: Macmillan and Co.

Russel, T. and Thaler, R., 1985. The Relevance of Quasi Rationality in Competitive Markets. *American Economic Review*, 75 (5), pp. 1071–1082.

Rutherford, M., 1984. Rational Expectations and Keynesian Uncertainty: A Critique. *Journal of Post Keynesian Economics*, 6 (3), pp. 377–387.

Samuelson, P. A. and Solow, R. 1960. Analytical Aspects of Anti-Inflation Policy. *American Economic Review*, 50 (2), pp. 177–194.

Shafir, E., Diamond, P., and Tversky, A., 1997. Money Illusion. *Quarterly Journal of Economics*, 112 (2), pp. 341–374.

Smith, V. L., 1962. An Experimental Study of Competitive Market Behavior, *Journal of Political Economy*, 70 (2), pp. 111–137.

Smith, V. L., 1982. Microeconomic Systems as an Experimental Science. *American Economic Review*, 72 (5), pp. 923–955.

Smith, V. L., Suchanek, G. L. and Williams, A. W., 1988. Bubbles, Crashes and Endogenous Expectations in Experimental Spot Asset Markets. *Econometrica*, 56 (5), pp. 1119–1151.

Stigler, G. J., 1961. The Economics of Information. *Journal of Political Economy*, 69 (3), pp. 213–225.

Taylor, J. B., 1979. Staggered Wage Setting in a Macro Model. *American Economic Review*, 69 (2), pp. 108–113.

Tobin, J., 1952. Money Wage Rates and Employment. In S. E. Harris (ed.) *New Economics*, New York: Knopf.

Tobin, J., 1971. *Essays in Economics*. Macroeconomics, Vol. 1. Amsterdam: North Holland.

Tobin, J., 1972. Inflation and Unemployment. *American Economic Review*, 62 (1), pp. 1–18.

Tobin, J., 1987. *Essays in Economics: Consumption and Econometrics*, Vol. 2. Cambridge, MA: MIT Press.

Tyran, J., 1999. *Money Illusion and Strategic Complementarity as Causes of Monetary Non-Neutrality*. Lecture Notes in Economics and Mathematical Systems. Berlin Heidelberg: Springer-Verlag.

Wood, J. C. and Woods, R. N., 1990. *Milton Friedman: Critical Assessments of Contemporary Economists*, Vol. 3. London: Psychology Press.

Wyplosz, Ch., 2001. Do We Know How Low Inflation Should Be? *CEPR Discussion Papers* No. 2722.

3 Renewal of interest in money illusion

> *In fact, I am persuadable–indeed, pretty much persuaded–that money illusion is a fact of life.*
>
> Blinder (2000, p. 54)

As mentioned in Chapter 2, the position of money illusion after the introduction of the natural rate theory and the rational expectations revolution has been dismissed as irrelevant, although it had been standard fare earlier. Notwithstanding, several economists claim that complete prohibition of money illusion in the standard formulation is overly restrictive. For instance, Klevorick and Kane (1967) assert that the complete absence of money illusion is an unlikely phenomenon where only the absence of extreme money illusion is necessary for prices to be determinate, and money neutral with reference to the Patinkin model. Erber (2010) also states that disregarding money illusion completely is not a good idea with respect to the imperfect world of financial markets. Akerlof and Shiller (2009, p. 41) claim that "money illusion is another missing ingredient in modern macroeconomics," and it was present (either explicitly or implicitly) in the views of the century's leading economists, such as John Maynard Keynes, Paul Samuelson, Robert Solow, Irving Fisher, Franco Modigliani, and James Tobin. Although they consider Fisher's and Keynes' money illusion as a notably naïve belief, they also point out that it is not necessarily true that there is no money illusion at all. Money illusion is under a need of serious revision, where the natural rate theory utterly banishes money illusion on the basis of little evidence. They assert that money cannot just be a veil, since much contracting is done in money terms. If people would see through inflation, it would have no effect on transactions. But since the adjustment is not perfect, something might be lost in translation from nominal to real values. Based on that, not only mistakes in discounting but also nominal representations lead to wrong decisions that imply the presence of money illusion.

This chapter will elaborate more thoroughly on the role of behavioral economics with regard to the resurrection of money illusion. Generally, economists suppose that individual effects of money illusion cancel out at the aggregate level. The second part of this chapter will show that this presumption might not necessarily be true and money illusion under certain conditions might have considerable implications at the aggregate level in terms of the non-neutrality of money.

This brings about an additional argument as to why money illusion should not be neglected in economics.

Behavioral economics account of money illusion

As Howitt (1987) mentions, the attitude of economists toward money illusion is rather equivocal. This concept is frequently invoked and resisted by economists, where economists' pervasive belief in rational expectations dictates the trend. However, some anomalous observations indicate that there is a deficiency in understanding the importance of money and the extent of nominal effects in the real world. There are a few classes of anomalous observations based on identification from Howitt (1987) and Akerlof and Shiller (2009):

- Indexing in contracts does not occur according to theoretical predictions.
- Prices are sticky.
- The behavior of individuals in talking and writing indicates confusion between nominal and real value of money.
- Accounting.

First, a frequently mentioned observation by, among others, Howitt (1985), Shafir et al. (1997), and Akerlof and Shiller (2009) is that indexing does not occur in contracts and laws as suggested by the theory. A small fraction of labor contracts includes indexation, that is, provides for COLA.[1] An illustrative example is the frequently discussed sample of Canadian labor contracts from 1976 to 2000 (Christofides and Peng, 2003). Only 19 percent of all the contracts were indexed and in a rather peculiar way. Indexation was far less than one-for-one and implemented in an asymmetric manner. While the introduction of indexed contracts when inflation went up was rather slow,[2] in the case of lowering inflation, indexation partially disappeared. If indexation does not occur, this does not automatically lead to the presence of money illusion. As Blinder (2000) argues, COLA indexation might not be evidence for money illusion, since firms may want to raise salaries more than inflation to reward good performance. However, Akerlof and Shiller (2009) note that it seems dubious for parties to reject the possibility of signing a contract that adjusts for inflation as it actually occurs (COLA indexation) and afterwards to make adjustments for inflation as it is expected to occur. As a result, rather imprecise or completely absent indexation indicates that exact adjustment for inflationary expectations in wage bargaining is not the case.[3] As already mentioned in Chapter 1, devoted to Keynes and Fisher, further evidence of money illusion is seen in the reluctance of the labor force to implement money wage cuts. Under these circumstances, labor unions withdraw from the indexing of contracts in times of deflation. The concept of fairness related to nominally deceived individuals seems to be responsible for the reluctant behavior of the labor force, as will be mentioned later in the chapter.

Very much the same holds for financial contracts and loans, which are also expressed in nominal terms without indexation. Unindexed contracts are often used by governments. Governments often have tax systems unindexed or incompletely indexed, which is also true of US tax law as noted by Shafir et al. (1997). Bonds are issued by the government at a fixed interest rate until maturity, with no interest rate change for most of the bond contracts when inflation changes.[4] Also, many mortgages are only partially indexed by means of adjustable rates. As a result, when inflation occurs, holders of mortgages are paying back at faster rate. Money illusion in this case seems to play a significant role as empirically proved by Brunnermeier and Julliard (2008). Courts are reluctant to revise contracts in response to inflation as indicated by Hirschberg (1976) or Leijonhufvud (1977). Incomplete indexation suggests again that the adjustment for inflationary expectations is imperfect, which may pose some considerations about money illusion.

In addition, another observation is the stickiness of prices. As Shafir et al. (1997) document, changes in the money supply have a first impact on quantities and a delayed impact on prices, and motivates research on the stickiness of prices and wages. Evidence of stickiness is provided by the existence of the lags in aggregate price equations or markets with large quantity movements and small price movements. Theoretical concepts such as overlapping contracts (Fischer 1977) or costs of price adjustment (Mankiw 1985) attempt to explain large quantity movements and small price movements by other forces than money illusion. Still money illusion in some sense is incorporated in Fischer's work as already demonstrated in Chapter 2.

Furthermore, not only are individuals resistant to cuts in money wages, but they are reluctant to price increases as well. As Akerlof and Shiller (2009) point out, consumers dislike price increases; this was also empirically investigated by Carlton (1986), who suggests that the prices of many industrial commodities are constant for significant periods. Anderson and Simester (2010) prove that customers are antagonized by price increases and respond by lowering subsequent purchases from the firm. Managers are therefore reluctant to change prices that much. This is also confirmed by Churchill (1982), who concludes that many businesses are reluctant to change old prices of goods from old stocks, despite the fact that replacement costs are higher due to inflationary pressures. This could have fatal consequences for small businesses, unable to pay the replacement costs, if selling the old stock at old prices. First, small businesses might be unaware of this danger when setting prices. Additionally, consumers, deceived by money illusion, may object to higher prices of goods from old stocks, as Shafir et al. (1997) suggest.

Akerlof and Shiller (2009) assume money illusion to be present in accounting also, which serves (among other capital decisions) as the basis for stock prices. Because accounts are in nominal terms and decisions made are based on nominal account, it seems that some nominal confusion might be present. The hypothesis of Modigliani and Cohn (1979), based on inflationary biases in corporate accounting, is aimed at investigating whether stock prices reflect profits adjusted for inflationary biases or whether profits remain unadjusted. They conclude that the stock market is not able to see through the veil of inflation. The fact that the stock market is prone to money illusion is also documented by Cohen, Polk and Vuolteenaho (2005). Problems in accounting are also demonstrated by Shafir et al. (1997) in an example of accounting methods like FIFO (first in, first out) and LIFO (last in, first out), which rely rather on historic prices instead of replacement cost. The problem of accounting is also closely related to the discussion by Churchill (1982) about businesses unaware of accounting dangers and selling the old stock at old prices.

Additionally, the behavior of individuals in talking and writing indicates confusion between the nominal and real value of money. As documented by Shafir et al. (1997) and Akerlof and Shiller (2009), money illusion is a widespread phenomenon documented by various situations, a good example being newspapers, where a comparison of salaries and donations is done across time with a failure to reflect the difference between nominal and real values. Furthermore, it is not evident that the ability to make a distinction between nominal and real values is better in the case of high inflation compared to low inflation. Paradoxically, in a highly inflationary environment, where it is expected that money illusion will be absent, some relics might be present. A good example is Fisher's (1928) woman with a mortgage debt denominated in marks, which evaluated her debt in dollars. Once her debt was discharged, she refused to benefit from the change in exchange rate, which altered the value of the debt from $7,000 to $250, but neglected to adjust for the decline in the value of the dollar. Fisher (1928) assumed the presence of money illusion even in a high inflationary environment.

This real fact of economic life is in contradiction with the theses of Keynes and Friedman that money illusion loses its relevance once inflation exceeds a particular threshold. Although there exists eventuality that people under high inflation may switch partially to evaluation based on real terms, they will go back to the nominal evaluation once inflation is lower. A good example is the aforementioned COLA indexation, which tends to cease from contracts when inflation falls, indicating inclination towards nominal evaluation.[5]

Psychological biases and money illusion

As the aforementioned anomalies indicate, the phenomenon of money illusion is not eliminated entirely. Renewal of interest in money illusion[6] emerged with the publication of Shafir et al. (1997). In order to support their statements governed by psychological bias, Shafir et al. (1997) conducted a survey questionnaire designed to detect the presence of money illusion in the decision-making of individuals. Questions were usually presented to large groups of people (100 or more). The responses of individuals differed substantially from standard assumptions free of money illusion, and the authors thus concluded that money illusion is a widespread phenomenon. In contrast, Boes, Lipp, and Winkelmann (2007) reached the opposite conclusion. Based on data from the German Socio-Economic Panel for the period 1993 to 2003, they could not reject the hypothesis of no money illusion at the individual level.

Generally, people are supposed to see through the veil of money in a perfect world of rational expectations and only real values matter. As an example, we can look again at the homogeneity postulate. If an individual's nominal income doubles and the prices of all goods and services consumed double as well the real income of our individual is unchanged and therefore buying power is the same as before. As Tyran (1999) notes, money illusion is not relevant if the objective situation of the individual, given by the real incentive structure, remains unchanged. In this case, the real actions of an illusion-free individual are not affected.[7] Two preconditions are fundamental for this statement. First, an individual's preferences are not dependent on nominal, but only on real magnitudes. Second, people should be aware of the fact that purely nominal changes don't affect their opportunity set.

However, psychological biases present in the behavior of individuals may allow for the violation of one or both of these conditions, which results in the violation of the homogeneity postulate. As a result, individuals might not be able to see through the veil of money. As Shafir et al. (1997) claim, individuals may base the evaluation of their income not solely on current buying power, but attribute greater importance to the evaluation of their money income. Thus, individuals subject to money illusion may be satisfied with the improvement in their well-being even when nominal income rises simultaneously with prices, keeping real income unchanged. This suggests that the explanation of money illusion is based on a psychological account, namely the interaction of nominal and real representations. In its pure form, the perception and decision-making of subjects is affected by the frame (nominal or real) in which the environment is presented. Thus, the basic corner stone, which is supposed to clarify proneness of subjects to money illusion, is a framing effect. Apart from the framing effect, Shafir et al. (1997) use other behavioral concepts to explain the occurrence of money illusion, such as the anchoring effect, mental accounting, or cognitive dissonance.

The framing effect

The framing effect, as outlined by Kahneman and Tversky (1981), states that the alternative framing of the same decision problem may generate a substantially different behavior. As already mentioned, this behavioral concept might be applied also to money illusion phenomenon. A more thorough explanation in the vein of Shafir et al. (1997) states that individuals are aware of the difference between real and nominal values, where the real representation represents true value. But the nominal representation seems to be simpler and more salient for decision-making and is sufficient for a short run. As a result, individuals tend to evaluate transactions prevalently in nominal terms in a single point of time or over a short moment. Then, economic decision-making is composed of real and nominal assessments, which implies the presence of money illusion. Thus, reliance on a particular frame (in this case a nominal one) that is simpler is a channel through which money illusion might be induced. This is in line with Kahneman and Tversky (1979), who documented that if individuals are given a choice between two logically equivalent representations, they tend to select the frame that is more natural and simplistic and continue to evaluate the option in that given frame. However, since aspects of options appear to be larger in one representation than in another, it might happen that alternative framings of identical options yield systematically different responses (Selten and Berg 1970; Kahneman and Tversky 1981). As a consequence, if the question is framed in nominal terms, people might prefer to select the nominally less risky option, which is, in fact, riskier in real terms. In fact, respondents might be subject to so called "high-number" illusion as noted by Tyran (1999), in which they tend to prefer the choice of higher nominal value. Based on the aforementioned statements, money illusion is defined from their stance as a "bias in the assessment of the real value of economic transactions, induced by a nominal evaluation" (Shafir et al. 1997, p. 348).

The framing effect and saliency of the real versus nominal term might be demonstrated also with help of a famous example from Shafir et al. (1997, p. 351):

> Consider two individuals, Ann and Barbara, who graduated from the same college a year apart. Upon graduation, both took similar jobs with publishing firms. Ann started with a yearly salary of 30,000 USD. During her first year on the job there was no inflation, and in her second year, Ann received a 2% (600 USD) raise in salary. Barbara also started with a yearly salary of 30,000 USD. During her first year on the job there was a 4% inflation, and in her second year, Barbara received a 5% (1500 USD) raise in salary.

One of the problems given to respondents was related to the salary two individuals receive.

As they entered their second year on the job, who was doing better in economic terms?

When the subjects had to evaluate the position of each individual in economic terms, the majority tend to evaluate the position in real rather than in nominal terms. As a result, 71 percent of respondents considered that Ann was doing better. However, the situation changed when respondents were asked under different frames incorporated in two questions below; which of the two was happier and which was more likely to leave a job for a better position.

As they entered their second year on the job, who do you think was happier?

As they entered their second year on the job, each received a job offer from another firm. Who do you think was more likely to leave her present job for another job?

When the emphasis was not purely economic, people opted for nominal over real evaluation. Although Ann had a higher salary based on higher real raises, she was considered to be less happy on the basis of lower nominal raises. Significantly, only 36 percent indicated that Ann was happier than Barbara. In addition, based on that frame 65 percent of people responded that lower happiness will have consequences for Ann in the form of her leaving her job for a better position. This shows how people perceive the value of money. Although they are able to make a distinction between nominal and real representation in economic terms, it is not usually the case. It is worth noting that the people in Shafir's example are not completely deceived by money illusion like Fisher (1928) claims, because they are able to correctly evaluate the situation, when it is made salient by framing in real terms. However, when the representation is made less salient, their decision-making is biased by nominal representation. They are even subject to high-number illusion and target the higher nominal income, although it is smaller in real terms.

The problem of alternative framing might be also documented by the resistance to indexation of long-term contracts, where money illusion also emerged as suggested by Shafir et al. (1997). In the decision-making process both buyers and sellers are expected to prefer an indexed contract, since its real value is protected. However, if the buyer or seller is risk averse in nominal terms, the indexation of contracts is considered to be riskier because the nominal value might be higher or lower in nominal terms than a fixed amount. Results show that most people try to avoid a primarily nominal risk, that is, evaluate contracts in nominal terms, and prefer non-indexed contracts. It appears that people are sensitive to framing. When the question was framed in real terms, more subjects preferred indexed contracts as opposed to when the question was framed in nominal or neutral terms. Thus, results show that people are prone to money illusion and fail to understand the importance of COLA.

Anchoring

Anchoring, as a special form of framing effect developed by Kahneman and Tversky (1974), refers to the human tendency to set some anchor (reference point) and rely too heavily on it, where evaluation generates information disproportionately consistent with the anchor value, thereby creating bias in subsequent judgements. If applied to money illusion phenomena, individuals can choose to rely either on a nominal or real anchor. However, they are more prone to use a nominal anchor as a reference point. The reason for such a choice is given by the saliency and naturalness of nominal values, as already suggested above. Anchoring is also related to the confusion of individuals from using a smallest nominal accounting unit as a yardstick for the evaluation of economic transactions. When the quantity of money doubles in an environment free of frictions, the same dollar bill will be worth half of its real value. However, people are not aware of the fact that the monetary yardstick shrank in real terms as suggested by Tyran (1999) in line with Fisher's (1928) thesis. Anchoring is, therefore, responsible for creating bias in the evaluation of nominal and real accounting units and might be connected with Fisher's (1928) example of the German shopkeeper during German hyperinflation in 1920s. The lady sold the t-shirt for a price that did not not reflect replacement costs under the new price level, since she was anchoring a prevalently nominal profit.

Anchoring may be even spotted in housing markets, as suggested by Brunnermeier and Julliard (2008) and Shafir et al. (1997). If we suppose an individual trying to sell a house in non-inflationary times when housing prices fell by 5 percent relative to other prices, this individual may set as a nominal anchor the historical price paid for the house and may be reluctant to sell it for less than this reference point. In times of relative price changes, an individual's decision will be driven by the change in the current price of goods and its historical anchor. Loss aversion might be identified relative to an anchor. Since the saliency of nominal values invites a choice of nominal anchor, this is another argument for money illusion. As a result, money illusion tends to arise even in case of relative change in prices without the need for a change in the price of money. This again confirms that money illusion represents "a bias in the assessment of the real value of economic transactions, induced by a nominal evaluation" (Shafir et al. 1997, p. 348).

This fact was further proved by investigation of Shafir et al. (1997), who argue that people put emphasis on nominal gains/losses rather than real ones. Again, we may find a connection with Fisher (1928). If individuals are governed solely by nominal values, the selling of the house appears a more attractive option following times of inflation, whereas buying is considered less favorable. Results also suggest that higher nominal prices (although real prices did not change) facilitated selling but were aversive to buying. Consumer aversion to increases in nominal prices is well utilized by the "buy-now-and-beat-inflation psychology" that is acting during times of high inflation, as proved by Maital (1982). This phenomenon might be best demonstrated by a quote from Maital and Benjamini (1980), cited by Shafir et al. (1997, p. 356): "All prices will probably go up including car prices. So, if you're thinking about a new car, think about buying now. There will probably never be a better time." Framing purchase decisions in terms of rising nominal prices will boost sales, neglecting the role of interest and whether the nominal interest rate is higher during inflation.

Loss aversion

We already mentioned that loss aversion occurs with respect to some anchor (reference point) in the case of money illusion with respect to a nominal anchor. Shafir et al. (1997) proved its existence in the housing market. Thaler, Tversky, Kahneman, and Schwartz (1997) prove the loss aversion in their study of financial investments. They claim that inflation has a significant impact on subjects' allocation to investment funds. In the case of a riskier fund, the mean allocation was 42.3 percent in no inflation conditions and 71 percent under 10 percent inflation. Subjects primarily perceived the reference point in nominal terms. As such, the nominal returns in an inflationary environment looked outstanding and they were less risk averse than in conditions of zero inflation. Loss aversion respectively meant that a real loss of 5 percent (which appeared as a 5 percent nominal gain) in the presence of 10 percent inflation was considered as less aversive than a 5 percent loss in conditions of no inflation (when the nominal and real values were identical).

Indirect channels—mental accounting and cognitive dissonance

The public tends to overlook inflation effects working through indirect channels. For instance, the public is not aware that nominal wages and inflation move together over the long run as documented by Shiller (1996). Furthermore, less than a third of respondents in Shiller's survey would expect higher nominal income in the case of higher inflation in the United States over the last five years. Brunnermeier and Julliard (2008) consider the effect of inflation to be of an indirect nature, where the connecting link between inflation and nominal wages are nominal profits.

People tend to be inattentive to these indirect effects, which is related to two psychological biases, one of them being mental accounting and other cognitive dissonance.

Mental accounting

Mental accounting outlined by Thaler (1980, 1999) refers to the situation in which people use multiple mental accounts to keep track of gains and losses. The link between multiple accounts is overlooked, leading to substantial biases.

Mental accounting bias, associated with money illusion, might be demonstrated with the help of the following example presented by Shafir and Thaler (2006, p. 697) to experienced wine collectors:

> *Suppose you bought a case of a good 1982 Bordeaux in the futures market for 20 USD a bottle. The wine now sells at auction for about 75 USD a bottle. You have decided to drink a bottle of this wine with dinner. Which of the following best captures your feeling of the cost to you of drinking this bottle?*

Results were as follows: 25 percent respondents evaluated the bottle at $75 (the value of replacement cost), 30 percent responded that it feels like it doesn't cost them anything because they paid for a bottle long time ago, not remembering even what they paid, and 25 percent of respondents reported that they feel like they saved $55 because they are able to drink a $75 bottle for only $20. Other versions, like breaking the bottle, yielded similar results.

As already demonstrated in the section devoted to anchoring, money illusion may arise because people tend to anchor the historic cost of the item and neglect the replacement cost. However, the replacement cost may differ due to changes in the value of money or changes in relative prices. Mental accounting induces people to behave in suboptimal way as they base their decision on multiple representations. Earning money, borrowing, saving, or investing is based on multiple accounts rather than on a single one.

Shafir et al. (1997) asked respondents to evaluate the behavior of sellers, who created inventories at different times and sold at the same time. The majority of respondents considered selling at a lower price as a better deal as long as the inventory was acquired at a lower price. However, they based their decision-making about the transaction solely on nominal differences and ignored inflation. It seems that mental accounting leads to erroneous outcomes; this is also valid in the case of accounting dangers, in which businesses tend to set the prices of their goods based on old stock prices.

Cognitive dissonance and self-attribution bias

Under these psychological biases, people tend to attribute higher nominal income to their achievements, rather than to the inflation effect. This fact was observed by Shiller (1996), who noted that none of the respondents mentioned that they benefited from the redistributive effect of inflation, which benefits creditors.

Fairness and morale

Fairness significantly affects the behavior of individuals. For instance, consumers do not consider fair that the grocery store owner has increased the price of the current stock of peanut butter due to the rise in the wholesale prices of peanut butter. The owner puts an emphasis on selling the peanut butter at current rather than historical price. We may refer again to accounting issues mentioned by Churchill (1982), but in this case the owner of the grocery store does not suffer from money illusion (Shafir et al. 1997). On the other hand, subjects evaluate the profits of the owner in nominal terms, not taking into account that real profit remains unchanged. It appears that consumers deceived by money illusion are reluctant to any rise in prices. As a result, the majority of consumers evaluate the pricing policy of the owner as unfair (Kahneman, Knetsch and Thaler 1986).

The perception of fairness and its relation to money illusion was explored in an example from a survey by Kahneman, Knetsch and Thaler (1986). A company, which makes a small profit is located in an economy experiencing a recession with substantial unemployment. Half of the respondents was presented with the situation of no inflation in the economy, in which the company decides to cut wages and salaries by only 7 percent. The other half was presented with the situation of a 12 percent inflation, in which the company decides to increase salaries by only 5 percent.

Although both situations were identical in terms of real income change, the former situation was considered to be unfair by 62 percent of respondents in the case of a nominal wage cut, but the latter was considered to be unfair only by 22 percent of respondents. This indicates the reluctance of workers toward downward money wage cuts because they are deceived by money illusion, as already pointed out by Fisher (1928). Agell and Bennmarker (2002) reached similar results to Kahneman, Knetsch, and Thaler (1986). Also, Bewley (1995) documents the fact that managers are convinced about the fact that workers consider wage cuts as highly unfair or even insulting.

Robustness of questionnaire survey

The behavioral research presented in the previous section is based on questionnaire surveys, which are associated with possible drawbacks. For instance, Shafir et al. (1997) refer to the obvious limitations of their study in the context of hypothetical questions. Still, they have been criticized for the fact that respondents were not paid anything for their effort and their incentives might not be sufficient, as pointed out by Duffy (1998). For instance, Smith and Walker (1993) note that experiments in which subjects are rewarded accordingly significantly affect the behavior of the tested subjects and might even reduce the variance of actions. Still, many findings of behavioral economics, even with respect to money illusion, based on questionnaire basis, proved to be empirically valid in laboratory experiments (Benartzi and Thaler 1995; Weber, Rangel, Wibral, and Falk 2009; Tyran and Stephens 2014; Fehr and Tyran 2001).

Summary

To sum up, if the objective function of the individual depends not on real but on nominal magnitudes, money illusion might emerge as a result. In other words, the individual is not able to perceive that an equiproportionate change in all nominal terms leaves the real magnitudes unchanged. Most of the economic transactions are framed in nominal terms, which causes nominal representation to be a natural representation for most people. Due to people's salient and simplistic decision-making, and their tendency to perceive nominal values without consideration of real ones, money illusion might be elicited. As a result, the non-homogenous character of labor supply, which generates money illusion, is reconfirmed by its inclusion into the framework of behavioral economics. Shafir et al. (1997) in reference to Tobin (1972) also recommend an extension of the analysis even to the demand side of the labor market, based on their analysis of money illusion within Solow's (1979) model of efficiency wages.

Although the views of Shafir et al. (1997) are not based on the complete blindness of subjects associated with change in purchasing power based on an unstable currency, they partially benefit from the legacy of Fisher's *Money Illusion* (1928). Similarly to Fisher, authors use illustrative examples based on real economic facts. Also, they admit the presence of relics of money illusion in a highly inflationary environment like Fisher. On the other hand, they are aware of the Lucas rationality postulate and don't deny that people might be aware of inflation. This especially holds in the world where everybody is "index-number conscious" as opposed to during Fisher times, when indexation was in the beginning.

Indirect channels of psychological judgment biases such as mental accounting and cognitive dissonance, however, might generate a counter-force, making subjects more prone to overlook inflationary effects as suggested also by Brunnermeier and Julliard (2008).

As already mentioned, the basic element for dissemination of the money illusion, even after rational expectations revolution occurred, is the framing effect, which causes deviations from rationality through psychological biases. It might seem that rational behavior could be restored if people are not confused by inflation. As Fisher (1928) and Fischer and Modigliani (1978) assume, individuals are considered to make optimal decisions if they are not deceived by inflation. However, the research of Shafir et al. (1997) proved that the response of individuals to nominal price and wage cuts, induced by nominal confusion, might generate an extension of money illusion even to non-inflationary settings.

It is worth mentioning that this aspect of money illusion was elaborated by Shafir et al. (1997) only from microeconomic point of view. Since the effects of individual money illusion tend to cancel out on average at the aggregate level, money illusion is considered to be negligible by opponents.

Money illusion back at the aggregate level

As already mentioned in Chapter 2, economists since the rational expectations revolution have sought to explain the short-run non-neutrality of money by factors other (informational frictions, staggering of contracts) than money illusion, which did not fit well in a fully rational framework and was largely dismissed by many economists like Tobin (1972).

However, the position of money illusion in economics has changed over time. Tyran (1999) outlined four reasons why money illusion should be reconsidered as a relevant concept in economics. First, there is strong empirical support for the existence of money illusion at the individual level due to research in behavioral economics. Specifically, a study by Shafir et al. (1997) proved that money illusion is caused by psychological bias in decision-making induced by the framing effect, mental accounting, or fairness and as such contributed to its resurrection in economics. Second, if the notion of money illusion as a pervasive phenomenon in individual decision making is accepted, it might be transferred to many economically relevant areas like financial markets, labor markets or macroeconomic aggregates. Third, recent contributions like Haltiwanger and Waldmann (1985, 1989) prove that very few agents affected by illusion may disproportionately affect market or aggregate outcomes under some conditions. The last reason for close attention to money illusion is associated with the question posed by Tyran (1999) as to whether the effect of individual mistakes might be translated to the aggregate level. Until that point, research concentrated only on the individual effects of money illusion induced by a psychological account. Critiques frequently pointed out that individual money illusion is not of great significance, since its effects might cancel out and may become irrelevant at the aggregate level. Thus, its potential role in macroeconomics was largely dismissed. However, experimental research by Fehr and Tyran (2001) brought money illusion back to the stage as an important phenomenon, which should not be omitted in the explanation of nominal inertia and non-neutrality of money.

Strategic interaction and money illusion

It is not sufficient to deduce from the presence of individual money illusion (i.e. Shafir et al. 1997) that money illusion might be of any importance at an aggregate level. Individual effects of money illusion might cancel out and may become irrelevant at the aggregate level. However, strategic interaction (Haltiwanger and Waldman 1985) as outlined in Chapter 2, is a crucial concept, which incorporates the effects of money illusion at the aggregate level as an important component of explanation of nominal inertia.

Haltiwanger and Waldman (1985, 1989) point out that in the case of heterogeneous agents, the effect of behavior of boundedly rational agents may be disproportionally large on the aggregate level under conditions of strategic complementarity. Strategic complementarity became a standard part of many Keynesian models[8] and was empirically proved even in real world economies as asserted by Cooper and Haltiwanger (1996) and Oh and Waldmann (1994). As a result, it is considered to be "typical or natural property of macroeconomics." The mechanism of strategic interaction is as follows in an environment described by monopolistic price competition: in the case of an increase in the aggregate price level, the firm tends to increase its own price in environment described by strategic complementarity, whereas it tends to decrease its own price in environment described by strategic substitutability.

A more thorough explanation might be provided with the help of the reduced form of real profit function[9] in the vein of Fehr and Tyran (2000):

$$\pi_i = \pi_i\left(\frac{P_i}{\overline{P}}, \frac{M}{\overline{P}}\right) \tag{1}$$

Where π_i is firm, i is profit, P_i is the nominal price of firm i, $\overline{P}$ stands for the aggregate price level, and M is the money supply. In this model, real money balances are proportional to real aggregate demand, where unique symmetric equilibrium $P_i = P_j$ is present for all i, j (i.e. the simplification of the model is made by the assumption of identical firms, where menu costs and informational frictions are absent). In equilibrium, each firm maximizes real profits when it sets its price equal to the average equilibrium price, $P_i^* = \overline{P}^*$. The real profit function is homogeneous of degree zero in P_i, $\overline{P}$, and M, where a change in M to λM ($\lambda \neq 1$) implies post-shock equilibrium values of λP_i^* and $\lambda \overline{P}^*$.[10]

Based on the aforementioned comments, one group of agents is supposed to not fully adjust their nominal prices, since it suffers from individual money illusion. Another group of agents, not prone to money illusion, is supposed to anticipate the behavior of the former group. As a result, the latter group expects a change in real aggregate demand $M/\overline{P}$, which will provide incentives for agents in this group to choose a price different from λP_i^*. *P*The interaction between these two groups may result in aggregate nominal inertia, which strongly depends on a strategic environment where agents' actions might be either strategic complements or strategic substitutes (Fehr and Tyran, 2001).

The strategic complementarity of Haltiwanger and Waldmann (1989) implies that the firm's profit maximizing nominal price P_i is positively related to the aggregate price level $\overline{P}$. This relationship is explained by the incentives of firms to select a nominal price close to the pre-shock equilibrium if they believe that the prices of other agents are kept close to the pre-shock equilibrium due to money illusion. As a result, non-rational firms might have a disproportionately large impact at the aggregate price level due to strategic complementarity. If strategic substitutability is assumed, then the real profit function would posit a negative slope (the negative relationship of the individual price to the aggregate price level), which would imply that rational firms would compensate for the non-rational behavior of some firms, making their impact on the aggregate level disproportionately small (Fehr and Tyran 2001). In other words, the best reply function under strategic complementarity has a positive slope, under strategic substitutability a negative slope.

Direct and indirect effects of money illusion

This discussion might provide arguments as to why money illusion should not be omitted in the explanation of nominal inertia together with the non-neutrality of money. The adjustment process of the economy after a fully anticipated monetary shock might be affected significantly through the failure of some agents to fully adjust to the nominal shock in an interactive situation. This may provide incentives for other agents to not fully adjust too. A so-called "snowball effect" might then affect the speed of the adjustment in the economy.

To explain more thoroughly this mechanism, it is crucial to distinguish between concepts of the "direct effects of money illusion" and "indirect effects of money illusion," introduced by Tyran (1999) and Fehr and Tyran (2000).

The "direct effects of money illusion" result from individual optimization errors based on the framing effect in line with the psychological account of money illusion introduced by Shafir et al. (1997). Sometimes such behavior is referred to as the individual effects of money illusion. People tend to adopt a particular frame and evaluate the options within this frame. Specifically, the salience of nominal values as natural units used in daily economic transactions causes people to take nominal values or changes in nominal values as a proxy for real values or changes in real values. This rule of nominal anchoring is also called by Tyran (1999) "Fisher's effect." Fehr and Tyran (2001) point out that such a rule might be appropriate in an environment with a given aggregate price level. However, if such behavior is applied in an environment of changing aggregate price level, this might constitute money illusion.

So, although these individual effects of money illusion are assumed to soon fade out and are considered to be negligible with respect to the aggregate level by opponents, its role might be strengthened under conditions of a changing aggregate price level. In particular, they might consequently be multiplied and result in indirect effects of money illusion as will be shown.

Apart from the Fisher's effect, the effect of high-number money illusion may be of substantial significance. As already mentioned, high-number money illusion, in the vein of Tyran (1999), is associated with the violation of the homogeneity postulate, where people fail to perceive that real buying power is unchanged or tend to target the higher nominal income, although it is smaller in real terms. The effect of high-number money illusion depends on the strategic environment. If the strategic complementarity is introduced, naive agents in the case of anticipated negative monetary contraction will reduce nominal prices only a little. This is given by the fact that the best reply function has a positive slope, in which case high nominal payoffs prevail at high individual prices. In other words, naive agents prone to high-number money illusion, consider high nominal payoffs associated with high nominal price levels as a proxy for real payoffs. As a result, they tend to choose high nominal prices. This generates sticky price choices in the case of negative anticipated monetary shock. In conditions of strategic substitutability, the best reply function has a negative slope, in which case high nominal payoffs prevail at low individual prices. Naïve agents prone to high-number money illusion in this case choose low nominal prices after negative anticipated monetary shock, leading to faster adjustment.

To clarify this discussion, nominal anchoring leads to inertial behavior of agents irrespective of strategic properties, whereas the effect of high-number illusion and consequent inertial behavior is induced by strategic complementarity. Subjects are considered to be prone to the so called first-order money illusion induced by representation bias.

Thus far, the strategic environment has only been introduced with respect to high-number money illusion and behavior of naive agents. However, the strategic environment might also shape expectations, in which "indirect effects of money illusion" become powerful with important macroeconomic consequences.

To explain the indirect effects of money illusion, other elements are added in line with Fehr and Tyran (2005a). First, agents in the economy are heterogeneous in terms of rationality. Some of them are naïve agents prone to money illusion; some of them don't suffer from such deception. Second, strategic complementarity in terms of following the crowd is introduced. Last, sophisticated and not super rational agents are present in an environment of uncertain expectations biased by money illusion.

The strategic complementarity elaborated in detail by Haltiwanger and Waldman (1989) implies that it is optimal for a rational agent to change his behavior (e.g. its price) if other agents change their behavior (their prices).[11] What is crucial is that a rational agent will change his behavior (price) in the same direction as other agents. This is based on the fact that a rational agent has an incentive to follow the crowd. In deciding which direction to follow, an agent has to form expectations in a strategic environment.

As already mentioned, the economy consists of heterogeneous agents regarding their ability to form expectations. Rational agents satisfy assumptions about rational expectations, whereas naïve agents are limited in their abilities by money illusion.[12] The mix of rational and naïve agents in the economy in the case of a one-time shock will result in an adjustment path similar to the pure naïve case adjustment with only slow movement to equilibrium in an environment of strategic complementarity, as shown by Haltiwanger and Waldmann (1985, 1989). This mechanism is enabled by the presence of a small number of naïve agents, whose effect on the adjustment process is disproportionally important for the first few periods after the shock. Under strategic complementarity, these naïve agents induce rational ones to hold non-equilibrium expectations, followed by a selection of non-equilibrium actions. In other words, rational agents have a tendency to behave in a complementary way, that is, to imitate the behavior of naïve agents and through that multiply the effect of non-equilibrium behavior at the aggregate level.[13]

So far, rational agents with perfect foresight have been part of our considerations. However, in reality it is difficult for decision-makers to form higher-order expectations. If we suppose the existence of rational agents with imperfect foresight (so called sophisticated agents) who are unable to form perfect expectations but able to choose rational action, we may expect that expectations might be biased under money illusion in a strategic environment. If sophisticated agents assume with some probability that other agents suffer from money illusion (or even assume that other agents expect others to suffer from money illusion), they may decide to adjust only imperfectly to an anticipated shock. Thus, only biased belief may cause the presence of nominal inertia leading to improper adjustment as Fehr and Tyran (2005a) note. This is sometimes called "higher-order money illusion" (Tyran 1999). The deviation from the equilibrium position is more than suggested by the relative number of sophisticated and naïve agents in the economy. As a result, only the existence of a small number of agents prone to money illusion may cause inertial adjustment at the aggregate level.

Based on the aforementioned explanation in the vein of Tyran (1999) and Fehr and Tyran (2001, 2005a), we may summarize the "indirect effects of money illusion," which come into effect under the assumption of heterogeneous agents and under the conditions of strategic complementarity.[14] Expectations of rational individuals are shaped in a way that after the shock they follow a group of naïve agents toward suboptimal outcomes in the vein of strategic complementarity, since it is profitable for them. Since rational sophisticated agents have imperfect foresight in an environment of uncertain expectations, their biased belief about others' money illusion is even intensified in conditions of strategic complementarity and money illusion is elicited at the aggregate level. Thus, strategic properties matter more when money illusion is prevalent, since expectations of sophisticated agents are systematically affected by expected or actual behavior of naive agents deceived by money illusion. The more naive agents are present, the more intensive are effects of strategic complementarity.

It is important to note that these indirect effects are multiplied through "direct effects of money illusion," in which naive agents prone to money illusion deviate from optimal outcomes. These naive agents deviate either due to nominal anchoring (Fisher's effect) or due to high-number money illusion in which case strategic complementarity is crucial and money illusion matters even more. As a result, considering behavior of both naive and sophisticated agents, money illusion matters more with strategic complements. Thus, only a negligible amount of individual money illusion is of great significance, since only a small group of individuals, who tend to mix nominal versus real payoffs, is sufficient to contribute to substantial nominal inertia at the aggregate level. More substantially, the individual behavior of very small group of subjects prone to money illusion is multiplied in conditions of strategic complementarity by the behavior of other sophisticated agents and their biased belief about other money illusion. Fehr and Tyran (2001) outline the so-called "snowball effect" to refer to behavior of sophisticated agents who follow a crowd to maximize profits. As a result, money illusion should be considered as a concept that after the nominal shock may have important indirect effects in the form of nominal inertia at the aggregate level under conditions of strategic complementarity, although individual money illusion is negligible.

Results of experimental investigation

Since it is rather challenging or impossible to evaluate the effects of money illusion based on field data, Fehr and Tyran (2001) opted for experimental investigation.

The role of money in nominal price adjustment was observed after a fully anticipated monetary shock with the help of a price-setting game based on strategic complementarity.

Results proved that individual money illusion may multiply and cause large indirect effects. Specifically, if individuals have to cope with the payoff represented in the nominal frame in conditions of strategic complementarity, the adjustment in nominal prices after a negative shock is rather slow. In contrast, the adjustment after a positive monetary shock under the nominal frame is rather quick, in line with positive slope of best reply function induced by strategic complementarity. This suggests rather asymmetric effects of money illusion across fully anticipated nominal shocks. The novelty of the Fehr and Tyran approach rests on delineation of indirect effects of money illusion, which are multiplied through the direct effects in an environment of strategic complementarity, in which case the shaped expectations generate substantial inertia at the aggregate level. In other words, although research rests partly on the individual effects of money illusion based on psychological account, a crucial contribution is the elaboration of money illusion effects at the aggregate level.

Aggregate-level effects of money illusion and motivation for future research

The aggregate-level effects of money illusion evidenced in Fehr and Tyran (2001) became widely influential and have been widely cited as important evidence of money illusion by many economists, among them Yellen and Akerlof (2006), Cannon and Cipriani (2006), Brunnermeier and Julliard (2008), and Basak and Yan (2010). Furthermore, it provided incentives for extension and continuation of research in this field as will be shown in Chapter 4.

The research of Fehr and Tyran (2001) is even replicated by Petersen and Winn (2012). They suggest that the effects of money illusion are of rather limited scope since the cognitive load under the nominal frame is heavy. Furthermore, they argue that the individuals in the post-shock phase exhibit rather adaptive best reply behavior, which is sufficient for the explanation of inertial behavior and alleviates again the hypothesis about money illusion effects.

Fehr and Tyran (2014) assert that Petersen and Winn (2012) rely in their argument on the incorrect definition of money illusion, which is rather narrow and psychologically implausible, and leads to seriously misleading claims. Furthermore, they argue that the price expectations show that the adaptive best reply strategy is of no predictive power for a subject's price decision-making. Indeed, expectations are significantly affected in the nominal treatment by money illusion effects. Strikingly, the research of Petersen and Winn (2012) generates (after proper explanation) rather similar outcomes regarding the effect of money illusion on nominal inertia.

Additionally, the aforementioned environment with heterogeneous agents with expectations that money illusion is built into the character of naïve agents, with the subsequent results for the adjustment, is similar to the analysis of informational frictions as Fehr and Tyran (2005b) note. Based on information constraint, Woodford (2002) and Mankiw and Reis (2002) distinguish between a share of agents fully informed about shocks and the share of agents who are not able to cope with information constraint, since they form their expectations based on outdated information. A money illusion-based account for nominal inertia is also based on an individual information constraint related to the confusion of nominal versus real values.

Notes

1 Cost of living adjustment.
2 That is, adjustment starts only after inflation has risen by more than a specified target.
3 Bewley (1998), with the help of the survey investigates to what extent labor markets suffer from a related illusion, i.e. resistance to wage cuts.
4 As mentioned in Chapter 1, already Fisher (1928) has proposed the so called "stabilized bond" based on proper indexation, which would account for a change in purchasing power.
5 Hendricks and Kahn (1985) document that percentage of the workers covered by COLA in United States was 50% in 1958, 20% in 1966, 61.2% in 1977, 57.3% in 1984.
6 Growing interest in money illusion is also demonstrated by several studies, Akerlof et al. (2000), Boes, Lipp and Winkelmann, (2007), Modigliani and Cohn (1979).
7 This is in line with Leontief's (1936) definition of money illusion mentioned in Chapter 1.
8 Tyran (1999), Cooper and John (1998), Oh and Waldman (1994) refer to research including monopolistic price competition (Hart, 1982, Kiyotaki, 1988), stock markets, (Shiller, 1984), coordination problems, (Summers, 1988) or labor markets, (Diamond, 1982, Howitt, 1985) and others.
9 Function already includes maximizing behavior of households and minimizing behavior of firms for given level of output, the equilibrium real wage, the equilibrium relation between real aggregate demand and real money supply. For more details see Akerlof and Yellen (1985) and Blanchard and Kiyotaki (1987).
10 As we can see, homogenous postulate is applied in line with Leontief (1936).
11 Their research is in line with the concept of near rationality of Akerlof and Yellen (1985).
12 Particularly, naïve agents suffer either from nominal anchoring independent of strategic properties or suffer from high-number money illusion, which depends on strategic properties. Even if the behavior of naïve agents is independent of strategic properties, still behavior of rational agents has a disproportional large impact on the aggregate level in conditions of strategic complementarity due to incentive of rational agents to follow the crowd, (Tyran 1999).
13 In environment characterized by conditions of strategic substitutability, rational agents would be motivated to set prices in the opposite directions than naïve agents prone to money illusion, thereby compensating for their suboptimal behavior. Similar to high-number illusion, the effect would be pretty fast adjustment to new equilibrium in case of negative anticipated nominal shock.
14 There are many studies, which prove that strategic complementarity is the case in the real economy. See for instance Cooper and Haltiwanger (1996), Oh and Waldman (1994).

References

Agell, J. and Bennmarker, H., 2002. Wage Policy and Endogenous Wage Rigidity: A Representative View from the Inside. *IFAU Working Paper* 2002–12.

Akerlof, G. A., Dickens, W. T., and Perry, G. L., 2000. Near-Rational Wage and Price Setting and the Long-Run Phillips Curve. *Brookings Papers on Economic Activity*, 31 (1), pp. 1–60.

Akerlof, G. A. and Yellen, J. L., 1985. A Near-Rational Model of the Business Cycle, with Wage and Price Intertia. *Quarterly Journal of Economics*, 100 (5), pp. 823–838.

Akerlof, G. A. and Shiller, R. J., 2009. *Animal Spirits, How Human Psychology Drives the Economy and Why It Matters for Global Capitalism*. Princeton, NJ: Princeton University Press.

Anderson, E. and Simester, D., 2010. Price Stickiness and Customer Antagonism. *Quarterly Journal of Economics*, 125 (3), pp. 729–776.

Basak, S. and Yan, H., 2010. Equilibrium Asset Prices and Investor Behavior in the Presence of Money Illusion. *Review of Economic Studies*, 77 (3), pp. 914–936.

Benartzi, S. and Thaler, R. H., 1995. Myopic Loss Aversion and the Equity Premium Puzzle. *Quarterly Journal of Economics*, 110 (1), pp. 73–92.

Bewley, T. F., 1995. A Depressed Labor Market as Explained by Participants. *The American Economic Review*, 85 (2), pp. 250–254.

Bewley, T. F., 1998. Why Not Cut Pay? *European Economic Review*, 42 (3–5), pp. 459–490.

Blanchard, O. J. and Kiyotaki, N., 1987. Monopolistic Competition and the Effects of Aggregate Demand. *American Economic Review*, 77 (4), pp. 647–666.

Blinder, A. S., 2000. Comment on Akerlof, Dickens and Perry, Near-Rational Wage and Price Setting and the Long-Run Phillips Curve. *Brookings Papers on Economic Activity*, 1, pp. 50–55.

Boes, S., Lipp, M., and Winkelmann, R., 2007. Money Illusion under Test, Socioeconomic Institute. *Economics Letters*, 94, pp. 332–337.

Brunnermeier, K. M. and Julliard, C., 2008. The Causes and Consequences of Recent Financial Market Bubbles, *Review of Financial Studies*, 21 (1), pp. 135–180.

Cannon, E. and Cipriani, G., 2006. Euro-Illusion: An Natural Experiment. *Journal of Money, Credit and Banking*, 38 (5), pp. 1391–1403.

Carlton, D., 1986. The Rigidity of Prices. *American Economic Review*, 76(4), pp. 637–658.

Christofides, L. and Peng, A. C., 2003. Contract Duration and Indexation in a Period of Real and Nominal Uncertainty. *CESifo Working Paper Series* 994, CESifo Group Munich.

Churchill, N., 1982. Don't Let Inflation Get the Best of You. *Harvard Business Review*, pp. 6–26.

Cohen, R. B., Polk, C., and Vuolteenaho, T., 2005. Money Illusion in the Stock Market: The Modigliani-Cohn Hypothesis. *Quarterly Journal of Economics*, 120 (2), pp. 639–668.

Cooper, R. W. and Haltiwanger, J., 1996. Evidence on Macroeconomic Complementarities. *Review of Economics and Statistics*, 78 (1), pp. 78–93.

Cooper, R. and John, A., 1988. Coordinating Coordination Failures in Keynesian Models. *Quarterly Journal of Economics,* 103 (3), pp. 441–63.

Diamond, P. A., 1982. Aggregate Demand Management in Search Equilibrium. *Journal of Political Economy*, 90 (10), pp. 881–894.

Duffy, J., 1998. Monetary Theory in the Laboratory. *Federal Reserve Bank of St. Louis Review*, 80, pp. 9–26.

Erber, G., 2010. The Problem of Money Illusion in Economics. *Journal of Applied Economic Sciences*, 5 (3(13)), pp. 196–216.

Fehr, E. and Tyran, J., 2000. Does Money Illusion Matter? *IEW – Working Papers* No. 045, Institute for Empirical Research in Economics, University of Zurich.

Fehr, E. and Tyran, J., 2001. Does Money Illusion Matter? *American Economic Review*, 91 (5), pp. 1239–1262.

Fehr, E. and Tyran, J., 2005a. Expectations and the Effects of Money Illusion. In B. Agarwal and A. Vercelli (eds.), *Psychology, Rationality and Economic Behavior. Challenging Standard Assumptions*. New York: Palgrave Macmillan/International Economic Association.

Fehr, E. and Tyran, J., 2005b. Individual Irrationality and Aggregate Outcomes. *Journal of Economic Perspectives*, 19 (4), pp. 43–66.

Fehr E. and Tyran, J., 2014. Does Money Illusion Matter? Reply. *American Economic Review*, 104 (3), pp. 1063–1071.

Fischer, S., 1977. Long-Term Contracts, Rational Expectations, and the Optimal Money Supply Rule. *Journal of Political Economy*, 85 (1), pp. 191–205.

Fischer, S. and Modigliani, F., 1978. Towards an Understanding of the Real Effects and Costs of Inflation. *Review of World Economics*, 114 (4), pp. 810–833.

Fisher, I., 1928. *The Money Illusion*. New York: Adelphi Publishers.

Haltiwanger, J. and Waldman, M., 1985. Rational Expectations and the Limits of Rationality: An Analysis of Heterogeneity. *American Economic Review*, 75 (3), pp. 326–340.

Haltiwanger, J. and Waldman, M., 1989. Limited Rationality and Strategic Complements: Implications for Macroeconomics. *Quarterly Journal of Economics*, 104 (3), pp. 463–483.

Hart, O., 1982. A Model of Imperfect Competition with Keynesian Features. *Quarterly Journal of Economics*, 97 (1), pp. 109–138.

Hendricks, W. E. and Kahn, L. M., 1985. *Wage Indexation in the United States: COLA or UnCOLA*. Cambridge, MA: Ballinger.

Hirschberg, E., 1976. *The Impact of Inflation and Devaluation on Private Legal Obligations*. Ramat Gan, Israel: Ban Ilan University Press.

Howitt, P., 1985. Transaction Costs and the Theory of Unemployment. *American Economic Review*, 75 (1), pp. 88–100.

Howitt, P., 1987. Money Illusion. In Eatwell J., Milgate M. and Newman, P. (eds.), *The New Palgrave: A Dictionary of Economics*, New York: W.W. Norton.

Kahneman D. and Tversky, A., 1974. Judgment under Uncertainty. Heuristics and Biases. *Science*, 185 (4157), pp. 1124–1131.

Kahneman, D. and Tversky, A., 1979. Prospect Theory: An Analysis of Decision under Risk. *Econometrica*, 47 (2), pp. 263–291.

Kahneman D. and Tversky, A., 1981. The Framing of Decisions and the Psychology of Choice. *Science*, New Series, 211 (4481), pp. 453–458.

Kahneman, D., Knetsch, J. L., and Thaler, R. H., 1986. Fairness as a Constraint on Profit Seeking: Entitlements in the Market. *American Economic Review*, 76 (4), pp. 728–741.

Kiyotaki, N. 1988. Implications of Multiple Expectational Equilibria under Monopolistic Competition. *Quarterly Journal of Economics*, 103 (4), pp. 695–713.

Klevorick, A. K. and Kane, E. J., 1967. Absence of Money Illusion: A Sine Qua Non for Neutral Money? *Journal of Finance*, 22 (3), pp. 419–423.

Leijonhufvud, A., 1977. *Costs and Consequences of Inflation*. In G. C. Harcourt (ed.), *The Microeconomic Foundations of Macroeconomics*. London: MacMillan.

Leontief, W., 1936. The Fundamental Assumptions of Mr Keynes' Monetary Theory of Unemployment. *Quarterly Journal of Economics*, 5 (4), pp. 192–197.

Maital, S., 1982. *Minds, Markets and Money*. New York: Basic Books.

Maital, S. and Benjamini, Y., 1980. Inflation as Prisoner's Dilemma. *Journal of Post Keynesian Economics*, 2 (1980), pp. 459–481.

Mankiw, N. G., 1985. Small Menu Costs and Large Business Cycles: A Macroeconomic Model of Monopoly. *Quarterly Journal of Economics*, 100 (2), pp. 529–537.

Mankiw, N. G. and Reis, R., 2002. Sticky Information versus Sticky Prices: A Proposal to Replace the New Keynesian Phillips Curve. *Quarterly Journal of Economics*, 117 (4), pp. 1295–1328.

Modigliani, F. and Cohn, A. F., 1979. Inflation, Rational Evaluation and the Market. *Financial Analyst Journal*, 35 (2), pp. 24–44.

Oh, S. and Waldman, M., 1994. Strategic Complementarity Slows Macroeconomic Adjustment to Temporary Shocks. *Economic Inquiry*, 32, pp. 318–329.

Petersen, L. and Winn, A., 2012. The Role of Money Illusion in Nominal Price Adjustment. Simon Fraser University *Discussion Papers* 12–19, Department of Economics, Simon Fraser University.

Selten, R. and Berg, C. C., 1970. Experimentelle Oligopolspielserien mit Kontinuierlichem Zeitablauf. In: H. Sauermann, (ed.), *Beitrage zur experimentellen Wirtschaftsforschung*, Vol. II. Tübingen: Mohr, pp. 162–221.

Shafir, E., Diamond, P., and Tversky, A., 1997. Money Illusion. *Quarterly Journal of Economics*, 112 (2), pp. 341–374.

Shafir, E. and Thaler, R. H., 2006. Invest now, Drink later, Spend Never: On the Mental Accounting of Delayed Consumption. *Journal of Economic Psychology*, 27, pp. 694–712.

Shiller, R. J., 1984. Stock Prices and Social Dynamics. *Brookings Papers on Economic Activity*, 2, pp. 457–510.

Shiller, R. J., 1996. Why Do People Dislike Inflation? *NBER* WP No. 5539.

Smith, V. and Walker, J., 1993. Monetary Rewards and Decision Cost in Experimental Economics. *Economic Inquiry*, 31 (2), pp. 245–261.

Solow, R. M., 1979. Another Possible Source of Wage Stickeness. *Journal of Macroeconomics*, 1, pp. 9–82.

Summers, L., 1988. Relative Wages, Efficiency Wages, and Keynesian Unemployment. *American Economic Review*, Papers and Proceedings, 78 (2), pp. 382–388.

Thaler, R., 1980. Toward a Positive Theory of Consumer Choice. *Journal of Economic Behavior and Organization*, 1 (1), pp. 39–60.

Thaler, R., 1999. Mental Accounting Matters. *Journal of Behavioral Decision Making*, 12, pp. 183–206.

Thaler, R. H., Tversky, A., Kahneman, D., and Schwartz, A., 1997. The Effect of Myopia and Loss Aversion on Risk Taking: An Experimental Test. *Quarterly Journal of Economics*, 112 (2), pp. 647–661.

Tobin, J., 1972. Inflation and Unemployment. *American Economic Review*, 62 (1), pp. 1–18.

Tyran, J. R., 1999. *Money Illusion and Strategic Complementarity as Causes of Monetary Non-Neutrality*. Lecture Notes in Economics and Mathematical Systems, Berlin and Heidelberg: Springer-Verlag.

Tyran, J. and Stephens, T. A., 2014. At Least I Didn't Lose Money: Nominal Loss Aversion Shapes Evaluations of Housing Transactions. University of Copenhagen, Department of Economics *Discussion Paper* No. 12–14. Available at: http://ssrn.com/abstract=2162415 [Accessed 19 September 2016].

Weber, B., Rangel, A., Wibral M., and Falk, A., 2009. The Medial Prefrontal Cortex Exhibits Money Illusion. *Proceedings of the National Academy of Science*, 106 (13), pp. 5025–5028.

Woodford, M., 2002. Imperfect Common Knowledge and the Effects of Monetary Policy. In P. Aghion, R. Frydman, J. Stiglitz, and M. Woodford (eds), *Knowledge, Information and Expectations in Modern Macroeconomics: Essays in the Honor of Edmund S. Phelps.* Princeton, NJ: Princeton University Press.

Yellen, J. and Akerlof, G., 2006. Stabilization Policy a Reconsideration. *Economic Inquiry*, 44 (1), pp. 1–22.

4 The money illusion and its applications

> *The term "money illusion" refers to a tendency to think in terms of nominal rather than real monetary values. Money illusion has significant implications for economic theory, yet it implies a lack of rationality that is alien to economists.*
>
> Shafir, Diamond, and Tversky (1997, p. 341)

Although early considerations about the potential relevance of money illusion date back to the 1970s, with the introduction of the Modigliani–Cohn hypothesis, its potential importance was registered by economists later. It was only with the arrival of behavioral economics and the work of Shafir et al. (1997), that the concept of money illusion was brought back to attention. Psychological accounts of money illusion were sufficient for its relevance at the individual level. However, the introduction of the aggregate-level effects of money illusion by Fehr and Tyran (2001) and their contribution to the non-neutrality of money were crucial.

Due to aforementioned research, money illusion became a matter of interest, although it does not fit well into the standard rational framework of economics and is considered rather peculiar in nature. This chapter is a complementary chapter to Chapter 3, since it further extends the knowledge of the pioneering studies, which resurrected the money illusion concept in various ways. The growing interest in money illusion is documented by a number of studies in various areas. The potential application of money illusion is discussed in the financial markets (Cohen, Polk, and Vuolteenaho 2005; Basak and Yan 2010) with the long tradition of the Modigliani–Cohn hypothesis. Money illusion is well investigated also in the housing markets (Brunnermeier and Julliard 2008; Genesove and Mayer 2001) and the labor markets (Bewley 1999; Agell and Lundborg 2003). A growing number of studies demonstrate its relation toward nominal rigidities (Vaona 2013; Fortin 2013) Also, the potential effect on consumer behavior is investigated (Hogan 2013; Blinder 1995), or its role after the introduction of the euro on altruistic attitudes (Cannon and Cipriani 2006; Bittschi and Duppel 2015).

Money illusion and financial markets

It has been already argued by Fisher (1928) that inflation might affect stock returns through money illusion. Modigliani and Cohn (1979) came back to this thesis mentioned by Fisher and formulated their famous hypothesis. In their view, investors are unable to be free from certain forms of money illusion and tend to price equities in a way that fails to reflect their real economic value. In particular, investors in times of inflation discount real stock cash flows at a rate which parallels the nominal interest rate, rather than real interest rate. Instead of considering real returns, they consider the nominal return on bonds. As a result, they undervalue equities in times of high inflation. In addition, Modigliani and Cohn (1979) state that investors fail to correctly report accounting profits for the gain to stockholders accruing from depreciation in the real value of nominal corporate liabilities. The portion of the company's interest rate bill should be seen rather as repayment of capital than an expense to the company, because it compensates creditors for the fall in the real value. The important implication of these two findings is that stock prices are too low during periods of high inflation.

Investors partially overlook inflation, since the cost of this negligence is small at first. However, it is supposed that if stakes are high at stock markets, actual cash flows are soon revealed by investors and money illusion should be quickly arbitraged away.

Cohen, Polk, and Vuelteenaho (2005) discuss in this sense, whether a small number of wealthy and rational arbitrageurs (compared to majority of stock investors who confuse nominal and real variables) might eliminate any potential mispricing induced by money illusion. They argue that a bet against the money illusion is expected to be relatively low, because of only a single bet at time and because of the slow correction of mispricing. Basically, any attempt by the investor to correct the mispricing exposes him to the uncertain development on the stock market. The slow correction of mispricing requires long holding periods for the arbitrage position. Along with that, the variance of the risk grows linearly in time as the investor is significantly exposed to volatility. As Modigliani and Cohn (1979) emphasize, if a rational investor had bet against money illusion in the early 1970s and could correctly assess the extent of the undervaluation of equities, he would suffer from substantial loss for more than a decade. As a result, arbitrage activity is prevented in this sense. In this case, we may identify the common link with the research of Fehr and Tyran (2001, 2005a, 2008). They empirically prove that in an environment of strategic complementarity it is profitable for rational agents to follow behavior of naïve ones affected by money illusion. Strategic complementarity is of substantial importance, because in this case even small number of naïve agents induces rational ones to copy their behavior, leading thereby to suboptimal outcomes. If we apply strategic complementarity in asset markets, it might intensify undervaluation of stock prices in the case of high inflation, despite the fact that the majority of investors are rational. Arbitrage activity is suppressed in this sense. As a result, even if there is a small amount of money illusion, it might have a first-order effect on the economy. Basak and Yan (2010) point out that this result is parallel with the New Keynesian idea of near rationality, where second-order decisions are of first order for the economy, leading to large fluctuations at the aggregate level. This is shown empirically in works like Basak and Yan (2010) or, as already mentioned, Fehr and Tyran (2001).

Similarly to the Modigliani–Cohn hypothesis, Lintner (1975), Gultekin (1983), and Schwert and Fama (1977) report a negative relationship between nominal stock returns and inflation, (realized and expected). If we bring back the Fisher's relationship mentioned in Chapter 1, (Fisher 1930; Thaler 1997) stating that nominal interest rate moves one-for-one with expected inflation, it is inconsistent with aforementioned negative relationship. However, it has already been argued that Fisher was well aware of the fact that this relationship might not be a good description of reality. Based on the empirical research conducted in five markets, the real interest rate was found to be much more variable than nominal interest rate. This indicates the unwillingness of individuals to adjust nominal interest rates to changing price level. Fisher points to the impact of money illusion, which might be responsible for rather imperfect working of this equation.

Modigliani and Cohn (1979) in line with Fisher claim that investors systematically discount future real payoffs at nominal rather than real rates. Svedsäter, Gamble, and Gärling (2007) emphasize through a series of experiments that investors are affected by nominal framing of stock prices in their decision-making and thereby their support for money illusion is strong.

However as even Modigliani and Cohn (1979) note, this conclusion is hard to swallow, especially in light of the knowledgeable people in efficient markets, who are not subject to systemic mistakes. Cohn and Lessard (1980) prove on a set of selected countries that stock prices are negatively correlated with nominal interest rates and inflation, but call for further investigation as to whether these relationships are caused by systematic errors in valuation by investors or by other factors. Opponents arrived with an alternative explanation for the negative relationship between capitalization rates and inflation. According to them, inflation affects the value of equity because it affects the risk premium. Modigliani and Cohn (1979) do not deny this possibility, but they naturally pose a question as to why profits should be riskier with a steady 6 percent inflation than with a steady 2 percent inflation. However, if changes in inflation change equity values because they change the risk premium, this explanation is identical to money illusion hypothesis. As a result, the only difference between these two hypotheses is that in the case of money illusion investors will start to see through the veil of nominal values and inflation will no longer depress market values.

This alternative hypothesis is sometimes explained as a part of the so-called "proxy effect." The proxy effect, first outlined by Fama (1981), states that inflation proxies for some unobservable or unidentified real macroeconomic variable, which drives fundamental stock values. In this particular case, high inflation or high inflation expectations are a bad signal about future economic development. Logically, higher inflation is associated with a riskier environment or higher risk aversion, generating a risk premium, which is correlated with inflation. In other words, inflation and or inflation expectations proxy for risk aversion.

Fama (1981) and Brunnermeier and Julliard (2008) claim that the proxy effect (risk aversion) might play a role in the negative relationship between inflation and the price of stocks. Cohn and Lessard (1980) admit that their attempt to control the risk premium factor is rather crude when investigating money illusion effects.

Still, in their view, money illusion effects overweigh the effect of the decline induced by a decline in after-tax profits. This latter effect called "tax-effects hypothesis" was outlined by Feldstein (1980) and might be another phenomenon considered part of the proxy effect. In principle, inflation depresses stock returns due to the imbalanced tax treatment of inventory and depreciation caused by a reduction in real after-tax profit by inflation.

The leading practitioner model of equity valuation ("the Fed model"), which has no official status within the Federal Reserve System, is worth attention with respect to money illusion. Sharpe (2002) and Asness (2003) empirically confirmed that the Fed model is a good description of aggregate stock prices behavior. In particular, it has been used by practitioners to value stocks versus bonds and it relates the dividend-price ratio (earnings yield) to the nominal bond yield. However, pricing of stocks by investors based on the Fed model exhibits the money illusion error, by projecting the same nominal growth rate during high and low inflation.

However, the research failed to isolate the proxy effect of the risk premium. As a result, even if investors do not suffer from money illusion, the inflation might affect stock prices due to the investors' attitude toward risk. Cohen, Polk and Vuolteenaho (2005) solved this puzzle by applying novel tests, which enable them to distinguish money illusion effects from the changing attitudes of investors toward risk.[1] Instead of testing the aggregate time-series predictions, they switched to cross-sectional predictions. In particular, they examined the pricing of treasure bills, safe stocks and risky stocks. Money illusion is expected to have a symmetrical effect (constant additive effect) on all stock returns regardless of their exposure to systematic risk. On the other hand, the impact of investors' risk attitude on stock returns is proportional to the level of riskiness. Their findings suggest that the role of money illusion on the stock market is indisputable. In particular, high (low) inflation is connected with higher (lower) stock returns than justified by an amount constant across stocks, regardless of the riskiness of the particular stock. This contrasts with impact of risk attitude of investors on future stock returns, since future returns of risky stocks are affected much stronger than returns of safe stocks. Still authors admit that the Sharpe–Lintner capital asset pricing model (CAPM) used in their analysis of investors' behavior might account for the acquired findings.

The research of Schmeling and Schrimpf (2011) represents a complement to the Cohen, Polk and Vuolteenaho (2005) asset pricing model, since it does not take money illusion hypothesis and the proxy hypothesis as the joint hypothesis, but rather discriminates between competing hypotheses. In particular, the authors suggest a model-free test, based on the relationship of investor's subjective expectations about future growth of output, inflation and stock returns. Findings suggest that the expected inflation does not proxy for future output movements or for the higher risk aversion. Rather it appears that subjective expectations are consistent with money illusion explanation, which is the main indicator of the predictive power of inflation for stock returns. In addition, they find that inflation expectations negatively affect subjective expectations of investors about stock returns, which contradicts with the risk aversion explanation, but is in line with money illusion.

Apart from money illusion, an alternative hypothesis is proposed by Chen, Lung, and Wang (2009) to explain investors' behavior. The so-called "resale hypothesis" suggests that the level and volatility of mispricing is positively related to heterogeneous beliefs of investors toward dividend growth rates.[2] These subjective beliefs are considered to be affected by the overconfidence of investors in their own private signals, as documented by Kyle and Wang (1997) or Hirshleifer and Subrahmanyam (1998). They empirically prove that both money illusion and resale hypothesis are relevant explanations in explaining the level of stock mispricing, but the resale hypothesis appears to have better explanatory power in the case of high or volatile price level.

As Modigliani and Cohn (1979) mention, there is much evidence that even knowledgeable investors find it surprising that the appropriate capitalization rate may become negative with sufficiently high inflation. If the Modigliani–Cohn hypothesis is accepted, it cannot be ruled out that in addition to investors, lending institutions and business managers are subject to money illusion as well. This has significant implications for the behavior of firms and their profits.

Furthermore, it appears that money illusion is highly probable in the case of price level fluctuations, which is in line with the results of Cohn and Lessard (1980) or Cohen, Polk, and Vuolteenaho (2005), whereas undervaluation will be noted by investors in the case of stable price level. Furthermore, the Modigliani–Cohn hypothesis proved to affect the stock market investors, but not bond market investors. The reason is that nominal bonds exhibit constant cash flows in nominal terms. Thus, the estimation of its long-term growth rate under a nominal frame is similar like under the real frame. On the other hand, the nature of stocks is rather different. If stock market investors erroneously expect constant long-term growth in nominal terms, they tend to use higher nominal interest rates to discount unchanged expectations of future nominal dividends. In other words, the investor fails to adjust the nominal growth rate of the stock toward the nominal discount rate. As a result, the dividend-price ratio moves with the nominal bond yield. If we assume constant expected long-term growth of the stock in real terms, but the investor expects it to be constant in nominal terms, the stock prices in equilibrium are undervalued when inflation is high and overvalued, when inflation is low.

This behavior of investors on the stock market was confirmed in the study of Campbell and Vuolteenaho (2004) who found out with the help of the vector autoregression model (VAR model) that the dividend-price ratio is positively related to inflation, leading to too low (high) stock prices in times of high (low) inflation. Many studies, such as Ritter and Warr (2002), Lee (2010), Acker and Duck (2013), Basu, Markov, and Shivakumar (2010), and Chordia and Shivakumar (2005), built their investigation of Modigliani–Cohn's money illusion on the interpretation about the positive relationship between the dividend–price ratio and inflation.

So far, the discussion has concentrated on the elaboration of money illusion effects that were inconsistent with expected direction of Fisher's effect. However, studies like Boudoukh and Richardson (1993) empirically prove that nominal market returns are at low frequency positively correlated with inflation and are thereby consistent with expected working of the Fisher effect. One might ask whether this finding is consistent with money illusion or not. Brunnermeier and Julliard (2008) claim that even though investors underestimate the nominal growth of earnings after an increase in inflation, they will soon find out their deception once the actual nominal earnings are known. King and Watson (1997) also confirm the existence of long-run Fisher effect, because the long-run real stock returns do not respond to a permanent inflation shock. Yeh and Chi (2009) confirm the existence of the short-run and partially long-run negative relationship between inflation and real stock returns, which is in line with the money illusion hypothesis but also in line with tax effects hypothesis.

In contrast to the previous research, Basak and Yan (2010) conducted their analysis not only for stock but also for the bond market. The authors designed an equilibrium asset pricing model (CRRA—constant relative risk aversion model) exposed to inflationary fluctuations, which incorporates money illusion. Money illusion is supposed to be partial in a sense that the investor partially overlooks the impact of inflation on his purchasing power, because it simplifies his decision-making process and implies negligible welfare loss. The Modigliani–Cohn hypothesis is thereby incorporated by assuming an investor who discounts future real payoffs by a combination of nominal and real interest rates. A crucial parameter is introduced, which represents a degree of money illusion by checking the bias toward nominal rates. This formulation enables a benchmark case to be built, which represents a combination of investor not subject to money illusion, and an investor deceived by money illusion. At the partial equilibrium level, the authors demonstrated that investors subject to money illusion tend to consume less with rising price level because they consider the consumption more expensive. However, rational investors are aware of the fact that real prices have not changed. At the aggregate level, they find a positive relationship between the dividend-price ratio and expected inflation under money illusion. The explanation of this result is based on outcomes obtained at partial equilibrium level. Since the money-illusioned investor is induced to consume less when the price level increases, higher expected inflation makes lower future demand for consumption. In other words, future consumption is less valuable.[3] Since long-term bonds and stocks represent claims to future consumption, higher expected inflation lowers their prices or leads to higher dividend price ratio and long bond yields. Furthermore, the basic model is extended by introducing heterogeneous agents with different degrees of money illusion, which further supports the robustness of the main results.

It is also worth noting that the stock market may suffer from money illusion, but not necessarily of the Modigliani–Cohn type. Engsted and Pedersen (2016) find a rather negative relationship between the dividend-price ratio and expected inflation. This finding is generated through modified methodology of Basak and Yan (2010) model.[4] Thus, findings are in contrast with previous studies like Basak and Yan (2010) or Campbell and Vuolteenaho (2004) who find a positive relationship. Their findings are in line with long-term development of the US stock market dividend yield, which is a very strong predictor of future long-horizon inflation.

The presence of money illusion in financial markets is also subject to investigation from the point of view of experimental economics. Noussair, Richter and Tyran (2012) conducted an experiment in which they proved that a purely nominal shock has substantial effects on real asset market prices because of investors affected by money illusion. In particular, there exists asymmetry in price adjustment, since after an inflationary shock prices adjust upwards relatively fast, but after a deflationary shock prices adjust only slowly. This slow inertial adjustment has substantial real effects in terms of mispricing in asset markets. Behavioral concepts of nominal loss aversion and mental accounting are utilized to explain the decision-making of investors, which has rather asymmetric effects. The nominal capital loss averse investor performs mental accounting, but fails to perceive that a capital gain occurs even if he sells a good first and then replaces is it with a purchase of an identical good at a lower nominal price. He does not perceive a capital gain when selling precedes purchase, and rather considers it as two separate transactions. As a result, a deflationary exogenous shock on an asset market,[5] composed of fundamental value traders and nominal capital loss averse agents, will generate the following behavior:

- A willingness to pay and accept of rational traders decreases by the same multiple as the increase in the value of the currency.
- Nominal capital loss averse investors (who have no units of assets) are willing to purchase units of assets at the new lower nominal price.
- Nominal capital loss averse investors (who have units of assets in inventory) are unwilling to sell units of assets at lower nominal price than the original purchase price.

This resistance to sell will create nominal price inertia and upward pressure on real prices. Thus, adjustment is slow and the effect of mispricing in asset markets strong. However, in the case of inflationary exogenous shock, the willingness of capital loss averse agents (who have units of assets) to sell at higher nominal market price is the same, like the willingness of capital loss averse agents (who have no units of assets) to purchase at the higher nominal market price. Capital loss averse agents who have units of assets are willing to purchase at the pre-shock market price. There is no reason for withholding, which leads to smooth adjustment. The aforementioned comments confirm rather asymmetric effects of inflationary and deflationary shocks in asset markets.

Recently there has been a new development in this field, which moves beyond stocks and bonds toward household finance literature to examine the effects of money illusion built on loss aversion and framing effects. The work of Tyran and Stephens (2016) represents a step forward since household finance is subject to substantial behavioral bias, including money illusion, which has not received attention yet. They subject to investigation a quasi-representative sample of the Danish population and examine money illusion features based on the combination of survey and official financial and sociodemographic data. A crucial role in the investigation is played by the money illusion index, constructed in the vein of prospect theory, which produces the illusion of certain gains despite a real loss being the case. Second, authors introduce nominal assets (bank deposits and bonds defined in money terms with nominal income stream) and real assets (including real estate and stocks with real income stream). In fact, nominal assets are associated with nominal gains, which are sometimes real losses hidden by inflation. In contrast, real assets are associated with nominal and real losses. Since nominal assets are "nominally safe," it might produce some degree of bias toward nominal representation associated with money illusion. The logic is simple. In times of high inflation, real losses will become nominal gains. In times of low inflation and volatile stock and real estate prices, investors subject to money illusion and loss aversion will be driven away from real assets toward nominal assets. This may happen even if nominal assets offer lower real returns, because of inflation. Empirical findings are in line with outlined theoretical framework. Results suggest that the money illusion is strongly associated with individual asset allocation. If individuals exhibit money illusion above average, they tend to invest 10 percent less in real assets compared to individuals with below average money illusion. Therefore, individuals prone to money illusion tend to allocate their wealth more in nominal assets rather than real assets, which is associated with substantial costs. Bias toward nominal representation is associated with lower rates of returns.

Money illusion and housing markets

As already argued, investors subject to money illusion value an asset inversely to the overall level of inflation, which leads to undervaluation/overvaluation of assets during periods of high/low inflation. Kearl (1979) and Follain (1982) empirically prove that the effects of higher inflation might be reflected even in the housing market in terms of lower demand for housing. This knowledge has been utilized in the work of Brunnermeier and Julliard (2008) who investigated the relationship between housing price movements and inflation that might be attributed to money illusion.

In particular, it is supposed that a rise in inflation can generate a substantial fall in housing prices in an environment composed of agents, which are prone to money illusion. Agents are considered to be subject to money illusion if they base their decision of renting or buying a house on a comparison between monthly rent and a monthly fixed nominal interest rate mortgage. In other words, they tend to take a nominal interest rate as a proxy for a real interest rate and suppose that they move in the lockstep. They wrongly attribute a rise in inflation to a rise in interest rate. As a result, they overestimate the real cost of future mortgage payments and cause a downward pressure on housing prices when inflation rises. In this aspect, a special form of money illusion may arise, if owners of homes are nominally risk averse to losses, which has been empirically examined by Genesove and Mayer (2001) and will be subject to investigation later in the chapter.

Still, the link between housing price movements and inflation might be not only due to money illusion but also due to financing frictions. First, some authors like Lessard and Modigliani (1975) or Tucker (1975) refer to the so-called "tilt effect." They empirically prove that under nominal fixed payment and with fixed interest rate mortgages, inflation may shift the real burden of mortgage payments toward the earlier years of the financing of a mortgage. This lowers the availability of the mortgages and consequently leads to a reduction in housing demand. Brunnermeier and Julliard (2008) point out that it is highly unlikely that the tilt effect plays the role since price level adjusted mortgage, or the graduate payment mortgage, have been available to house buyers since 1970s. Instead, "lock-in effect" might be the case. If inflation and nominal interest rate are higher, then households who have lock-in a non-portable mortgage with a low fixed nominal interest rate, might be reluctant to sell their house to buy a new house of better quality. This leads to a fall in demand for high-quality residential properties and reduces the supply of low-quality residential properties. However, lock-in effect evaporates when inflation and nominal interest rate fall.

The presence of money illusion in the housing market might be verified by investigating the link between inflation and the price-rent ratio. As Brunnermeier and Julliard (2008) suggest, the price-rent ratio appears as a good predictor of future price and rent changes, since it isolates analysis from fundamental movements (changes in construction cost, demographic changes and changes in housing quality), which have had symmetrical effects on housing prices and rents. Although renting and buying house are not perfect substitutes, long-run movements in the rent level should capture the long-run movements in service flow.

Second, the proxy effect is another important element through which inflation could affect the price-rent ratio. Either inflation may drive up the riskiness of the environment and risk aversion of agents, followed by an increase in risk premium and fall in real estate prices, or inflation, disruptive for the economy, might represent a proxy for future downturns and a consequent fall in housing prices. Brunnermeier and Julliard (2008), with the help of the price-rent ratio, decompose rational channels through which inflation could affect housing-price movements and an implied mispricing component. Their findings suggest that there is neither supportive evidence for the proxy effect nor for market frictions (tilt effect or lock-in effect). Furthermore, the large share of variation in the mispricing component is explained by inflation variability and nominal interest rate movement. As a result, the link between inflation and housing market mispricing seems to be attributed to an aggregate money illusion phenomenon.

The housing market is also subject to substantial nominal loss aversion, which might be considered as a special form of money illusion outlined in Chapter 3. Genesove and Meyer (2001) examined the presence of this phenomenon in the housing market of downtown Boston in the 1990s. Whereas in a boom houses sell quickly at prices close to the sellers asking prices or even above, in a bust, houses stay on the market for a long period of time with asking prices well above the selling prices. The authors suspect that the seller's reservation price may be less flexible than the buyer's due to money illusion. Their findings suggest that sellers exhibit substantial nominal loss aversion in the residential real estate market, which seems to confirm money illusion phenomena. Specifically, this explanation is based on a prospect theory of Kahneman and Tversky (1979, 1992), which claims that individuals are much more sensitive to losses than to equivalent gains. Additionally, sellers tend to nominally anchor the nominal purchase price as the reference point. As a result, when house prices fall after a boom, nominally averse sellers, whose expected selling price falls below original purchase price, tend to set an asking price well above the level of the asking price of other sellers, and thereby stay longer on the market. Additionally, sellers facing a smaller loss tend to set a much higher marginal mark-up of price over the expected selling price, compared to sellers facing a larger loss. Also, Einiö, Kaustia and Puttonen (2008) confirm the reluctance of apartment owners in the Helsinki area to sell at a nominal loss, with disproportional number of apartments sold at the nominal buying price.

Nominal loss aversion in the housing market was also proved by experimental surveys. Tyran and Stephens (2012) subjected a large heterogeneous sample to an experimental investigation and discovered that the individual's evaluation of a housing transaction is systematically biased by nominal loss aversion, in which real losses loom larger. Results show that the interaction of money illusion and loss aversion is undisputable and may be well applied to other areas like nominal rigidity in labor markets, and so on.

The investigation of money illusion in housing markets is also topical in the context of the Fisher equation. The study of Piazzesi and Schneider (2008) might be of particular attention in this sense. Their model yields interesting outcomes in which investors, prone to money illusion, confuse nominal interest rates with changes in real interest rate. In contrast, rational investors keep in line with development, where nominal interest rates move together with expected inflation. Particularly interesting are the implications for the housing market in terms of a housing boom. This follows from a disagreement of illusionary and rational investors about real interest rates. If for instance inflation expectations of rational investors rise above the historical level, a rise in nominal interest rate will follow. Investors prone to money illusion mistakenly perceive a rise in nominal interest rates as a rise in real interest rates. As a result, their subjective real rate is higher than the actual real interest rate of smart investors. On the other hand, if inflation expectations of rational investors are unusually low, followed by fall in nominal interest rates, investors prone to money illusion perceive a lower real interest rate than is the actual rate. In the former case, like times of expected high inflation in 1970s, rational investors tend to borrow and move to the real estate market, while individuals prone to money illusion are deterred from borrowing and housing by the high nominal rates. In the latter case, individuals prone to money illusion increase their demand for housing and mortgages due to the false notion of a low real interest rate. Rational investors instead invest into bonds. Notwithstanding, in both cases of a high or low nominal interest rate, borrowing and lending is stimulated and a housing boom occurs.

Money illusion and nominal rigidity

The revolution in rational expectations suppressed the view that nominal wages and prices play a role in economic decisions. However, as documented by

Shafir et al. (1997), Fehr and Tyran (2001), Modigliani and Cohn (1979), and others, this premise is too extreme and it appears that money illusion seems to be widespread phenomena not only at the individual level but also at the macroeconomic level.

This view was emphasized by Tobin (1972), as mentioned in Chapter 1, when he admitted that under certain circumstances money illusion might account for downward nominal rigidity with important aggregate-level effects in the form of a permanent trade-off between inflation and unemployment. This view is sometimes called "Tobin's theorem." Tobin's view was affirmed by Eckstein and Brinner (1972), who claim that low inflation is ignored by workers and firms during wage bargaining. As soon as inflation rises, workers and firms become more aware of its effects, which will be reflected more in nominal wage contracts. This will create a permanent negative trade-off between inflation and unemployment at low rates of inflation. Once inflation reaches a particular threshold, workers and the firm will be fully aware of inflation and incorporate it into their expectations, leading to a disappearance of the trade-off between inflation and unemployment and return to the classical version of the Phillips curve. In this sense, this explanation is very close to the concept of near-rationality formulated by Akerlof and Yellen (1985) and utilized later by Akerlof, Dickens, and Perry (1996) and Akerlof (2002), with respect to first-order effects at the aggregate level.

The investigation of nominal rigidities with respect to money illusion has received considerable attention in many more recent studies like Vaona (2013), Hogan (2013), Fortin (2013), Habu (2011), or Fehr and Goette (2005). Specifically, the work of Akerlof et al. (1996, 2000), which received considerable attention in Chapter 3, represents a substantial challenge by proving downward nominal wage rigidity, implying a negative relationship between inflation and unemployment.[6] The existence of downward nominal rigidity is a rather empirical question, but it seems that its existence is extensive and persistent in advanced countries as pointed out in many empirical studies (Fortin 2013, among others).

The pervasive presence of downward nominal rigidity seems to be controversial especially with respect to the existence of money illusion, which seems to be in contradiction with the rational expectations hypothesis. Economists are reluctant to accept the fact that money illusion might play role, since it is hard to believe that it would persist in the long run. The long-run effects of money illusion are addressed by Vaona (2013), Miao and Xie (2013), and Fehr and Tyran (2005a), and will be subject to evaluation later in this chapter. Still persistent but transitory changes in aggregate demand might have a permanent influence on output and employment due to the path dependency in the economy, as suggested by Fontana and Palacio-Vera (2007). In contrast, Akerlof et al. (2000) in their analysis remain cautious about the evidence in favor of downward nominal-wage rigidity, since it is not clear that such a rigidity is a pervasive feature and further empirical investigation is required.

However, as already suggested in Chapter 3, trends in behavioral economics (Shafir et al. 1997; Akerlof 2002; Akerlof and Shiller 2009) together with theories, which allow for potential deviation from full rationality (Haltiwanger and Waldman 1989, Akerlof and Yellen 1985), resurrected the concept of the money illusion as a potential explanation for aggregate-level effects. Therefore, it is worth addressing its possible role in the investigation of nominal rigidities.

If we briefly summarize the relation of money illusion to nominal rigidities, based on our knowledge from previous chapters, the issue might be outlined as follows: downward nominal rigidity is related to psychological costs, which leads to the failure of workers, who resist money wage cuts but voluntarily accept real wage cuts during inflation times, which alleviates their purchasing power. Also, Akerlof et al. (1996) admit that individuals are concerned about relative wages, with resistance toward nominal wage cuts, where inflation, eroding all wages simultaneously, creates space for real wage cuts. There is a clear connotation with Keynes (1936), who claimed that it would be impracticable for workers to resist every reduction of real wages when inflation evaporates the purchasing power of money, unless this reduction reaches an extreme degree. This has been further elaborated on by many others like Tobin (1972), as already mentioned in Chapter 1, Schultze (1959) or Samuelson and Solow (1960).

Psychological aspects appear to be crucial in an explanation for the role of money illusion in occurrence of nominal rigidities. The concept of fairness and the loss aversion, introduced in Chapter 3 in the pioneering work of Shafir et al. (1997), represent fundamental behavioral aspects with respect to money illusion together with non-indexing of contracts, as they might play a significant role in downward nominal rigidity, leading to suboptimal outcomes.

Fairness and nominal rigidity

Fairness is acknowledged as an important element in perception of well-being. Fisher (1928) emphasized that social injustice may be dangerous as it may lead to strikes, riots or violence. The concept of fairness might also be witnessed implicitly in the work of Keynes (1925) with respect to nominal rigidity. Based on one of his examples, he concluded that in conditions of distrust, individual groups of labor perceive the pressure for a nominal wage cut as attack on them and are resistant to money wage cuts. In contrast, labor is less resistant to money wage cuts in the case of an increase in general cost of living. In modern economic theory, the importance of fairness is emphasized by equity theory and relative deprivation theory.

The equity theory mentioned in Adams (1963) states that motivation and positive outcomes may be preserved only when employees find their treatment to be fair in terms of a fair balance between their inputs (hard work, skill level, acceptance, enthusiasm, etc.) and an employee's outputs (salary, benefits, recognition, etc.). If fair treatment is not the case, employees become demotivated, which results in reduced effort and disruptive behavior.

Equity theory goes hand in hand with relative deprivation theory. As stated by Runciman (1966, p. 10): "The magnitude of relative deprivation is the extent of the difference between desired situation and that of the person desiring it." As a result, people deprived of things valuable in society evaluate what they should have compared to others and join social movements.

As a result, both theories suggest that fairness plays a substantial role, with possible negative implications. The working of the concept of fairness has been already confirmed in the labor market in the previous chapter within the studies of Shafir et al. (1997), Kahneman, Knetsch, and Thaler (1986), or Agell and Bennmarker (2002). Generally, findings indicate a reluctance of workers toward downward money wage cuts, because they are deceived by money illusion. Furthermore, these studies suggest that there exists a wide application of fairness with respect to an explanation of downward nominal rigidities.

However, the concept of fairness is subject to discussion.

First, survey findings might be unreliable measures. It seems that they rely too much on an individual's perception of hypothetical events, not taking into account how individuals would respond to actual events. For instance, the response to question such as: "Do you consider this situation to be fair?" is subject to the context in which the circumstances would arise as noted by Yates (1998). As a result, although findings based on a survey bring useful information as mentioned by Hogan (2013), direct empirical evidence based on observed wage changes is highly desirable.

Second, the concept of fairness itself is subject to criticism. Specifically, it is difficult to distinguish between workers, who are concerned about their wage relative to the highest earners, and workers who are simply happier with a higher level of income. For instance, Clark and Oswald (1996) surveyed 5,000 employees as part of the "British Household Panel Study." They concluded that respondents are happier when having higher wages relative to a benchmark. Cappelli and Sherer (1988) provide survey results of 600 airline employees in the United States, which indicate increased satisfaction with pay as wages rise relative to the market wages.

Moreover, the situation of a worker who is concerned about fairness might be observationally equivalent to a worker who is simply comparing his wage relative to alternative options. A worker who is comparing the costs and benefits of staying in a current job is in line with the theory of competitive behavior on labor markets. As Yates (1998) notes fairness concerns might not be the case and thereby the reason for downward nominal rigidity of wages evaporates.

Third, the literature on fairness based solely on self-interest does not seem to match the findings of experimental research. For instance, people in experimental competitive games often give up income if it leads to fairer distribution, despite the whole "pie" is smaller as documented by Fehr and Schmidt (2006), Smith (2006), or Bolton (1991). As a result, alternative models of distribution decisions were formulated. For instance, Charness and Rabin (2002), based on their results, refer to the existence of charity social preferences in which individuals tend to place emphasis on outcomes for those being worse off than they. This suggests interesting implications for the labor market because certain groups might reject a money wage increase or even might accept a money wage cut. This may alleviate the notion of downward nominal wage rigidity.

Last, many experimental studies in settings with incomplete contracts (especially labor contracts) identify the phenomenon of reciprocal behavior based on the notion of fairness, which leads to a rejection of unfair offers and induces to make fair offers, for instance Fehr, Kirchsteiger, and Riedl (2002), Charness (2004), and Falk and Fischbacher (2006). In particular, Fehr and Fischbacher's (2004) analysis suggests that participants tend to punish those individuals who acted unfairly. This implies that people may prefer policies aimed at punishing unfair behavior. This might be applied in the labor market, where individuals judge a wage to be unfair relative to the market wage on related labor market as a reference. This is utilized by Green and Harrison (2009) in their fairness model of minimum wage setting.[7] They examine the data in ten Canadian provinces from 1969 to 2005, and conclude that the minimum wage is set according to standards of fairness, which may eliminate inequality and especially ban unfair transactions like unfairly low wages of unskilled labor. In particular, the mix of the societal notion of justice, reflection of self-interest, or charity, appears to play a role in the labor market, suggesting that fairness may take different forms, supporting or alleviating the argument for downward nominal wage rigidity and related money illusion.

Still, many studies prove that fairness is an issue in downward nominal wage rigidity. Agell and Lundborg (2003) present a survey on wage rigidity in a sample of 159 Swedish firms in period of very low inflation and high unemployment. Their results suggest a strong role for pervasive nominal wage rigidity, given by institutional features of the Swedish labor market (setting wage contract, the structure of bargaining institutions, etc.). They also admit the importance of fairness and the concept of relative wages. In particular, they document the virtual absence of nominal wage cuts over several years. Although Bewley (1998) argues that Keynes relative wage theory is outdated, since surveyed workers have little knowledge about the wage rates at other firms, Agell and Lundborg (2003) have a different opinion. According to them, the Swedish environment exhibits great awareness of employees of the wage distribution inside and outside the company's environment. They find support for their claims in the replies of managers, of which 40 percent suggested the importance of Keynes theory of nominal wage rigidity. Also, Brown et al. (2008) finds evidence for relative wage considerations based on a sample of 16,000 British workers. Clark and Oswald (1996), based on sample of 5,000 British workers, also conclude that workers consider not absolute income but income relative to some reference level. As a result, we may admit that workers' concern about relative wages might constitute an important reason for nominal rigidity. This creates a strong argument in favor of money illusion, which was implicitly assumed in Keynes theory, as noted in Chapter 1.

Particularly interesting is an investigation of the extent of downward nominal rigidity associated with concept of fairness and nominal loss aversion in an environment of low nominal wage growth. As opposed to the initial presumption, it shows that related real effects are substantial even in low inflation environment. Fehr and Goette (2005) base their research on the Swiss experience between 1991 and 1997, when inflation was reaching very low levels over several consecutive years. Nominal wage growth fell rapidly from 7 percent to 1 percent between 1991 and 1994, and nominal wage remained at low level for four years. The presumption was that agents had enough time to adjust to this environment and nominal wage cuts should be considered as nothing unusual and the kind of necessity in the face of structural changes induced by low inflation environment. In contrast, results show that the low inflation environment only slightly alleviated the reluctance to cut nominal wages, and over time the relevance of nominal wage rigidity intensified. The authors admit that behavioral features like fairness standards and nominal loss aversion a play significant role in the downward nominal wage rigidity, even in times of low inflation. The model introduces heterogeneous individuals with regards to fairness standards and the degree of money illusion, leaving some with flexible wages and some with rigid wages.

Results show that fairness standards render nominal wage cuts costly. Fairness standards are closely linked to job movers versus stayers, with results suggesting that it is easier to apply money wage cuts in the case of job movers than in case of job stayers. Also, the loyalty and work morale of full-time workers is more important than of part-time workers, suggesting a strong case for nominal wage rigidity in the case of the former. Additionally, job stayers and full-time workers have more firm-specific human capital than job movers and part-time workers. This implies that nominal wage rigidity is stronger for full-time workers and job stayers. An interesting phenomena is that a fraction of workers with uncut wages rises, whereas the frequency of wage cuts remains the same. This implies that despite the greater need for wage cuts at a time of low inflation, the impact of nominal rigidity is substantial. To sum up, the evidence based on behavioral features associated with money illusion, suggests that nominal wage rigidity also persists in periods of low nominal wage inflation, indicating important real effects in terms of unemployment.

It appears that fairness issues together with money illusion are associated with a strong negative relationship between work morale and unilateral nominal wage cuts, as reported by Blinder and Choi (1990), Campbell and Kamlani (1997), or Bewley (1998). A weaker relationship was found between wage levels and work morale. In addition, people prefer a rise in nominal wages rather than an unchanged wage, although both options are identical in real terms (Loewenstein and Sicherman 1991). Based on the experimental survey of Haldane (1999), 30 percent of respondents consider nominal wage rise to positively affect their sense of job satisfaction.

Downward nominal wage rigidity is also connected with fairness issues on the side of employers who are not subject to money illusion, but who are aware of the fact that employees consider cuts unfair. Bewley (1999) conducts research based on 336 interviews with business leaders, union officials, employment counsellors and business advisors in Connecticut during the recession of the early 1990s. He finds that employers are unwilling to cut nominal wages of employees because it is considered by workers as unfair. Furthermore, it is associated with significant aversion to nominal losses, which undermines the morale of employees. As a result, the nominal wage rigidity is result of nominally deceived employees, in which case managers are rationally reluctant to cut money wages and rather cut jobs. The fact that firms are concerned with the perceived fairness and consistency of their internal wage structures is also documented by Katz (1986) and Doeringer and Piore (1971). A particularly interesting feature is that fairness judgements seem to be affected by nominal but also by real wage cuts triggering a strong negative response as proved by Goette and Huffman (2007) on a student sample entering the labor market.

Furthermore, it is worth mentioning the rather asymmetric effects of fair versus unfair treatment. As Fehr, Goette and Zehnder (2009) point out, the positive effects of fair treatment on behavior are small, whereas negative effects of unfair behavior loom larger. This might be applied straightly on labor market. Employees will react positively to 10 percent rise in nominal wages by increasing effort, whereas in the case of a10 percent nominal wage cut, they will be substantially antagonized by unfairness and the effect will be much stronger with significant reduction in effort. This is in line with Kahneman et al. (1986), who state that a small cut in wage harms much more fairness judgements than a small increase in wage stimulates fairness perceptions. This is in line with loss aversion as discussed later in the chapter. The asymmetric effects of fair and unfair treatment were also proved empirically.[8] Kandil (2006, 2010) provides evidence at the aggregate level for a large variety of industrialized countries, where wages generally respond stronger to positive shocks than to negative shocks of similar magnitude, indicating the presence of downward nominal rigidity.

Loss aversion and nominal rigidity

As already mentioned, we may question the relevance of survey results in terms of consistency of hypothetical and actual events. Paradoxically, research shows that loss aversion in terms of money illusion, in which agents exhibit significant loss aversion toward nominal losses, might not be that improbable. As already mentioned in Chapter 3, Thaler, Tversky, Kahneman and Schwartz (1997) prove the existence of loss aversion in their study of a subject's allocation to investment funds, and Shafir et al. (1997) and Stephens and Tyran (2012) in the housing market, empirical studies like Lintner (1956) or Fama and Babiak (1968) confirm that managers of joint-stock companies adopt such dividend policies to minimize the probability of dividend cut, since they fear that markets will react more adversely to a cut in dividends compared to rise in dividends.

Nominal loss aversion is heavily utilized in the labor market. For instance, Kahneman, Knetsch and Thaler (1986) report in their survey that 78 percent of respondents would prefer a 7 percent money wage increase when inflation was 12 percent to a 5 percent money wage cut when prices were stable. The reduction in real wages was identical in both cases, indicating thereby the proneness of subjects to money illusion. On the one hand, these findings indicate satisfaction of workers from having an increase in money wage (although real wage was constant), on the other hand, it indicates the respondents' loss aversion to money wage cut. Elsby (2005) tests the model of downward nominal wage rigidity based on workers' resistance to nominal wage cuts, concluding that behavioral implications of loss aversion remain significant. The importance of the loss aversion with respect to the presence of downward nominal wage rigidity was proven even in conditions of low inflation as already outlined in research of Fehr and Goette (2005).

Workers' behavior is nicely summarized in the vein of empirical evidence of Ahrens, Pirschel and Snower (2014). Workers tend to attribute larger weight to perceived utility loss from a wage decrease than the perceived utility gain from a wage increase of equal magnitude. Empirical results prove that wages are completely rigid with respect to small labor demands shocks, relatively downward rigid for large shocks, but downward rigid and upward flexible for medium sized labor demand shocks. Therefore, nominal wage rigidity is rather asymmetric.

We may find further extensive evidence that money illusion, fairness and loss aversion go hand in hand as a possible explanation for downward nominal wage rigidity. Dunn (1996) provides evidence of loss aversion based on wage data from seven US labor markets, which is in line with the studies of Thaler (1980), Knetsch and Sinden (1984), and Kahneman, Knetsch, and Thaler (1990). As already mentioned, Bewley (1999) finds evidence for the nominal loss aversion on the part of employees, based on which firms are reluctant to cut wages. Also, Bewley (1995) conducted a survey in Connecticut, the results of which imply that employees prone to money illusion exhibit significant loss aversion together with fairness considerations.

Non-indexed contracts and dislike of going first

In Chapter 3, the survey of Shafir et al. (1997) proved that nominally risk-averse individuals, subject to money illusion, may perceive indexed contracts as riskier, since the indexed amount which they get might be lower or higher in nominal terms than a fixed dollar amount. As noted by Akerlof and Shiller (2009), non-indexed contracting is widely applied and might be considered as indicator of nominal deception leading to nominal wage rigidity. Another interesting feature worth a note is a dislike of going first. If workers are confronted with a wage cut of 10 percent, they may resist to go first although they know that others will follow, because they are afraid of losing out in the meantime. On the other hand, workers are more than willing to go first in the case of a 10 percent nominal wage increase, because they can gain relative to others.

Money illusion, nominal wage rigidity and Phillips curve

The study of Akerlof et al. (1996) and (2000) mentioned in Chapter 3, was one of the fundamentals, which found support for the long-run trade-off between inflation and unemployment by incorporating money illusion. Other studies emerged, aiming to verify the macroeconomic relevance of nominal wage rigidity related to the Phillips curve and find stronger or weaker support for the existence of nominal wage rigidity.

Djoudad and Sargent (1997) applied the same methodology to Canadian macroeconomic data between 1956 and 1989, and obtained similar results in favor of downward nominal rigidity. Lundborg and Sacklén (2006) adopted the model of Akerlof, Dickens and Perry to Swedish data and found the case for inflation and unemployment trade-off. Maugeri (2010), working from Italian data, concluded that a long-run trade-off between inflation and unemployment is the case at low and moderate rates of inflation. Gottschalk and Fritsche (2005) examined the German Phillips curve with the help of multivariate cointegration analysis in the 1980s and 1990s and found a negative relation between inflation and unemployment.

Vaona (2013) arrived with an innovative approach and estimated the long-run Phillips curve in the New Keynesian model of sticky wages, in which agents are subject to money illusion. The money illusion concept is based on the nominal anchoring of Shafir et al. (1997), where individuals are aware of the difference between nominal and real values. In addition, money illusion in Vaona's study builds on a numerosity effect, which is rather similar to high-number money illusion introduced by Tyran (1999). Based on this effect, individuals tend to judge quantity on the basis of the number of units, without considering other factors. Results show that if agents tend to over-perceive real economic variables, the impact of a monetary shock is less severe. This is given by the fact that individuals believe that their real wage is higher than their actual real wage and thereby change their nominal wage by a lower amount, leading to more positive money non-superneutralities. However, if agents under perceive real economic variables, the impact of monetary shock is more serious, because they change their nominal wage by a substantial amount, leading to more negative money non-superneutralities.

Another set of studies aimed to investigate money illusion effects with the help of a wage Phillips curves within Tobin's theorem.[9] Fortin (2013) estimated that a wage Phillips curve based on Canadian macro data in period 1956 to 2011, in line with Tobin's theorem, described the resistance of workers toward nominal wage cuts. Results indicate a pervasive presence of downward nominal wage rigidity and thereby a strong case for money illusion, with significant aggregate-level effects. Furthermore, the model with money illusion features exhibits superior performance compared to the classical model with full wage flexibility.

However, Card and Hyslop (1997) and Farés and Lemieux (2001) failed to find the presence of downward nominal wage rigidity in the US and Canadian Phillips curves at the aggregate level. Downward nominal wage rigidity was only found at microeconomic level. However, as Fortin (2013) notes, their research suffers from deficiencies of blind linear trends and year dummies, and a rather simple explanation of higher unemployment by a constant upward trend. Stark and Sargent (2003) corrected the model of Card and Hyslop (1997) by accounting explicitly for changes in structural unemployment, and found that the slope of the Phillips curve based on Canadian data falls significantly after 1991.

Crawford and Wright (2001) aimed to estimate Tobin's type wage Phillips curve with incorporated money illusion based on Canadian dataset in the period 1978 to 1999. Results confirm that the long-run Phillips curve was convex, but at very low rates of inflation, implying that the downward nominal rigidity was the case, but was quantitatively small. This would speak in favor of the presence of money illusion only below some threshold limit in line with Keynes as suggested in Chapter 1. Additionally, the authors estimated that menu costs play a role in the replacement of nominal wage increases of 0.6 percent or less by wage freezes. In other words, measured zero-wage changes can arise, because employers do not adjust wages given the menu costs of changing wages as noted by Card and Hyslop (1997) and Crawford and Harrison (1998). Further, some small wage increases or decreases might be rounded at zero. As a result, the spike of the wage change distribution at zero would also include cases in which the actual wage would be zero instead of positive. Based on this, it cannot be deduced that all wage freezes are related to cases in which employees receive a wage change of zero rather than a wage cut as noted by Fortin (2013). Otherwise, the upward effect of downward nominal wage rigidity on wage growth might be overstated. Economically significant convexity of the Phillips curve at only low rates of inflation has lead the Bank of Canada to cite it as evidence that downward nominal wage rigidity is negligible for the economy (Bank of Canada 2011). However, the authors are criticized for their reliance on the universe of large unionized firms, which account for only 7 percent of private employment, and therefore cannot be considered as representatives of the Canadian labor market. As a result, their conclusion might not be relevant as evidence for negligible downward nominal rigidity at macroeconomic level.

Stark and Sargent (2003) also aim to verify a Tobin's wage Phillips curve with incorporated money illusion for Canadian cross-province data from 1981 to 1999. In contrast to Fares and Lemieux (2001), they model thoroughly determinants of structural unemployment like changes in social programs. They demonstrate that Tobin's model of the downward nominal rigidity has much better explanatory power than the classical model. The authors were motivated in their research by the failure of the classical Phillips curve to explain development in Canadian economy after 1991. Specifically, missing deflation was the problem to be explained. In period of 1992 to 1998, the unemployment equaled on average 10 percent, but the inflation rate remained unchanged around 1.5 percent. The similar trend was observed in the United States between 2009 and 2012, with unemployment at 9 percent on average and a steady inflation rate of around 1.6 percent (see, for instance, Gali 2011). Various explanations of this trend emerged in line with the classical model, such as supply side shocks, structural developments, inflation targeting policy, or flatter short-run Phillips curve, but appeared to be irrelevant. The available literature aims to re-estimate the classical model with a full set of time-varying parameters on a continuous basis (Demers 2003 or Khalaf and Kichian 2003), or to develop alternative options like Tobin's downward nominal wage rigidity hypothesis with incorporated money illusion (Fortin 2013; Stark and Sargent 2003; Fares and Lemieux 2001).

Money illusion and strategic environment

In Chapter 3 we tackled the experiment of Fehr and Tyran (2001), in which subject price choices differed after negative nominal shock with respect to the frame, in which they were displayed. The large difference in the post-shock phase between the adjustment under nominal frame compared to choices under the real frame revealed considerable nominal inertia, which was attributed to money illusion effects in strategic environment. The nature of strategic interaction appeared as crucial for money illusion to have pronouncing effects at the aggregate level. A crucial finding was that a mere biased belief about others money illusion is responsible for nominal rigidities although the money illusion might be negligible. Many studies got inspired by their research, such as Yellen and Akerlof (2006), Cannon and Cipriani (2006), Brunnermeier and Julliard (2008), and Basak and Yan (2010).

Strategic interaction with respect to money illusion was elaborated thoroughly in other studies of Fehr and Tyran (2005a, 2005b, 2007, 2008). The nature of strategic interaction affects not only the magnitude of nominal inertia but also expectation formation, which is rather sticky under strategic complementarity. Sticky expectations are translated into sticky price setting in this environment and consequently into the aggregate level. This nature of behavior is given by the costs resulting from the expectation error. Under strategic complementarity the rational player expects suboptimal money illusion behavior of other agents and tends to imitate their behavior and follows the crowd. In contrast under strategic substitutability, the rational player tends to compensate behavior of money illusion prone agents and chooses action farther away from theirs. However, it also appears that strategic substitutability provides incentives for players to be more rational and forward-looking. In contrast, exactly the opposite holds for strategic complementarity, the effect of which is intensified even by the biased belief about others having money illusion or even of those others expectation that others suffer from money illusion. As a result, subjects prone to money illusion appear to have a disproportionately large aggregate-level effect in case of strategic complementarity, but a disproportionally small effect in case of strategic substitutability.

Asymmetric effects of money illusion represent very interesting findings related to strategic complementarity. Asymmetric behavior is attributed to the effect of high number money illusion. In the case of a negative nominal shock one might expect that firms will adjust their prices respectively. However, experimental studies of Fehr and Tyran (2001, 2005a) prove that the adjustment is rather inertial. The mere biased belief about the attractiveness of nominal payoffs induced by high number money illusion in a strategic environment leads to a reluctance of subjects to adjust prices downwards. In other words, even rational subjects under conditions of strategic complementarity tend to choose high nominal payoffs (as a proxy for real payoffs) that are connected with higher price levels. In contrast, the adjustment of prices in the case of a positive shock is much faster. Subjects are willing to adjust their prices upwards, in line with a higher equilibrium price level after the shock, because this adjustment is associated with higher nominal payoffs. Asymmetric effects and especially downward rigidity of prices might also be attributed to nominal loss aversion, in which individuals tend to attribute greater weight to the size of losses than to the size gains of equal magnitude. Asymmetry in nominal inertia given by experimental evidence of the aforementioned studies might be of great importance in terms of the real economic effects of positive and negative monetary shocks.

A second important line of research is the investigation of permanent effects of money illusion. These effects are addressed with the help of experimental design containing multiple equilibria (Fehr and Tyran 2005b). In previous research on the short-run effects of money illusion, the design consisted of unique equilibrium to which nominal prices converged. To investigate permanent effects,[10] a conflict is created between the principle of nominal payoff dominance and the principle of real payoff dominance. In particular, the real payoff is highest and nominal payoff low in the first equilibrium. Thereby this equilibrium is Pareto-efficient. In contrast, the nominal payoff is highest, but the real payoff low in the second equilibrium. If a nominal payoff dominates in the decisions of individuals, they take nominal payoff as a proxy for real payoff. In other words, they are prone to money illusion and choose the second equilibrium. But if real payoff dominates, they are not prone to money illusion and they will choose the first Pareto-efficient equilibrium, where the real payoff is the highest. The studies of Fehr and Tyran (2005a, 2005b) provide striking evidence for the permanent effects of money illusion, since subjects tend to choose the second equilibrium with nominal payoff dominance.

Opponents argue that individual anomalies like money illusion tend to dissipate through learning. However, as was already demonstrated, learning in a strategic environment is rather difficult. Even if the individual effects of money illusion are temporary, there are large permanent effects in strategic environment. Especially in strategic environments with multiple equilibria it is impossible or too late to affect aggregate outcome. This is given by the fact that once individuals coordinate on inferior equilibria, they are locked and experience losses relative to efficient equilibrium as based on evidence of Fehr and Tyran (2005a, 2005b).

To sum up, the failure of rational agents to coordinate under strategic complementarity toward optimum outcomes, given the beliefs about money illusion, might generate substantial nominal rigidities. Also, Blinder, Canetti, Lebow, and Rudd (1998) provide evidence on a coordination failure as a source of nominal inertia. Especially inertial adjustment toward equilibrium after the negative nominal shock given by experimental evidence suggests, that money illusion might account for non-neutrality of money. Additionally, money illusion effects are not supposed to vanish over time, but seem to have long-run effects as individuals coordinate on inferior equilibria.

Efficiency wages

Money illusion is also applied in efficiency wage models. The survey results of Agell and Lundborg (2003) document that efficiency wage considerations still apply, with resulting real rigidities. In this aspect, the incorporation of money illusion into efficiency wage model might account for the presence of nominal rigidity.

Shafir et al. (1997) extend their research by introducing the model of efficiency wages in line with Solow (1979) and incorporate considerations about real wages affecting the willingness to supply effort. Apart from that they built into the model concerns regarding nominal wage increases. The resulting model represents an interaction of real and nominal rigidities. The authors admit that the resistance of workers to nominal wage cuts might be responsible for the fact that the continuous relationship between the cost of raising wages and the workers' effort no longer holds. In fact, employers are sensitive to the implications of fairness issues for workers' morale. As a result, the scope for nominal wage cuts is rather limited. The resulting compressed wage schedule of firms has substantial consequences even for workers who receive wage increases. As a result, money illusion affects not only the allocation of workers on the labor market, but also an aggregate level of employment. Authors propose a modification of the Tobin's model, which in its original version allows for no nominal wage cuts, which is too artificial situation. They also suggest that to utilize a theory of the determination of wage structure in a firm, which is capable of identifying money illusion on the part of workers and on the part of a firm and consequently explore possible institutional amendments to reduce some money illusion effects. Habu (2011) in his study aims to follow the research of Shafir et al. (1997) and extend the efficiency wage model to incorporate money illusion. He models separately the labor market with respect to nominal and real wages, coming to conclusion that unemployment in the real frame is higher than in the nominal frame, the difference for which is a direct consequence of money illusion. The study also proposes a possibility for the role of authority, which may indicate the fairness of the wage through signaling. This can substantially eliminate money illusion and the resulting unemployment under the nominal frame.

Relevance of nominal wage rigidity

Research about the nominal wage rigidity is rather extensive[11] and beyond the scope of this book. We focus solely on whether money illusion might account for nominal wage rigidity, about which many economists remain skeptical. It is worth making a few comments regarding this.

First, the literature provides rather mixed empirical findings. Some studies confirm that nominal rigidity and especially downward nominal wage rigidity, based on money illusion explanation, is a genuine phenomenon, for example, Shafir et al. (1997), Fortin (2013), Stark and Sargent 2003, Djoudad and Sargent (1997), Lundborg and Sacklén (2006), Maugeri (2010), Vaona (2013), Elsby (2005), Agell and Lundborg (2003), Bewley (1999), and many others mentioned in this chapter. In contrast, many studies find unconvincing evidence in favor of this hypothesis, like Card and Hyslop (1997), Farés and Lemieux (2001), McLaughlin (1994), or Lebow, Stockton, and Wascher (1995). Yates (1998) finds, in his study, the loss aversion and money illusion to be in line with experimental evidence, however, it is highly improbable that these factors prevail in the long run. The case for downward nominal rigidity is thereby theoretically and empirically unconvincing or not proven.

Second, the model of Akerlof et al. (1996) and (2000) built on money illusion, is subject to criticism. In particular, the long-run Phillips curve is computed with the help of the short-run estimated parameters, which suggests potential model misspecification by not accounting for shifts in the long-run non-accelerating rate of unemployment (NAIRU). Additionally, Blinder (2000) finds it inappropriate to use the neoclassical framework if labor demand is negatively sloped function of the real wage, because firms prone to money illusion would under-deflate the money wage, behaving like the real wage was higher than it is. As a result, firms in the case of the downward sloping labor curve would hire fewer workers in equilibrium. However, as Stiernstedt (2011) notes, the model of Akerlof, Dickens, and Perry does not contain any such conditions as neoclassical framework. Third, the model assumes that money illusion dissipates at higher rates of inflation, but it is persistent at low levels of inflation. Many economists like Svensson (2001) remain skeptical about the population being fooled by inflation with consequent real effects, especially due to a transparent monetary policy, which helps people to avoid money illusion. Additionally, we may also subject to scrutiny Tobin's money illusion hypothesis, which is applied to job stayers and not job switchers. Also, the inconsistent development of Tobin's theory might be subject to attention, where later in his work he rather does not admit the existence of money illusion.

Fourth, other forces might account for nominal wage rigidity rather than money illusion or fairness issues as noted by Fehr, Goette, and Zehnder (2009). For instance, some models of Malcomson (1999) show that a fixed wage contract may generate efficient levels of relationship specific investment. The incumbents' wages within these models respond solely to exogenous conditions if the external development becomes binding. Thus, the nominal wage won't be adjusted to change in real external options, as soon as the real wage is strictly within the intervals of the real external option. Once the external options become binding, the wage is adjusted. The resulting implications are that wage cuts will be less frequent during inflation and more frequent during deflation. However, this is not confirmed by empirical evidence. As Fehr and Goette (2005) show in the Switzerland case, there is a rather substantial impact of downward nominal rigidity despite the greater need for wage cuts at a time of low inflation. Additionally, no evidence suggests that nominal wage cuts became frequent during the Great Depression in the United States (Akerlof et al. 1996).

Money illusion and consumer behavior

As already mentioned in Chapter 3, money illusion effects might be utilized even in case of consumer behavior with respect to the substantial psychological costs of inflation. As suggested previously, consumers are said to be prone to money illusion if having difficulty between the change in a relative price and a general increase in prices. If consumers are not aware about the true nature of change in relative prices, inflation governs their behavior to suboptimal outcomes.

Consumption-saving decisions

First, money illusion seems to play a substantial role in the consumption-saving decisions of individuals. As already argued in Chapter 1, money illusion in the view of Tobin (1971) is expected to operate in a way that there is negative relationship between money income and real consumption expenditure, with real income constant. This relationship is intensified by the inelasticity of price expectations, because if the current prices are well above expected future prices, consumers tend to reduce present consumption in favor of future consumption and create savings. As a result, with higher money income and prices, there are higher savings out of the same real income. The additional effect, which intensifies the effects of money illusion, is related to the volume of accumulated savings, which affects the marginal propensity to save. In the case of a rise in money income and prices, the real value of accumulated savings is lower and consumers are supposed to consume less. Money illusion effects might be applied even to savings up to retirement as pointed out by Hogan (2013). If inflation rises, individuals subject to money illusion tend to anchor a nominal interest rate, assuming it moves in lockstep with the real interest rate. As a result, they overestimate the real value of the interest and save less for retirement than desirable. As a result, money illusion might significantly affect the particular living standard in retirement. Furthermore, given the long-time horizon, even a small overestimate of the real interest rate might generate a substantial effect. Gemma (2016) proves the effects of money illusion on consumption-saving decisions with the help of a laboratory experiment. Subjects deal with an environment, in which nominal values are displayed differently, but real values exhibit no difference. This setting implies an unchanged optimal real consumption path. Results suggest that higher rates of inflation induce subjects to consume more in early periods and less in later periods of the experiment. In deflationary situations, subjects also tend to consume more in early periods and less in later periods of the experiment. These striking results are explained by the fact that in the former case, subjects tend to anchor rising inflation, whereas in the second case they anchor decreasing nominal interest rate.

Inflation dislike

It is well known that the public expresses a dislike for inflation. As pointed out in Chapter 3, individuals are not only resistant to money wage cuts, but also dislike price increases. Shiller (1996) in his survey documents that distaste among the public for inflation is larger than it is among economists and is perceived to reduce the standard of living.

First, price cuts are one issue in which consumers exhibit a significant dislike for inflation either due to confusion or due to consequent doubts about the quality of the product. If we consider the former, it is argued that customers cannot calculate relative price changes when there are price cuts, since they are confused. This holds for an environment in which consumers were used to rising prices and price cuts are expected as something highly improbable. However, this statement seems to be counterintuitive with respect to frequent discount actions of which consumers must be necessarily aware. As documented by Yates (1998) and Warner and Barsky (1995), prices are frequently discounted in retail prior to Christmas and occur especially during weekends. This might alleviate the notion that customers are not used to price cuts.

If we consider the latter, price cuts might be evaluated by some consumers as a sign of a fall in a quality. This might be based on imperfect observations of consumers about the quality of a good before purchase. If they suppose that firms set the price of their product with respect to marginal cost, they deduce that the fall in price is associated with a fall in quality of inputs used to produce it. Consequently, a discontinuous relationship between the expected quality of the good and utility derived from buying it, signifies that the good is useless below a certain quality threshold. Implications for a firm might be substantial because the reduction in price might lead to disproportionate fall in demand. This idea of consumers having limited information about the quality of variety of products was outlined by Allen (1988). Blinder (1995) and Hall and Yates (1996) conducted surveys and found only a limited role for this effect. For instance, Blinder (1995) asked firms whether their customers associated a reduction in price of a good with a reduction in its quality. This was considered relevant only by 18 percent of respondents. Nevertheless, quality signaling should not be neglected since it might be pervasive enough to lead to suboptimal outcomes. As argued by Yates (1998), another possibility is that consumers derive their utility from consuming an expensive product. A crucial condition for money illusion to hold is that consumers believe that the general price level is unchanged and thereby a cut in the nominal price is translated into a cut in the real price.

Second, it is well known that consumers prone to money illusion are averse toward increases in nominal prices as already demonstrated in Chapter 3. This phenomenon was confirmed by various authors such as Akerlof and Shiller (2009), Shafir et al. (1997) or Carlton (1986). Aversion toward higher nominal prices is then directly translated into lower subsequent purchases by customers. As a result, managers are thereby reluctant to change prices that much as documented by Churchill (1982). Additionally, consumer aversion to increases in the nominal prices is well utilized by the "buy-now-and-beat-inflation psychology."

However, as Hogan (2013) points out, the dislike for inflation may be due to a different form of money illusion, in which consumers attribute any increase in wages to their own capabilities or good fortune, and consider inflation to be responsible for the increase in prices of goods.

Money as unit of account

Another aspect of money illusion is related to the role of money as a unit of account. The expression of wages and prices in terms of the monetary unit simplifies decision-making. However, usefulness of this measure depends on the consumer's ability to assess the value of a given amount of money in terms of its buying power. In terms of a complete deception formulated by Fisher (1928), consumers are not able to assess the real value of the currency when the price level is changing. In contrast, the contemporary theory of money illusion, based on behavioral features, suggests that people are not completely deceived. Rather when prices rice, the real value of money falls and they lose the nominal anchor against which all prices can be compared.

Money illusion and other applications

There are many other applications of money illusion, some of which we tackled in Chapter 3, suggesting that it might me a potentially relevant phenomenon. We have seen that money illusion might play role in financial markets, labor markets, in business accounting, in consumption-saving decisions, indexation of contracts, in goods markets, in the explanation of nominal rigidities, in coordination issues, in the short-run non-neutrality of money, and many others. A few of the lesser known applications of money illusion will be now be addressed.

The introduction of the euro is considered as sort of illustrative natural experiment, in which money illusion effects might be examined, as noted by Fehr and Tyran (2005a). The change in the nominal frame after euro introduction significantly affected the behavior of specific markets. As ECB (2003) notes, in January 2002:

> The month-on-month increases in prices charged by restaurants and cafés in the euro area … was more than three times higher than the average increase in the same month during the period 1996-2001 … Similar price movements were noted for hairdressing … and other service items. For most of these items, price increases in the euro area were also rather high compared with those in non-euro area EU countries.
>
> (ECB 2003, p. 40)

The effects of money illusion after the introduction of the euro might be substantially translated into consumer behavior. Some authors refer rather to the term "euro illusion" than money illusion, such as Gamble (2007), where the subjective value of money is influenced by the nominal representation of a currency. Empirical evidence on this issue is rather mixed. For instance, the findings of Desmet (2002) and Gamble et al. (2002) show that the biased evaluation in favor of the nominal value in foreign currency does not occur systematically in all affected countries. In contrast, many recent studies, like Mathieu and Riera (2010) and Del Missier, Bonini, and Ranyard (2007), suggest that the effect of euro illusion might be substantial. To discuss more thoroughly these consequences, it is worth emphasizing that money illusion can take two forms in this sense, either "nominal anchoring" or "different assessment."

First, if consumers tend to apply nominal anchoring, they mix lower nominal prices with lower real prices. As a result, after the introduction of the euro, individuals may continue to evaluate prices and budget in terms of their original national currency. The conversion in most countries led to lower numbers, which induced people to value their income more and spend more. This sort of effect is empirically confirmed in the studies of Raaij and Rijen (2003), who document a case in the Netherlands, where consumers might be victims of money illusion effect, since they consider prices cheaper than they are due to nominal anchoring effect, or they inaccurately convert euro to the Dutch guilder by forgetting to add 10 percent. However, the effect is only temporary, since customers get accustomed to the new currency and will anchor euro instead of the former currency.

Second, money illusion might be explained by "different assessment" based on the numerosity heuristic rather than nominal anchoring (Pelham, Sumarta, and Myaskovsky 1994). In the case of numerosity heuristic, consumer's evaluation is based on the difference between prices and budget. This was empirically proved in the experimental study of Soman, Wertenbroch, and Chattopadhyay (2006) as another sort of money illusion. If prices and budgets are quoted in different currencies, the numerosity effect produces similar outcomes, like the one based on nominal anchoring as Cannon and Cipriani note (2006). In contrast, if prices and budgets are quoted in the same currency, the numerosity effect based on heuristic produces opposite results of the nominal anchoring. Soman et al. (2006) prove that if numerosity decreases proportionately (including fall in all nominal values like price of goods and nominal income), then with lower nominal values the total spending decreases. As a result, the introduction of the euro, which resulted in smaller numbers in the majority of countries, should decrease the spending.

An interesting line of research aims to examine money illusion effects after euro introduction with regards to the altruistic behavior of individuals. There are a few studies, which focus on the impact of the introduction of euro on charitable giving, and provide particularly interesting results. It appears that donors prone to money illusion increased their donations after the currency change to keep their donations at the previous level. This is shown in the study of Kooreman, Faber, and Hofmans (2004), who provide evidence of money illusion in a large Dutch charity, when donations to the charity increased by 11 percent in the year after introduction of euro. The exchange rate at that time between the Dutch guilder and the euro equaled 2.20371. Donors, however, applied the rule of thumb that the exchange rate is roughly one euro for two guilders. Thus, a rise in donations by a bit more than 10 percent might be attributed to the currency change.

Also, Cannon and Cipriani (2006) conducted a natural experiment to verify the presence of money illusion after the introduction of the euro in Italy in 2002. They evaluated data on Sunday collections in churches in Italy and other European churches and considered whether the euro introduction affected church giving. They investigated the presence of two forms of money illusion, nominal anchoring and the numerosity effect based on difference assessment. The conversion rate in most countries like Italy led to lower numbers, which in the case of nominal anchoring should induce people to value their income more and spend more. Results confirmed a strong case for money illusion type of nominal anchoring in Italy, where church giving rose substantially after the introduction of the euro. A lower degree of money illusion was found in case of Ireland. Results proved that different assessments also prevailed over nominal anchoring in France, Germany, Belgium and Spain, leading to lower church giving. Still the data is less significant due to a lower number of observations than in the case of Italy.

To sum up, results revealed rather asymmetric effects of money illusion on church giving after the introduction of the euro. In general, when nominal anchoring prevails over difference assessment, it leads to higher church giving, whereas if difference assessment prevails it leads to lower church giving. This holds for the case when the conversion to the euro leads to lower numbers. The aforementioned study of Kooreman, Faber and Hofmans (2004) indicated a positive effect on charitable donations after the introduction of the euro. We may attribute these results to the stronger nominal anchoring effect of money illusion.

The recent study of Bittschi and Duppel (2015) confirms the positive effect of money illusion after the introduction of the euro on declared donations from German administrative income tax data. Although their results indicate considerable weaker effects, still the positive effect of nominal anchoring prevails.

Another interesting application, which accounts for the long-run effects of money illusion is the study by Miao and Xie (2013). The authors presented a stochastic continuous time monetary model of endogenous growth with incorporated money illusion. Agents prone to money illusion maximized utility based on both nominal and real quantities. The authors demonstrated that money illusion has distorting effects because the misperception of the growth and riskiness of the real wealth leads to suboptimal consumption/saving decisions. The resulting consumption/saving behavior is affected by two opposite effects, wealth effect and substitution effect. When the risk aversion parameter is higher than one, the wealth effect prevails over the substitution effect. This implies that an agent at higher expected inflation perceives growth of the nominal wealth as real growth and consumes more. In contrast if the risk aversion parameter is lower than one, the substitution effect prevails and the agent consumes less. The former effect is consistent with an explanation of money illusion provided by Tobin (1972). If the risk aversion parameter equals one, both effects cancel out and the agent does not react to change in expected inflation rate.

Whereas money illusion effects are of the second order to its participants, they are of the first order for the economy. A crucial result is that the presence of negligible money illusion may substantially affect the long run growth. The model suggests various topics for future research such as modelling of money illusion to examine price and wage rigidities in a multi-agent model with business cycle implications.

Money illusion has been recently re-examined with respect to its effects in a small open economy. In particular, Lai (2015) examines the effect of money illusion on exchange rate dynamics in a model of small open economy. Previous attempts, like the study of Murphy and Das (1976), argue that money illusion might be the factor which hinders effective balance of payments adjustment through exchange rates, but the discussion is a static one. In contrast, in view of the Mundell–Corden hypothesis, money illusion is regarded as prerequisite for the efficacy of exchange rate adjustment (Corden 1972, p. 12). These different views regarding the effect of money illusion on balance of payments adjustment, result from different criteria as outlined by Lehment (1978). Lai (2015) goes further and implements money illusion within the New Keynesian open economy model. Results show that money illusion is the main determining factor for the exchange rate overshooting regardless of the consumption elasticity of money demand or the share of traded goods. Money illusion in this model is supposed to weaken the relationship between money demand and consumption behavior. As a result, the adjustment to the exchange rate must be of a significant degree to equilibrate the money market, followed by exchange rate overshooting. The higher the extent of money illusion, the higher the degree of activity in capital, consumption and money demand, which leads to substantial welfare improvement. However, the analysis is restricted solely to the discussion of the relation between money illusion, consumption, and demand—neglecting the production behavior. Additionally, money illusion is given exogenously rather than endogenously, which suggests motivation for future research.

Additionally, money illusion has been examined from point of view of neuroeconomics by Weber, Rangel, Wibral, and Falk (2009). They examine with the help of functional magnetic resonance imaging (fMRI), whether the brain's reward circuitry (more specifically areas of the ventromedial prefrontal cortex) exhibits money illusion. Subjects received rewards, which differed in nominal terms but were identical in real economic terms. Findings revealed that the level of activity of reward-related brain areas increased and exhibited money illusion in response to nominal price increases. This happened despite the fact that subject's real purchasing power remained unchanged.

Notes

1 It is worth to note that Cohen et al. (2005) use the term money illusion, but Campbell and Vuolteenaho (2004a, 2004b) use the term inflation illusion. Practically these two terms refer to the same phenomenon.
2 This represents an improvement compared with Campbell and Vuolteenaho (2004), who suppose that investors are not heterogeneous and set the same dividend-price ratio.
3 This is in line with Tobin's view of money illusion outlined in his *Essays in Economics* (1971).
4 Modified methodology of Engsted and Pedersen (2016) adopts recursive preferences instead of constant relative risk aversion (CRRA) preferences and also non-independent and identically distributed consumption growth, implying variable dividend price ratio. The asset pricing model with recursive preferences and exogenous consumption growth is well applied, for instance by Piazzesi and Schneider (2006) to examine the effects of inflation on the pricing of nominal bonds. Their finding suggests that as soon as inflation is bad news, the nominal yield curve slopes up. Additionally, when it is difficult to interpret inflation news, the level of nominal interest rates and term spreads are high.
5 In case of the nominal deflationary shock there is no effect on the real fundamental value of the currency, but the conversion rate of the currency after the shock decreases, increasing thereby the value of each unit of the nominal currency, followed by fall in the value of asset, (In particular, $k = 14$ in experiment of Noussair et al. (2008) represents a factor which determined rise in the value of each unit of the nominal currency after deflationary shock, followed by fall in the value of asset).
6 As thoroughly discussed, this analysis is based on near-rationality with behavioral features, which suggests the role for money illusion.

7 The fairness model does not specify, whether nominal or real wages are relevant for fairness judgments. But evidence of Kahneman (1986), Shafir et al. (1997), or Goette and Huffman (2007) suggests relevance of nominal wage cuts.

8 Kahneman and Tversky (1986) do not mention whether they discuss nominal or real wage, however literature provides significant proof of nominal loss aversion, (Shafir et al. 1997).Since the literature related to behavioral account of labor market is rather extensive, please refer to Fehr, Goette, and Zehnder (2009), who evaluate the concept of fairness from various points of view.

9 Tobin's theorem is based on explanation of the nature of money illusion associated with the nominal rigidities and its resulting implications for the shape of Phillips curve as already discussed above.

10 An experimental price setting game with strategic complementarity is used, where individuals set a price in every period and form expectations about the average price in their own group. There is no monetary shock during the experiment. Individual payoffs depend on their own price and the average price of the other players, about which they receive feedback in each period. Payoffs are designed in such a way that multiple equilibria exist.

11 For more extensive research on nominal wage rigidity and downward nominal wage rigidity please refer to the contract theory (Fischer 1977; Taylor 1979), the implicit contract theory (Akerlof 1980; Baily 1974; Azariadis 1975; Gordon 1976; Sargent 1979, Holmstrom 1980; Stiglitz 1986, Altmann 2010), the efficiency wage theory (Shapiro and Stiglitz 1984; Akerlof et al. 1982; Weiss 1980, 1990; Yellen 2001; Menezenes 2014), the fair wage hypothesis (Akerlof and Yellen 1990, Gachter and Thoni 2010; Gun 2000), or the insider-outsider theory (Lindbeck and Snower 2002).

References

Acker, D. and Duck, N. W., 2013. Inflation Illusion and the Dividend Yield: Evidence from the UK. *European Journal of Finance*, 4 (2013), pp. 1–16.

Adams, J. S., 1963. Toward an Understanding of Inequity. *Journal of Abnormal and Social Psychology*, 67, pp. 422–436.

Agell, J. and Bennmarker, H., 2002. Wage Policy and Endogenous Wage Rigidity: A Representative View from the Inside. *Research Papers in Economics*, 2002 (12), Stockholm University, Department of Economics.

Agell, J. and Lundborg, P., 2003. Survey Evidence on Wage Rigidity and Unemployment: Sweden in the 1990s. *Scandinavian Journal of Economics*, 105 (1), pp. 15–30.

Ahrens, S., Pirschel, I., and Snower, D. J., 2014. A Theory of Wage Adjustment Under Loss Aversion. *CEPR Discussion Paper* No. DP10288. Available at: http://ssrn.com/abstract=2535425 [Accessed 19 September 2016].

Akerlof, G. A., 2002. Behavioral Macroeconomics and Macroeconomic Behavior, *American Economic Review*, 92 (3), pp. 411–433.

Akerlof, G. A. and Shiller, R. J., 2009. *Animal Spirits, How Human Psychology Drives the Economy and Why It Matters for Global Capitalism*, Princeton, NJ: Princeton University Press.

Akerlof, G. A. and Yellen, J. L., 1985. A Near-rational Model of the Business Cycle, with Wage and Price Inertia. *Quarterly Journal of Economics*, 100 (5), pp. 823–838.

Akerlof, G. A., Dickens, W. T., and Perry, G. L., 1996. The Macroeconomics of Low Inflation [including comments by Gordon and Mankiw]. *Brookings Papers on Economic Activity*, 27 (1), pp. 1–59.

Akerlof, G. A., Dickens, W. T., and Perry, G. L., 2000. Near-Rational Wage and Price Setting and the Long-Run Phillips Curve. *Brookings Papers on Economic Activity*, 31 (1), pp. 1–60.

Allen, F., 1988. A Theory of Price Rigidities when Quality is Unobservable. *Review of Economic Studies*, 55 (1), pp. 139–151.

Asness, C., 2003, Fight the Fed Model. *Journal of Portfolio Management*, 30 (1), pp. 11–24.

Bank of Canada, 2011. Renewal of the Inflation-Control Target, Background Information, Ottawa, November. Available at: www.bankofcanada.ca/wp-content/uploads/2011/11/background_nov11.pdf [Accessed 19 September 2016].

Basak, S. and Yan, H., 2010. Equilibrium Asset Prices and Investor Behavior in the Presence of Money Illusion. *Review of Economic Studies*, 77 (3), pp. 914–936.

Basu, S., Markov, S., and Shivakumar, L., 2010. Inflation, Earnings Forecasts, and Post-Earnings Announcement Drift. *Review of Accounting Studies*, 15 (2), pp. 403–440.

Bewley, T. F., 1995. A Depressed Labor Market as Explained by Participants. *American Economic Review*, 85 (2), pp. 250–254.

Bewley, T. F., 1998. Why Not Cut Pay? *European Economic Review*, 42 (3–5), pp. 459–490.

Bewley, T. F., 1999. *Why Wages Don't Fall During a Recession*. Cambridge, MA: Harvard University Press.

Bittschi, B. and Duppel, S., 2015. Did the Introduction of the Euro Lead to Money Illusion? Empirical Evidence from Germany. *ZEW Discussion Papers* No. 15-058, ZEW – Zentrum für Europäische Wirtschaftsforschung/Center for European Economic Research.

Blinder, A. S., 1995. On Sticky Prices: Academic Theories Meet the Real World. In N. G. Mankiw (ed.), *Monetary Policy*, Vol. 28. Chicago and London: University of Chicago Press.

Blinder, A. S., 2000. Comment on Akerlof, Dickens and Perry, Near-Rational Wage and Price Setting and the Long-Run Phillips Curve. *Brookings Papers on Economic Activity*, 1, pp. 50–55.

Blinder A. S. and Choi, D. H., 1990. A Shred of Evidence on Theories of Wage Stickiness. *Quarterly Journal of Economics*, 105 (4), pp. 1003–1015.

Blinder, A. S., Canetti, E. R. D., Lebow E. D., and Rudd J. B., 1998. *Asking About Prices: A New Approach to Understanding Price Stickiness*. New York: Russell Sage Foundation.

Bolton, G., 1991. A Comparative Model of Bargaining: Theory and Evidence. *American Economic Review*, 81 (1), pp. 1096–1136.

Boudoukh, J. and Richardson, M., 1993. Stock Returns and Inflation: A Long-Horizon Perspective. *American Economic Review*, 83 (5), pp. 1346–1355.

Brown, G. D. A., Gardner, J., Oswald, A. J., and Qian, J., 2008. Does Wage Rank Affect Employees' Well-Being? *Industrial Relations*, 47 (3), 355–389.

Brunnermeier, K. M. and Julliard, C., 2008. The Causes and Consequences of Recent Financial Market Bubbles. *Review of Financial Studies*, 21 (1), pp. 135–180.

Campbell, C. and Kamlani, K. S., 1997. The Reasons for Wage Rigidity: Evidence from a Survey of Firms. *Quarterly Journal of Economics*, 112 (3), pp. 759–789.

Campbell, J. and Vuolteenaho, T., 2004. Bad Beta, Good Beta. *American Economic Review*, 94 (5), pp. 1249–1275.

Cannon, E. and Cipriani, G., 2006. Euro-Illusion: A Natural Experiment. *Journal of Money, Credit and Banking*, 38 (5), pp. 1391–1403.

Cappelli, P. and Sherer, P. D., 1988. Satisfaction, Market Wages, & Labor Relations: An Airline Study. *Industrial Relations*, 27 (1), pp. 56–73.

Card, D. and Hyslop, D., 1997. Does Inflation 'Grease the Wheels of the Labor Market'? In *Reducing Inflation: Motivation and Strategy*, Christina D. Romer and David H. Romer (eds.), Cambridge, MA: National Bureau of Economic Research, pp. 71–122.

Carlton, D. W. 1986. The Rigidity of Prices. *American Economic Review*, 76 (4), pp. 637–658.

Charness, G., 2004. Attribution and Reciprocity in an Experimental Labor Market. *Journal of Labor Economics*, 22 (3), pp. 665–688.

Charness, G. and Rabin, M., 2002. Understanding Social Preferences with Simple Tests. *Quarterly Journal of Economics*, 117 (3), pp. 817–869

Chen, C., Lung, P. P., and Wang, F. A., 2009. Stock Market Mispricing: Money Illusion or Resale Option. *Journal of Financial and Quantitative Analysis*, 44 (5), pp. 1125–1147.

Churchill, N., 1982. Don't Let Inflation Get the Best of You. *Harvard Business Review*, pp. 6–26.

Clark, A. and Oswald, A., 1996. Satisfaction and Comparison Income. *Journal of Public Economics*, 61 (3), pp. 359–381.

Cohen, R. B., Polk C., and Vuolteenaho, T., 2005. Money Illusion in the Stock Market: The Modigliani-Cohn Hypothesis. *Quarterly Journal of Economics*, 120 (2), pp. 639–668.

Cohn, R. A. and Lessard, D. R., 1980. The Effect of Inflation on Stock Prices: International Evidence. *WP No.11470 of University of Illinois at Chicago Circle and Massachusetts Institute of Technology*, presented at the September 1980 Meetings of the American Economic and American Finance Associations in Denver, CO.

Chordia, C. and Shivakumar, L., 2005. Inflation Illusion and Post-Earnings-Announcement Drift. *Journal of Accounting Research*, 43 (4), pp. 521–556.

Corden, W. M., 1972. *Monetary Integration*. Essay No. 93. Princeton, NJ: International Finance Sec., Princeton University.

Crawford, A. and Harrison, A., 1998. Testing for Downward Rigidity in Nominal Wage Rates. In T. Macklem (ed.), *Price Stability, Inflation Targets and Monetary Policy*. Proceedings of a Conference held by the Bank of Canada in May 1997.

Crawford, A. and Wright, G., 2001. Downward Nominal-Wage Rigidity: Microevidence from Tobit Models. *Bank of Canada WP 2001-7*, May.

Del Missier, F., Bonini, N., and Ranyard, R., 2007. The Euro Illusion in Consumer's Price Estimation: An Italian-Irish Comparison in the Third Year of the Euro. *Journal of Consumer Policy*, 30, pp. 337–354.

Demers, F., 2003. The Canadian Phillips Curve and Regime Switching. *Bank of Canada Working Paper 2003–32*, October.

Desmet, P., 2002. A Study of the Potential Effects of the Conversion to Euro. *Journal of Product and Brand Management*, 13 (1), pp. 134–146.

Djoudad, R. and Sargent, T. C., 1997. Does the ADP Story Provide a Better Phillips Curve for Canada? *WP Economic Studies and Policy Analysis Division*, Department of Finance, Ottawa, October.

Doeringer, P. B. and Piore, M. J., 1971. *Internal Labor Markets and Manpower Analysis*. Lexington, MA: Heath.

Dunn, L. F., 1996. Loss Aversion and Adaption in the Labour Market: Empirical Indifference Functions and Labour Supply. *Review of Economics and Statistics*, 78 (3), pp. 441–450.

Eckstein, O. and Brinner, R., 1972. The Inflation Process in the United States. *A Study Prepared for the Use of the Joint Economic Committee*, February.

Einiö, M., Kaustia, M., and Puttonen, V., 2008. Price Setting and the Reluctance to Realize Losses in Apartment Markets. *Journal of Economic Psychology*, 29 (1), pp. 9–34.

Elsby, M. W. L., 2005. Evaluating the Economic Significance of Downward Nominal Wage Rigidity. *Journal of Monetary Economics*, 56 (2), pp. 154–169.

Engsted, T. and Pedersen, T. Q., 2016. The Predictive Power of Dividend Yields for Future Inflation: Money Illusion or Rational Causes? *CREATES Research Papers* 2016–11, Department of Economics and Business Economics, Aarhus University.

European Central Bank (ECB), 2003. *Annual Report 2002*, Frankfurt. Available at: www.ecb.europa.eu/pub/pdf/annrep/ar2002en.pdf?c203255db568d0eb3d4e6e0699f80fb0 [Accessed 19 September 2016].

Falk, A. and Fischbacher, U., 2006. A Theory of Reciprocity. *Games and Economic Behavior*, 54 (2), pp. 293–315.

Fama, F. E., 1981. Stock Returns, Real Activity, Inflation, and Money. *American Economic Review*, 71 (4), pp. 545–565.

Fama, F. E. and Babiak, H., 1968. Dividend Policy: An Empirical Analysis. *Journal of the American Statistical Association*, 63 (324), pp. 1132–1161.

Fares, J. and Lemieux, T., 2001. Downward Nominal-Wage Rigidity: A Critical Assessment and Some New Evidence for Canada. In Price Stability and the Long-Run Target for Monetary Policy. Proceedings of a seminar held at the Bank of Canada, June 2000, Ottawa: Bank of Canada.

Fehr, E. and Fischbacher, U., 2004. Third Party Punishment and Social Norms. *Evolution and Human Behavior*, 25 (2004), pp. 63–87.

Fehr, E. and Goette, L., 2005. Robustness and Real Consequences of Nominal Wage Rigidity. *Journal of Monetary Economics*, 52 (2005), pp. 779–804.

Fehr, E., Goette, L., and Zehnder, C., 2009. A Behavioral Account of the Labor Market: The Role of Fairness Concerns. *Annual Review of Economics*, 1 (1), pp. 355–384.

Fehr, E., Kirchsteiger, G., and Riedl, A., 2002. Does Fairness Prevent Market Clearing? *European Economic Review*, 42 (1), pp. 1–34.

Fehr, E. and Schmidt, K. M., 2006. The Economics of Fairness, Reciprocity and Altruism – Experimental Evidence and New Theories. In Kolm and J. M. Ythier (eds.), *Handbook of Giving Altruism and Reciprocity*, Vol. 1. Amsterdam: Elsevier.

Fehr, E. and Tyran, J., 2001. Does Money Illusion Matter? *American Economic Review*, 91 (5), pp. 1239–1262.

Fehr, E. and Tyran, J., 2005a. Expectations and the Effects of Money Illusion In: B. Agarwal and A. Vercelli (eds.), *Psychology, Rationality and Economic Behavior*. Challenging Standard Assumptions. New York: Palgrave Macmillan/International Economic Association.

Fehr, E. and Tyran, J., 2005b. Individual Irrationality and Aggregate Outcomes. *Journal of Economic Perspectives*, (19) 4, pp. 43–66.

Fehr, E. and Tyran, J., 2007. Money Illusion and Coordination Failure. *Games and Economic Behavior, Elsevier*, 58 (2), pp. 246–268.

Fehr, E. and Tyran, J., 2008. Limited Rationality and Strategic Interaction: The Impact of the Strategic Environment on Nominal Inertia. *Econometrica*, 76 (2), pp. 353–394.

Feldstein, M., 1980. Inflation and the Stock Market. *American Economic Review*, 70 (5), pp. 839–847.

Fisher, I., 1928. *The Money Illusion*. New York: Adelphi Publishers.

Fisher, I., 1930. *The Theory of Interest*. London: Macmillan.

Follain, J. R., 1982. Does Inflation Affect Real Behavior? The Case of Housing. *Southern Economic Journal*, 48 (3), pp. 570–582.

Fontana, G. and Palacio-Vera, A., 2007. Are Long-Run Price Stability and Short-Run Output Stabilization All That Monetary Policy Can Aim For? *Metroeconomica*, 58 (2), pp. 269–298.

Fortin, P., 2013. The Macroeconomics of Downward Nominal Wage Rigidity: A Review of the Issues and New Evidence for Canada. *Cahiers de recherche WP No. 1309*. Available at: www.cirpee.org/fileadmin/documents/Cahiers_2013/CIRPEE13–09.pdf [Accessed 19 September 2016].

Gali, J., 2011. The Return of the Wage Phillips Curve. *Journal of the European Economic Association*, 9 (3), pp. 436–461.

Gamble, A. Garling, T., Charlton, J., and Ranyard, R., 2002. Euro Illusion: Psychological Insights into Price Evaluations with a Unitary Currency. *European Psychologist*, 7, pp. 302–311.

Gamble, A., 2007. The Euro Illusion: Illusion or Fact? *Journal of Consumer Policy*, 30 (4), pp. 323–336.

Gemma, Y., 2016. Money Illusion Matters for Consumption-Saving Decision-Making: An Experimental Investigation. *Discussion Paper No.2016–E–6, Institute for Monetary and Economic Studies*, Bank of Japan.

Genesove, D. and Mayer, C., 2001. Loss Aversion and Seller Behavior: Evidence from Housing Market. *NBER WP* No. 8143.

Goette, L. and Huffman, D., 2007. Do Emotions Lead to Better Labor Market Outcomes? In L. Goette and D. Huffman (eds.), *Do Emotions Lead to Better or Worse Decisions?* New York: Russell Sage.

Gottschalk, J. and Fritsche, U., 2005. The New Keynesian Model and the Long-Run Vertical Phillips Curve: Does it hold for Germany? *German Institute for Economic Research, Discussion Papers 521*, DIW Berlin.

Green, D. A. and Harrison, K., 2009. Minimum Wage Setting and Standards of Fairness. *W10/09 of Economic and Research Social Council*. Available at: www.ifs.org.uk/wps/wp1009.pdf [Accessed 19 September 2016].

Gultekin, B. N., 1983. Stock Market Returns and Inflation: Evidence from Other Countries. *Journal of Finance*, 38 (1), pp. 49–65.

Habu, T., 2011. Money Illusion and its Implication on Unemployment. *Undergraduate Economic Review*, 7 (1), Article 10.

Haldane, A., 1999. Pursuing Price Stability, Evidence from United Kingdom and other Inflation Targeters. In: Andrew P. Fischer (ed.), *Workshop on Inflation Targeting*. Prague: Czech National Bank.

Hall, S. W. M. and Yates, A., 1996. How do UK Companies Set Prices? *Bank of England Quarterly Bulletin*, May, pp. 180–92.

Haltiwanger, J. and Waldman, M., 1989. Limited Rationality and Strategic Complements: Implications for Macroeconomics. *Quarterly Journal of Economics*, 104 (3), pp. 463–483.

Hirshleifer, K. D. D. and Subrahmanyam, A., 1998. Investor Psychology and Security Market Under and Overreactions. *Journal of Finance* 53 (6), pp. 1839–1886.

Hogan, S., 2013. What Does Downward Nominal – Wage Rigidity Imply for Monetary Policy? *Bank of Canada WP 97 (13)*, Bank of Canada. Available at: http://publications.gc.ca/collections/Collection/FB3–2–97–13E.pdf [Accessed 19 September 2016].

Kahneman, D. and Tversky, A., 1979. Prospect Theory: An Analysis of Decision under Risk. *Econometrica*, 47 (2), pp. 263–291.

Kahneman, D. and Tversky, A., 1992. Advances in Prospect Theory: Cumulative Representation of Uncertainty. *Journal of Risk and Uncertainty*, 5 (4), pp. 297–323.

Kahneman, D., Knetsch, J. L., and Thaler, R. H., 1986. Fairness as a Constraint on Profit Seeking: Entitlements in the Market. *American Economic Review*, 76 (4), pp. 728–741.

Kahneman, D., Knetsch, J. L., and Thaler, R. H., 1990. Experimental Tests of the Endowment Effect and the Coase Theorem. *Journal of Political Economy*, 98 (6), pp. 1325–1348.

Kandil, M., 2006. Asymmetric Effects of Aggregate Demand Shocks across U.S. Industries: Evidence and Implications. *Eastern Economic Journal*, 32 (2), pp. 259–283.

Kandil, M., 2010. The Asymmetric Effects of Demand Shocks: International Evidence on Determinants and Implications. *Applied Economics*, 42 (17), pp. 2127–2145.

Katz, L. F., 1986. Efficiency Wage Theories: A Partial Evaluation. In S. Fischer (ed.), *NBER Macroeconomics Annual*, Vol. 1. Cambridge, MA: MIT Press.

Kearl, J. H., 1979. Inflation, Mortgages, and Housing. *Journal of Political Economy*, 87 (5), pp. 1–29.

Keynes, J. M., 1925. The Economic Position in England, 14 September 1925. Available at: http://la.utexas.edu/users/hcleaver/368/368keynespositiontable.pdf [Accessed 19 September 2016].

Keynes, J. M., 1936. *The General Theory of Interest Employment and Money*. London: Macmillan.

King, R. G. and Watson, M. W., 1997. Testing Long-Run Neutrality. *Economic Quarterly*, 83 (3), pp. 69–101.

Khalaf, L. and Kichian, M., 2003. Testing the Stability of the Canadian Phillips Curve Using Exact Methods. *Working Paper* No. 2003–7, Bank of Canada, March.

Knetsch, J. L. and Sinden, J. A., 1984. Willingness to Pay and Compensation Demanded: Experimental Evidence of an Unexpected Disparity in Measures of Value. *Quarterly Journal of Economics*, 99 (3), pp. 507–521.

Kooreman, P., Faber, R., and Hofmans, H., 2004. Charity Donations and the Euro Introduction: Some Quasi–Experimental Evidence on Money Illusion. *Journal of Money, Credit and Banking*, 36, pp. 1121–1124.

Kyle, A. S. and Wang, A. F., 1997. Speculation Duopoly with Agreement to Disagree: Can Overconfidence Survive the Market Test? *Journal of Finance*, 52 (5), pp. 2073–2090.

Lai, C., 2015. Money Illusion and Exchange Rate Dynamics in a Small Open Economy. *Research in World Economy*, 6 (1), pp. 199–207.

Lebow, D. E. and Stockton, D. J. and Wascher, W., 1995. Inflation, Nominal Wage Rigidity, and the Efficiency of Labor Markets, Federal Reserve Board of Governors Finance and Economics Discussion Series No. 95-45. Available at SSRN: http://ssrn.com/abstract=3032 [Accessed 19 September 2016].

Lee, B. S., 2010. Stock Returns and Inflation revisited: An Evaluation of the Inflation Illusion Hypothesis. *Journal of Banking and Finance*, 34 (6), pp. 1257–1273.

Lehment, H., 1978. Money Illusion and Balance-of-Payments Adjustment: A Comment. *Journal of Political Economy*, 86 (1), pp. 151–153.

Lessard, D. and Modigliani, F., 1975. Inflation and the Housing Market: Problems and Potential Solutions. In D. Lessard and F. Modigliani (eds.), *New Mortgage Designs for Stable Housing in an Inflationary Environment*, Boston, MA: Federal Reserve Bank of Boston.

Lintner, J., 1956. Distribution of Incomes of Corporations among Dividends, Retained Earnings, and Taxes. *American Economic Review*, 46 (2), pp. 97–113.

Lintner, J., 1975. Inflation and Security Returns. *Journal of Finance* 30(2), pp. 259–280.

Loewenstein, G. and Sicherman, N., 1991. Do Workers Prefer Increasing Wage Profiles? *Journal of Labor Economics*, 9 (1), pp. 67–84.

Lundborg, P. and Sacklén, H., 2006. Low-inflation Targeting and Long-run Unemployment. *Scandinavian Journal of Economics*, 108 (3), pp. 397–418.

McLaughlin, K. J., 1994. Rigid Wages? *Journal of Monetary Economics*, 34 (3), pp. 383–414.

Malcomson, J. M., 1999. Individual Employment Contracts. In: O. Ashenfelter and D. Card (eds.), *Handbook of Labor Economics*, 1(3), Ch. 35, pp. 2291–2372.

Mathieu, P. and Riera, P., 2010. Contingent Valuation Method and the Changeover to the Euro: An Empirical Application. *Revue d'Economie Régionale and Urbaine*, No. 5, pp. 987–1000.

Maugeri, N., 2010. Macroeconomic Implications of Near Rational Behavior: An Application to the Italian Phillips Curve. *Working Paper* 587 (2010). Siena: Università Defli Studi di Siena, Quaderni del Dipartimento di Economica Politica.

Miao, J. and Xie, D., 2013. Economic Growth under Money Illusion. *Journal of Economic Dynamics and Control*, 37 (1), pp. 84–103.

Modigliani, F. and Cohn, A. F., 1979. Inflation, Rational Evaluation and the Market. *Financial Analyst Journal*, 35 (2), pp. 24–44.

Murphy, J. C., and Das, S. K., 1976, Money Illusion and Balance-of-Payments Adjustment. *Journal of Political Economy*, 84 (1), pp. 73–82.

Noussair, C., Richter, G., and Tyran, J., 2012. Money Illusion and Nominal Inertia in Experimental Asset Markets. *Journal of Behavioral Finance*, 13 (1), pp. 27–37.

Pelham, B. W., Sumarta, T. T., and Myaskovsky, L., 1994. The Easy Path from Many to Much: The Numerosity Heuristic. *Cognitive Psychology*, 26, pp. 103–133.

Piazzesi, M. and Schneider, M., 2006. Equilibrium Yield Curves, *NBER Working Paper* No. 12609.

Piazzesi, M. and Schneider, M., 2008. Inflation Illusion, Credit and Asset Pricing. *NBER Working Paper* No. 12957.

Ritter, J. R., and Warr, R. S., 2002. The Decline of Inflation and the Bull Market of 1982–1999. *Journal of Financial and Quantitative Analysis*, 37 (1), pp. 29–61.

Runciman, W. G., 1966. *Relative Deprivation and Social Justice*. London: Routledge.

Samuelson, P. A. and Solow, R., 1960. Analytical Aspects of Anti-Inflation Policy. *American Economic Review*, 50 (2), pp. 177–194.

Schmeling, M. and Schrimpf, A., 2011. Expected Inflation, Expected Stock Returns, and Money Illusion: What Can We Learn from Survey Expectations? *European Economic Review*, 55 (5), pp. 702–719.

Schultze, C., 1959. Recent Inflation in the United States. In Joint Economic Committee (ed.), *Employment, Growth and Price Levels*. Study Paper No. 1, Washington, DC: US Government Printing Office.

Schwert, G. and Fama, F., 1977. Asset Returns and Inflation. *Journal of Financial Economics*, 5 (2), pp. 115–146.

Shafir, E., Diamond, P., and Tversky, A., 1997. Money Illusion. *Quarterly Journal of Economics*, 112 (2), pp. 341–374.

Sharpe, S., 2002. Reexamining Stock Valuation and Inflation: The Implications of Analysts' Earnings Fore-casts. *Review of Economics and Statistics*, 84 (4), pp. 632–648.

Shiller, R. J., 1996. Why do People Dislike Inflation? *NBER Working Paper* No. 5539.

Smith, J., 2006. How Costly is Downward Nominal Rigidity in the United Kingdom? Warwick University, Available at: www2.warwick.ac.uk/fac/soc/economics/staff/jcsmith/publications/agg_cost.pdf [Accessed 19 September 2016].

Solow, R. M., 1979. Another Possible Source of Wage Stickiness. *Journal of Macroeconomics*, 1 (1), pp. 79–82.

Soman, D., Wertenbroch, K., and Chattopadhyay, A., 2006. On the Perceived Value of Money: The Reference Dependence of Currency Numerosity Effects. *Journal of Consumer Research*, 34 (1), pp. 1–10.

Stark, A. and Sargent, T., 2003. Is there Downward Nominal Wage Rigidity in the Canadian Phillips Curve? *Department of Finance Working Paper 2003 (01)*, Ottawa, March.

Stiernstedt, H., 2011. Money Illusion and the Optimal Long–Run Rate of Inflation. Doctoral dissertation, Lund University. Available at: http://lup.lub.lu.se/luur/download?func=downloadFile&recordOId=2154721&fileOId=2154723 [Accessed 19 September 2016].

Svedsäter, H., Gamble, A. and Gärling, T., 2007. Money Illusion in Intuitive Financial Judgments: Influences of Nominal Representation of Share Prices. *Journal of Socio–Economics*, 36, 698–712.

Svensson, L. E. O., 2001. Comment on Wyplosz, Charles. Do We Know How Low Inflation Should Be? *Why Price Stability?* First ECB Central Banking Conference, ECB, Frankfurt, 2001.

Thaler, R. H., 1980. Toward a Positive Theory of Consumer Choice. *Journal of Economic Behavior and Organization*, 1 (1), pp. 39–60.

Thaler, R. H., 1997. Irving Fischer: Modern Behavioral Economist. *American Economic Review*, 87 (2), pp. 439–441.

Thaler, R. H., Tversky, A., Kahneman, D., and Schwartz, A., 1997. The Effect of Myopia and Loss Aversion on Risk Taking: An Experimental Test. *Quarterly Journal of Economics*, 112 (2), pp. 647–661.

Tobin, J., 1971. *Essays in Economics, Vol. 1, Macroeconomics*. Amsterdam: North–Holland.

Tobin, J., 1972. Inflation and Unemployment. *American Economic Review*, 62 (1), pp. 1–18.

Tucker, D. P., 1975. The Variable–Rate Graduated–Payment Mortgage. *Real Estate Review*, pp. 71–80.

Tyran, J. R., 1999. *Money Illusion and Strategic Complementarity as Causes of Monetary Non–Neutrality*. Lecture Notes in Economics and Mathematical Systems, Berlin and Heidelberg: Springer-Verlag.

Tyran, J. and Stephens, T. A., 2012. At Least I Didn't Lose Money: Nominal Loss Aversion Shapes Evaluations of Housing Transactions, University of Copenhagen, Dept. of Economics *Discussion Paper* No. 12–14. Available at: http://ssrn.com/abstract=2162415 [Accessed 19 September 2016].

Tyran, J. and Stephens, T. A., 2016. Money Illusion and Household Finance. University of Copenhagen, Dept. of Economics *Discussion Paper* No. 16–14. Available at: www.economics.ku.dk/research/publications/wp/dp_2016/1614.pdf/ [Accessed 6 January 2017].

Van Raaij, W. F., and van Rijen, C. L. A., 2003. Money Illusion and Euro Pricing. Presented at the IAREP Euro–workshop, Vienna, July 3–5, 2003. Available at: http://homepage.univie.ac.at/stephan.muehlbacher/euro/papers/vanRaaij%26van.Rijen.pdf [Accessed 19 September 2016].

Vaona, A., 2013. Money Illusion and the Long–Run Phillips Curve in Staggered Wage–Setting Models. *Research in Economics*, 67 (1), pp. 88–99.

Warner, E. J. and Barsky, R., 1995. The Timing and Magnitude of Retail Store Markdowns: Evidence from Weekends and Holidays. *Quarterly Journal of Economics*, 110 (2), pp. 321–352.

Weber, B., Rangel, A., Wibral, M., and Falk, A., 2009. The Medial Prefrontal Cortex Exhibits Money Illusion. *Proceedings of the National Academy of Science*, 106 (13), pp. 5025–5028.

Yates, A., 1998. Downward Nominal Rigidity and Monetary Policy. *Bank of England Working Paper* No. 82.

Yeh, C. and Chi, C., 2009. The Co-Movement and Long-Run Relationship between Inflation and Stock Returns: Evidence from 12 OECD Countries. *Journal of Economics and Management*, 5 (2), pp. 167–186.

Yellen, J. and Akerlof, G., 2006. Stabilization Policy a Reconsideration. *Economic Inquiry*, 44 (1), pp. 1–22.

5 Economic literacy and money illusion

If ignorance paid dividends, most Americans could make a fortune out of what they don't know about economics.

Luther H. Hodges, US Secretary of Commerce
(*Wall Street Journal*, March 14, 1962)

The previous chapter demonstrated that money illusion might be relevant in many areas. This chapter aims to introduce more thoroughly the rising interest in an economically literate public, highlighted with regards to research on the uptrend, which is related to the investigation of the potential effects of economic education. This interest is intensified by the fact that significant resources have been given by the Reserve Banks of the Federal Reserve System (the FED) and other central banks across the rest of the world to promote economic literacy. The second part of the chapter outlines the educational hypothesis, where the level of economic literacy is put in the context of money illusion. The question is addressed as to whether acquired economic education might not eventually suppress the indirect effects of money illusion and therefore weaken nominal inertia based on successful coordination in the strategic environment.

Delineation of basic terms

It is worth focusing on the proper delineation of basic concepts, since some studies refer to the term "economic literacy," some to the term "financial literacy," or those terms are intermingled.

Economic literacy might be broken down into two components, the former being conceptual literacy, the latter factual literacy (Roberts and Polley 2005). Factual literacy is related to the knowledge of basic economic concepts, which every literate person should know. In contrast, conceptual literacy comprises not only economic knowledge, but also the ability to utilize this knowledge in the form of economic thinking to make better decisions in relevant situations. An economic way of thinking is just a system of logical economic decisions using economic concepts and generalizations.

Winick (2006) notes that economic literacy is an important area that individuals should learn and know about as citizens and as the participants of worldwide economies that have been increasingly dependent on each other. Jacob (1995, p. 11) defines economic literacy as an "ability to understand, discuss and respond to the events that shape our economic environment, which is essential not only to the economists but to everyone from child to adult."

If we focus on financial literacy, it might be defined in many ways. For instance, Lusardi and Mitchell (2013, p. 6) define financial literacy as "the ability to process economic information and make informed decisions about financial planning, wealth accumulation, debt and pensions." Atkinson and Messy (2012, p. 7) define financial literacy as "a combination of awareness, knowledge, skill, attitude and behavior necessary to make sound financial decisions and ultimately achieve individual financial wellbeing." According to Huston (2010) financial knowledge is a necessary component of financial literacy, but there is an additional dimension of financial literacy. An individual must be also capable of applying his financial knowledge to make financial decisions. This is consistent with the definition of Ali et al. (2014, p. 336), who define financial literacy as "the knowledge and understanding of financial concepts, and the skills, motivation and confidence to apply such knowledge and understanding in order to make effective decisions across a range of financial contexts."

Perhaps the most accurate delineation of financial literacy, which summarizes different definitions of financial literacy in terms of "theoretical," "applied," and "awareness," is provided by Oanea and Dornean (2012, p. 116):

> Financial literacy is defined as a person's minimal knowledge about financial terms such as money, inflation, interest rate, credit and others, but besides this the abilities and skills of that person to use all this information in personal life, being aware about the consequences of its financial actions.

Based on this delineation of financial and economic literacy, a frequently debated topic is the specification of financial literacy with respect to economic literacy. Does economic literacy include only personal finance or general economics? This problem was also discussed throughout the Symposium on Economic Literacy held at the Federal Reserve Bank (FED) of Minneapolis on May 13–14, 1999. A major consideration focused on whether attention should be focused on one at the exclusion of the other. The debate finally ended with the suggestion of Arthur Rolnick, senior vice president and director of research at the Minneapolis FED that "Personal finance and economics should be considered as part of a continuum" (Fettig, 1999, p. 1). Moreover, according to him, personal finance should be supportive in a way that it enables individuals to apply basic economic principles. Since financial tasks provide a clear application of economic concepts, economic and financial literacy go hand-in-hand with each other.

The central benefit of economic and financial literacy is represented by economic education, which should develop the ability to conduct objective and reasoned analysis of economic problems. "Economic education" sometimes also called "economics education" is divided into two crucial streams. The former focuses on the current state of economic education, its improvement and methods

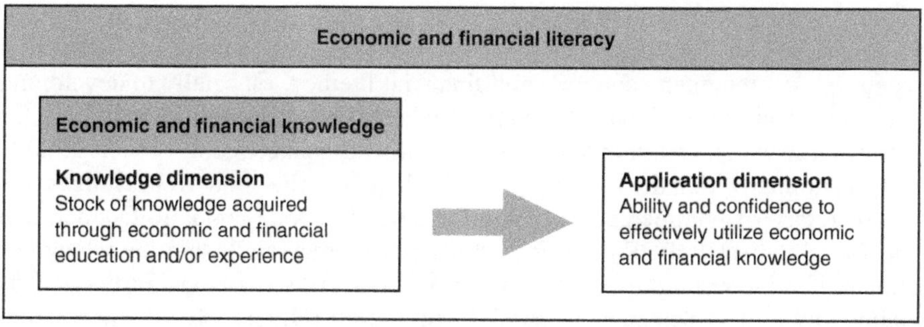

Figure 5.1 Connection between economic literacy, financial literacy, and economic education.

Source: Own elaboration. Adapted from Huston (2010).

and techniques used to teach economics at various educational levels. The latter aims to analyze the effectiveness of alternative educational techniques in economics, the level of economic literacy across various groups, and factors which affect the level of economic literacy. Economic education is quite distinct from "economics of education," which concentrates on the economics of the institution of education. Economic education in its pure form of educating, has undisputable value added for economic and financial literacy, since it develops the capability to conduct objective, reasoned analysis of economic problems. Acquisition and use of knowledge of economic concepts and generalizations allows for informed decision making with consequences at the individual level but also in terms of economic policy. As summarized by Witt and Kotte (1995, p. 165), economic education should foster the development of economic thinking, which leads also to special kind of knowledge, which is understood as "knowledge about knowledge, or meta knowledge, in the sense of knowledge about the structure and validity of economic knowledge, as well as knowledge about the ways to use this knowledge."

The delineation of economic, financial literacy and economic education, and the connection between them might be summarized with help of Figure 5.1. As already suggested, economic and financial knowledge are not equivalent to economic and financial literacy. An individual is supposed not only to be endowed by knowledge, but also apply this knowledge to make respective decisions.

Significance of economic and financial literacy

In the last few years, there has been a growing tendency of central banks and other institutions to promote economic education by running a variety of educational programs. Significant resources have been given by Reserve Banks of the Fed and other central banks across the world to promote economic and financial literacy. Additional organizations in the United States assess and target economic and financial literacy like the US National Center for Research in Economic Education, the Council for Economic Education, or the Foundation for Teaching Economics and Junior Achievement. The European Central Bank (ECB) devotes significant resources to its financial education program to increase awareness about the Eurosystem and Eurosystem monetary policy. The UK Department for International Development (DFID) and the World Bank Group devote substantial resources to strengthen economic and financial literacy, especially in developing countries. The International Monetary Fund (IMF) also promotes economic literacy in line with its mission to promote a healthy global economy, and its attitude is well summarized in the beginning of this chapter in the quote from Hodges, the US secretary of commerce. Also, the Organization for Economic Cooperation and Development (OECD) considers financial literacy skills and knowledge as critical with increasing responsibility for financial risks at an ever earlier age, as claimed by OECD Secretary-General Angel Gurría (OECD 2014b). As a result, the OECD implements various programs for international evaluation of financial literacy across the adult and youth population.

Factors accountable for increased attention to financial literacy

The question arises as to the underlying motives of central banks to promote economic education. Technological advances and globalization of economies transformed the economic environment, which is more vulnerable and fast-changing. In a more complex world, this creates a demand for sufficient economic literacy because, not only is access to information required, but subjects must also be able to use it in an appropriate way. This development is confirmed by the Federal Reserve Bank of San Francisco (2005), and in other studies like Guidolin and La Jeunesse (2007) or Mandell and Klein (2009).

First, technological advancement has made financial delivery and processing of financial products and services more efficient. Also, consumers are able to choose from a wide variety of products without geographic limitation based on available information. However, this requires a sufficient amount of financial knowledge, in order to utilize the value of information in appropriate way. Technological advancement has also created space for targeted marketing where databases are able to match consumer preferences with product offerings. This promotes competition and enhances customer services, but at the same time makes consumers more vulnerable to unscrupulous lending practices. Furthermore, the lender-borrower interaction has been diminished due to sophisticated credit-scoring technology, which produces a risk profile of consumers with respective pricing of credit. The lack of personal interaction limits decision-making of financially illiterate consumers and thereby weakens guidance on the course of action. Competition resulting from technological advancement has brought up a wide variety of products, like highly specialized deposit and credit products. Also, there has been a development of nonbank providers of financial services like payday lenders or check cashers. In addition, deregulation of the banking industry has led to the expansion of new non-conventional lending options such as longer term and interest only loans. On the one hand, consumers have more opportunities, on the other, they are more vulnerable and their decision-making is affected by low financial experience and may be highly costly in terms of monthly fees or excessive transactions.

Predatory lending practices are popular since they are more affordable for some borrowers, but at the same time liquidating. Although not technically illegal, they might be highly inappropriate for consumers. A good example is a loan structured with relatively small fixed payments in the beginning but with a large payment at the end of the term, which might be not affordable for those earning fixed income. Regulatory protections are important, but at the same time consumer education is important to combat predatory lending.

The economic profile of households has also changed. Households have become more consumption-oriented and less savings-oriented, which raises doubts about having sufficient resources in retirement. Consumer debt levels and non-business bankruptcies have risen.

Also, demographical change plays a significant role, with the population being more diverse and unfamiliar with financial practices. Language, educational and cultural barriers may lead to a switch by financially illiterate groups to alternative providers of financial services, which charge higher fees.

In light of recent developments, consumer's responsibility for credit, investment and retirement management has increased. This is certainly demanding. Suboptimal decisions of financially illiterate consumers may have negative implications on the entire economy.

As a result, banking institutions consider economic and financial literacy of prime importance for individuals to behave efficiently. Furthermore, Bernanke (2006a) points out that not only is economic literacy essential for consumers to make informed financial decisions, but also for business in healthy financial decision making.[1] In addition he emphasizes that conducting monetary policy and maintaining a stable financial system depends among other factors in the support of an educated public:

> The Federal Reserve's mission of conducting monetary policy and maintaining a stable financial system depends upon the participation and support of an educated public. Accomplishing this mission involves trade-offs and tough decisions. As the Fed pursues the monetary policy objectives that have been set out for us by Congress—to pursue price stability, maximum employment, and moderate long-term interest rates—it is essential that the public understand our objectives and our actions. Educating the public about the reasoning behind our decisions helps build confidence in our economic system—another critical factor in keeping our economy running smoothly.
>
> (Bernanke, 2006b, p. 1)

Also, Blinder (1994) points out the basic or low level of economic literacy in the country and world is one of the things that leaves the political process vulnerable to this malady. This suggests that economic literacy might contribute to better informed public as suggested by Mishkin (2008).

As pointed out by Stark (2006) and many others, the direct impact of economic and financial education might be beneficial since it helps to maintain the primary goal of price stability. The public might better accept price stability as the goal if it understands the complexity of real and nominal effects of monetary policy in a sense that price stability protects the economy and contributes to economic efficiency and welfare. It also helps the public understand the importance of a central bank's independence, and the fact its goals of price stability are not undermined by the government. Financial and economic literacy may also play a substantial role in the formation of inflation expectations. Bruine de Bruin et al. (2010) found that higher inflationary expectations in the United States are correlated with lower levels of financial literacy. In addition, the communication of central banks is also easier because educated individuals might understand the information provided by central banks regarding their decisions more quickly. This further promotes a central bank's transparency. The effectiveness of the conduct of monetary policy, enhanced by economic and financial literacy might then provide better guidance, not only for individual consumers but also for firms, which might make more efficient financial choices. This might indirectly foster economic and financial stability, because uncertainty and volatility might be significantly reduced. This discussion may be summarized in the view of Minehan (2006), Bernanke (2006a; 2006b), Fettig (1998, 1999), where economic literacy might provide a positive effect, as follows:

- For an individual, generally more effective knowledge, analytical skills, better use of information, which then implies a higher probability of achieving optimum outcomes.
- Enhance the effectiveness of monetary policy.
- Smooth functioning of financial markets.
- Built reputation and promote acceptance for CB's actions followed by increased transparency.
- Promote economic and financial literacy as a public good.
- Support sustainable economic policies.

To enhance literacy, economic education activities became the cornerstone of central banks' communication strategies. Central banks target various groups depending on type of knowledge transferred. The first targeted group are primary school children, who are made familiar with basic money concepts in an entertaining way (for instance the Bank of England and its special educatory course "Pounds and Pence Package," or the Netherlands Bank and its "Money Box"). Special education packages, which focus on money management and economic concepts, are addressed to the secondary school children target group (for instance the Bundesbank and its study material "Unser Geld," "Geld und Geldpolitik," or the online game "Mission Bundesbank," or the Bank of England and its study material "Made of Money"). The college and university students, as a third target group, are given special attention. Central banks like the ECB or Bundesbank prepare advanced economic packages, which include a mix of academic literature, presentations, workshops or courses. The fourth group is composed of secondary school teachers, who participate in economics seminar series organized in cooperation with other institutions. Also, this group is endowed with teacher training materials on economics (for instance the information brochure of the ECB "Price stability: why is it important for you" for students and teachers in cooperation with Eurosystem, or the iconomix package devised by The Swiss National Bank, which contains innovative teaching strategies and online strategic games). Last, central banks run information campaigns to inform the general public with an aim to increase financial literacy (for instance the FED and its campaign "There is a lot to learn about money" in 2003, or exhibitions like the National Bank of Belgium). The initiative and strategy of central banks regarding financial literacy differ substantially and a good overview is provided by Fluch (2007) and Apostoaie (2010).

Measurement of economic and financial literacy

The measurement of economic and financial literacy is not a trivial issue. Lusardi and Mitchell (2011c, p. 2) note that "while it is important to assess how financially literate people are, in practice it is difficult to explore how people process economic information and make informed decisions about household finances." Also, there are not any standardized instruments to measure economic and financial literacy as suggested by Huston (2010).

Economic literacy

The fundamental cornerstone for measuring economic literacy emerged in the context of a press conference, organized by the newly established Joint Council on Economic Education (JCEE) in 1989. Paul Volcker, former Federal Reserve chairman, stressed at this conference that "the news is not good" (JCEE 1989, pp. 1–2). This claim was encouraged by William B. Walstad, who added that "The level of economic knowledge among most high-school students is shocking." JCEE 1989, pp. 1–2). The JCEE outlined twenty standards that define what secondary school graduates should know about economics. The widespread discussion about economic literacy finally culminated in the development of the Test of Economic Literacy (TEL), which was designed by Walstad and Soper (1989). It appeared that this framework turned out to be good instrument for the assessment of student performance with respect to economic abilities. The TEL was recently upgraded and represents a nationally normed, standardized, valid and reliable measure (Walstad, Rebeck and Butters 2013). The TEL is widely accepted by central banks (for instance Federal Reserve Bank of Minneapolis) and some states like New York, granted to it the official status of an economic course ending with an exam.

In a Minneapolis Federal Reserve Survey, only 30 percent knew that a reduction in government expenditure and money growth helps reduce inflation, which suggests the case for economic education (Fettig 1998). Walstad and Rebeck (2001) examined 7,261 high school students at the end of the fall and spring semesters of in 1999 to 2000 and found out that participation in an economic course improved the economic knowledge of participating over non-participating students by 20 percentage points. Butters and Asarta (2011) used the TEL data based on a survey of 2,149 high school students and confirmed previous findings that additional economic training was associated with better outcomes. The TEL was not only successfully applied by Shen (1993) and Beck and Krumm (1990) to cross-validate the TEL in other countries, but also applied to target various populations (Beck and Krumm 1991).[2]

Since 1995, the IMD[3] World Competitiveness Yearbook (WCY) has published an indicator of economic literacy known as the "WCY index." The construction of this indicator is based on a survey of internationally experienced senior business leaders, ranging from top and middle managers to nationals or expatriates, located in domestic or foreign enterprises. The survey included 4,000 business leaders in 55 countries. Respondents were required to assess the level of economic literacy among the population on a scale of 0 to 10. Also, they were required to assess the statement whether education in finance does meet the needs of the business economy. This suggests a potential caveat of this indicator as noted by Jappelli (2010), where the level of economic literacy is based on business leaders' responses rather than a general audience.

This indicator might be compared with the Survey of Health, Assets, Retirement and Expectations (SHARE) numeracy variable based on the SHARE survey. The proxy for economic literacy is represented by the variable, which measures the ability to perform basic computations and understanding of basic financial principles. Despite the fact the SHARE variable contains only a few economic concepts, there are numerous studies, which provide evidence that numerical skills affect financial outcomes. For instance, Christelis, Jappelli and Padula (2010) found that direct and indirect investment in stocks are positively related to mathematical ability, verbal fluency and recall skills. McArdle, Smith and Willis (2009) suggest that numerical skills are associated with complex decision-making and higher probability of savings and investment. As proved by Jappelli (2010), WCY and SHARE indicators are well aligned and provide a reasonable proxy for economic literacy.

Financial literacy

The most commonly used measurement of financial literacy is a set of three questions developed by Lusardi and Mitchell (2008, 2011a). The set of three questions was already utilized before in a survey of US citizens aged fifty and older as a part of the American Health and Retirement Study (HRS), 2004. These three financial literacy questions test compounding of interest rate, understanding of inflation, and knowledge about stocks, stock mutual funds and risk diversification (with the correct answer given in bold):

- *Suppose you had $100 in a savings account and the interest rate was 2 percent per year. After five years, how much do you think you would have in the account if you left the money to grow: [**more than $102**; exactly $102; less than $102; do not know; refuse to answer.]*
- *Imagine that the interest rate on your savings account was 1 percent per year and inflation was 2 percent per year. After one year, would you be able to*

buy: [more than, exactly the same as, or ***less than today*** *with the money in this account; do not know; refuse to answer.]*

- *Do you think that the following statement is true or false? "Buying a single company stock usually provides a safer return than a stock mutual fund." [true;* ***false****; do not know; refuse to answer.]*

The results of a special module of the 2004 HRS indicated high prevailing financial illiteracy among older US population. Only one third could answer all three questions correctly despite their engagement in numerous financial decisions and transactions over their lifetime. Various other surveys added these three questions such as the 2007 to 2008 National Longitudinal Survey of Youth (NLSY) for population between the age of twenty-three and twenty-eight (Lusardi, Mitchell and Curto 2010), the RAND American Life Panel (ALP) covering all ages, (Lusardi and Mitchell 2009), and the 2009 and 2012 National Financial Capability Survey covering adult population (Lusardi and Mitchell 2011d). These financial literacy measures were extended by more sophisticated concepts. For instance, National Financial Capability Study (NFCS), measuring financial literacy of the adult population, extends the survey by two additional questions about asset pricing and understanding of mortgage interest and bond prices, known as the "Big Five." Only 39 percent of respondents answered the standard set of three questions. Additionally, only 21 percent knew about the negative relationship between bond prices and interest rates (Lusardi 2011).[4] In general, findings confirm that most US respondents exhibited a considerable level of financial illiteracy.

The Jumpstart Coalition for Personal Financial Literacy introduced financial literacy as a construct in its study of Jumpstart Survey of Financial Literacy Among High School Students in 1997. The aim is to provide view about the performance of high school seniors at the start of their working career. Results show that over the period of increasing attention to public school training in personal finance, the performance of high school seniors exhibited a declining trend. Still, the 2002 Jumpstart Survey shows substantially higher performance of students who participated in an interactive market stock game compared to those who did not or who took another form of training (Mandell, 2008).

However, as Lusardi and Mitchell (2014) note, this evaluation does not provide a clear-cut picture of the knowledge of young people due to the long list of survey questions (more than fifty). In addition, other studies provided evidence about low financial literacy among youth. For instance, Chen and Volpe (1998) found that the performance of business majors substantially outweighs the performance of non-business majors, but in general the level of financial literacy of college students is low. This is also supported by Shim et al. (2010) for college students and Mandell (2008) for high school students.

International evidence on financial literacy

This method of three questions forms a useful basis of international comparison. Various national surveys have been conducted in other countries: Beckmann

(2013) in Romania; Fornero and Monticone (2011) in Italy; Bucher-Koenen and Lusardi (2011) in Germany; Behrman, Mitchell, Soo and Bravo (2012) in Chile; Cole, Sampson and Zia (2011) in India and Indonesia; Sekita (2011) in Japan; Crossan, Feslier and Hurnard (2011) in New Zealand; Klapper and Panos (2011) in Russia; Almenberg and Säve-Söderbergh (2011) in Sweden; Alessie, van Rooij and Lusardi (2011) in the Netherlands; and Arrondel, Debbich and Savignac (2013) in France. An international comparison of survey results is displayed in Table. 5.1.[5]

Lusardi and Mitchell (2011a) show that in the United States, only 30 percent of people can answer all three questions. Comparable surveys in Table 5.1 show that the level of financial literacy is quite low and similar to the pattern in the United States. However, financial literacy is still lower in low-income countries like India. Still, well-developed countries like Germany, the Netherlands, Japan and Austria don't over perform substantially countries like Russia and Romania, where financial markets exhibit rapid change. In contrast, Romania and Russia as past planned economies, display low knowledge of the inflation question. Interestingly, the performance of Japanese people in answering the question about inflation was also significantly lower compared to the Germans or Dutch. This was probably due to the historical experience with deflation. Striking are the results of Sweden and Chile regarding the interest rate question. Such a low performance could, however, be caused by a substantially more difficult question posed, which, however, yielded the exact answer like in the case of more simple question. The majority of people in all countries reported zero knowledge of the risk diversification question.

It is worth emphasizing the findings of the OECD, which was a pioneer in international comparison of financial literacy. Its report in 2005 highlights the lack of financial literacy in Europe, Australia and Japan. Low financial literacy scores were also confirmed across Europe in the study of Christelis, Jappelli and Padula (2010). Atkinson and Messy (2011, 2012) analyzed the performance across fourteen countries using a set of eight financial literacy questions (including the standard set of three questions) and arrived at a similar conclusion about low financial literacy.

The OECD took it a step further in the evaluation of financial literacy across the youth (high school students) with its Program for International Student Assessment (PISA), which in 2012 added a module on financial literacy to modules in mathematics, science and literacy. This created an opportunity for the evaluation of financial literacy of fifteen years old around the world, which is considered as necessary skill for participation in ever-changing and complex market environment. The findings cover eighteen countries and economies. Results show that students have only basic skills in financial literacy. Only one in ten students is a top performer in terms of financial literacy in the set of ten OECD countries, which participated in the survey. In addition, more than 15 percent of students from OECD countries exhibited a performance below the baseline level of proficiency. Furthermore, large disparities exist across countries. In the highest performing—Shanghai-China, the Flemish community of Belgium, Estonia, Australia, New Zealand and the Czech Republic—students could solve

Table 5.1 International comparison of responses based on financial literacy surveys

Authors	*Country*	*Year of data*	*Interest rate*	*Inflation*	*Risk diversification*	*Survey sample*
Alessie, VanRooij and Lusardi (2011)	Netherlands	2010	84.8%	76.9%	51.9%	1,665
Almenberg and Save-Soderbergh (2011)	Sweden	2010	35.2%	59.5%	68.4%	1,302
Arrondel, Debbich and Savignac (2013)	France	2011	48%	61.2%	66.8%	3,616
Beckman (2013)	Romania	2011	41.3%	31.8%	14.7%	1,030
Behrman (2010)	Chile	2006	2%	26%	46%	13,054
Bucher-Koenen and Lusardi (2011)	Germany	2009	82.4%	78.4%	61.8%	1,059
Cole, Sampson and Zia (2010)	Indonesia	2007	78%	61%	28%	3,360
Cole, Sampson and Zia (2010)	India	2006	59%	25%	31%	1,496
Crossan, Feslier and Hurnard (2011)	New Zealand	2009	86%	81%	27%	850
Fornero and Monticone (2011)	Italy	2007	40%	59.3%	52.2%	3,992
Klapper and Panos (2011)	Russia	2009	36.3%	50.8%	12.8%	1,366
Lusardi and Mitchell (2011d)	USA	2009	64.9%	64.3%	51.8%	1,488
Sekita (2011)	Japan	2010	70.5%	58.8%	39.5%	5,268

Source: Own elaboration.

moderately difficult tasks (at least one in three and up to three in four students were successful). In contrast, in the lowest performing countries, students could solve only simple tasks (OECD 2014a).

We have outlined some common measures of financial literacy ranging from a standard set of three questions to longer survey batteries. The question remains—how effective is each approach in terms of testing financial literacy. Hung, Meijer, Mihaly and Yoong (2009) performed a validation of seven different financial literacy measures, calculated from various question batteries, which were given to the same respondents in four different sessions of the RAND ALP. Results suggest that financial literacy measures based on different performance tests[6] are highly correlated with each other, but are more variable with respect to planning for retirement, saving and wealth accumulation.

Subjective versus objective literacy

Apart from the objective measures of financial and economic literacy, a subjective measure of literacy has been operationalized. The so-called "self-reported" financial literacy measures an individual's self-assessment of their knowledge. The literature shows that there is sometimes a substantial mismatch between self-assessed knowledge and actual financial knowledge (Hastings and Mitchell 2011; Collins et al. 2009). In addition, respondents are too confident about their financial knowledge (Agnew and Szykman 2005). As Lusardi (2011) notes 70 percent of respondents in the US Financial Capability Study overestimated their knowledge, but only 30 percent replied correctly. Bucher-Koenen, Lusardi, Alessie and van Rooij (2012) report similar findings for Germany and the Netherlands. Still, general literature reports a positive correlation between self-reported financial knowledge and objective measures of financial literacy, and independent predictive power of self-reported financial knowledge relative to objective measures of financial literacy. Allgood and Walstad (2013) confirm this view in the 2009 NFCS. In particular, the state-by state survey was based on the big five questions, where both subjective and objective measures are predictive of financial outcomes in various areas like credit cards, investments, loans, insurance coverage. Similar results were reached by Parker et al. (2012). Alessie et al. (2011) reports that both subjective and objective measures of financial literacy predict stock market participation.

Disaggregating the effects of economic and financial literacy

Although studies differ in terms of the targeted audience and in the approach to measuring economic and financial literacy, some common findings might be identified.

Financial literacy and age

We already tackled this issue when discussing financial literacy measures. Basically studies suggest that financial literacy follows an inverted U-shape with respect to age, being lowest among the elderly and young people. Lusardi and Mitchell (2011a) document that cross-sectional data make it difficult to distinguish age from cohort effects, but in general the hypothesize is that individuals tend to accumulate knowledge, which deteriorates with age. Finke, Howe and Huston (2011) ruled out cohort effects and other demographic characteristics and explained lower financial literacy of older people by a decline in cognitive processes. Also, they identified a substantial gap between self-reported and actual knowledge. As Lusardi and Mitchell (2014) and Deevy et al. (2012) noted, this might explain higher exposure of old people to financial scams.

The financial literacy of young people, which is substantially low, is subject to attention by various studies. The OECD (2014a) together with the Jumpstart coalition (cited by Mandell, 2008), Williams-Harold (1999), Huddlestone-Casas et al. (1999) report that US high school students exhibit a basic sort of financial literacy. Lusardi and Tufano (2009b) obtained similar results for American teenagers. Mandel (2008) documented failing financial literacy for high school students. Beal and Delpachitra (2003) and Ali et al. (2014) found low levels of financial literacy for Australian students. There are several reasons for different levels of financial literacy among youth, such as participation in a business major versus a non-business major (Chen and Volpe 1998), working ten to twenty hours per week or having a savings account (Valentine and Khayum 2005).

Economic and financial literacy, education and income

It has been argued that education might play a substantial role in literacy differences. Those with a lower educational attainment are much less likely to be knowledgeable, which is a pattern found across several countries (Lusardi and Mitchell, 2011c). In addition, poor numeracy seems to be associated with low education attainment (Christelis, Jappelli and Padula 2010).

Cognitive ability is an additional phenomenon, which must be controlled in order to examine the pure impact of financial literacy. Lusardi, Mitchell and Curto (2010) found a positive relationship between financial literacy and cognitive abilities based on the NLSY survey measures. Still, cognitive factors are only partially capable of explaining the substantial heterogeneity in financial literacy. These issues are related to the endogeneity problem, which will be discussed more thoroughly later in the chapter.

Some studies identified a possible connection between financial literacy and income and especially a causal effect of financial literacy on wealth accumulation. Most of the studies prove a positive effect of financial literacy on wealth accumulation like Monticone (2010), Behrman et al. (2012), and Hastings and Mitchell (2011). Jappelli and Padula (2013) show that financial literacy and wealth are jointly determined and correlated over the life-cycle. Behrman et al. (2012) concluded that the effects of financial literacy on wealth accumulation are stronger than effects of educational attainment.

Jappelli (2010) examined the dataset of fifty-five countries. The results suggest that economic and financial literacy is positively related to human capital endowment, but negatively associated with generous social security system in particular country.

Economic and financial literacy by gender

Several studies also report a large gender gap difference in financial literacy regardless of age. It appears that males generally score better in terms of financial knowledge than females and these differences prevail not only in more sophisticated questions, but also in basic ones, (Lusardi and Mitchell 2011b; Lusardi, Mitchell and Curto 2010; Lusardi and Tufano 2009a, 2009b; Hung, Parker and Yoong 2009). In addition, women are more likely to say that they do not know the answer, which indicates their awareness about the lack of knowledge across developed and developing countries (Lusardi and Mitchell 2011c). In contrast, Bucher-Koenen and Lusardi (2011) find no gender differences in East Germany.

MasterCard Worldwide (2011) evaluated the financial literacy of 10,500 women in twenty-four countries across Asia, the Middle East, North and Sub-Saharan Africa. The results suggested that the financial literacy of women in African and Middle Eastern countries is generally lower than that of Asian women. Also, financial literacy might not be correlated with income necessarily, since women in Thailand scored the highest and women in Japan and Korea the lowest.

Several authors aimed to find an explanation for the gender gap. Some gender differences might be rational due to traditional specialization within the family, where married women acquire financial knowledge later as pointed out by Hsu (2011). This, however, does not explain why low financial literacy prevails among single women, which is witnessed in studies of gender difference at high school and college (Chen and Volpe 2002, Mandell 2008). Fonseca et al. (2012) argues that the traditional model of specialization in financial decision-making within couples by gender might not be accountable for the gender gap in financial literacy. Instead he admits that the financial literacy gap might be substantially reduced by education, income, and current and past marital status. Also, the gender gap in the US is not explained by difference in characteristics of men and women, but by the way literacy is created. In addition, the decision-making role within couples is allocated more by relative level of education than by gender.

Also, the varying self-confidence across gender might represent an important factor for differences in financial literacy (Bucher-Koenen et al. 2012). Furthermore, a longer life span of women in the US might make them more vulnerable to poverty in old age with a lower level of financial literacy than the older population on average (Lusardi and Mitchell 2008). Particularly of interest might be the finding of Mahdavi and Horton (2014), which suggests no role for higher economic education in terms of improving economic literacy. In particular, well educated women were not that much financially literate.

Financial literacy and geographic/ethnic disparities

The literature suggests the presence of strong regional disparities in financial literacy. The performance of those living in rural areas is significantly lower than of those living in urban areas, as noted by Klapper and Panos (2011). Also, the center-north region of Italy exhibits higher financial literacy compared to the south of Italy (Fornero and Monticone 2011) and west Germany exhibits higher performance then the east, (Xu and Zia 2012). Similar differences in financial literacy were reported across the United States by Bumcrot, Lin and Lusardi (2013). However, as opposed to initial demographical predictions, South Dakota and Idaho had higher levels of financial literacy, while the opposite held for Pennsylvania, New Jersey or New York.

Also, a substantial difference in financial literacy exists by race and ethnicity. Hispanics and African-Americans score lower in terms of financial literacy than whites, Lusardi and Mitchell (2007a, 2007b, 2011 b). Also, they are less likely to own checking accounts or hold high-return assets and face higher costs in terms of information and planning (Lusardi, 2005). Other studies, like Crossan et al. (2011), confirm lower financial literacy of Maori than of the general population in New Zealand, excluding Maori participating in financial education courses. Also, lower levels of financial literacy of religious minorities, such as Muslims, is observed in the Netherlands (Alessie et al. 2011).

How does literacy matter?

There is a vast amount of literature, which concentrates on the relationship between economic, financial literacy, and consequent economic behavior. This has become topical in the wake of financial crisis in 2008 to 2009, where, in particular, the less financially literate, like the elderly, became exposed to financial scams.

Financial illiteracy seems to be correlated with financial mistakes, which is documented by several studies. The majority of US households exhibit low financial literacy and tend to adopt a rule of thumb behavior when making decisions about saving, as noted by Bernheim et al. (2001). Also, it appears that financial mistakes might be attributed more to younger and older consumers. In addition, it is hypothesized that financial mistakes, high interest rates, and financial fees follow a U-shaped pattern, with cost-minimizing performance at about the age of fifty-three (Agarwal et al. 2011).

It is confirmed that financial literacy enhances day-to-day financial management skills, (Hilgert, Hogarth and Beverly 2003). Several studies indicate that financial literacy is associated with more sophisticated investment behavior. For instance, financially literate individuals tend to participate more in the stock market as proved by Dutch survey data, (Alessie et al. 2011). In addition, German investors with lower levels of financial literacy not only participate less in stock markets but also are more likely to sell assets, which lost value during a crisis (Bucher-Koenen and Ziegelmeyer 2011). Also, investors with higher levels of financial literacy tend to better diversify their portfolio, as proved in a survey of Portuguese investors (Abreu and Mendes 2010) and in a survey of Italian investors (Jappelli and Guiso 2009). If we refer back to the subjective perception of knowledge, where respondents are often too confident, Xia, Wang and Li (2014) find positive association between financial literacy overconfidence and stock market participation.

Financial literacy is also linked to retirement planning. Lusardi and Mitchell (2011a) found that financial literacy is associated with the lack of planning for retirement in the United States. Similar and quite robust results were found by other studies in Germany (Bucher-Koenen and Lusardi 2011; Pahnke and Honekamp 2010), in the Netherlands (Alessie et al. 2011), in Japan (Sekita 2011), in Italy (Fornero and Monticone 2011), in Canada (Boisclair, Lusardi and Michaud 2014), in Russia (Klapper and Panos, 2011), and on the dataset for nine European countries (Ashok and Spataro 2015).

Financial literacy also influences mortgage and debt outcomes. Research suggests that households, which exhibit low levels of financial literacy, tend to engage in high-cost borrowing. Lusardi and de Bassa Scheresberg (2013) investigated various areas, including payday loans, pawn, shops and refund anticipation loans, and confirmed this trend of high-cost borrowing in the United States. High-cost borrowing together with higher fees and transaction costs is also the case for the least financially savvy, who are often unaware of their debt position or find their debt position to be excessive (Lusardi and Tufano 2009a). Financially illiterate consumers also tend to choose alternative mortgage products with back-loaded payment over a standard repayment mortgage (Gathergood and Weber 2015). Low financial literacy is also associated with engagement in mortgage equity withdrawals (MEWs) via first or second mortgages, without knowledge of the risk (Duca and Kumar 2014). Borrowers with low financial literacy are also more willing to accept riskier mortgages with disadvantageous characteristics and are less likely to use advantageous prepayment opportunities and exhibit high default rate (An, Bostic and Yao 2015). Low financial literacy is also associated with costly credit card behavior (Mottola 2013) and both self-perceived and actual knowledge have an effect on credit card behavior over the life cycle (Allgood and Walstad 2013). Inaccurate self-assessment of creditworthiness appears to play a role, since it might lead to suboptimal decisions like mortgage priced by higher interest rate (Courchane et al. 2008). It appears that many individuals are not aware about the interest rate charged on their credit cards or mortgage balances (Lusardi 2011; Gathergood 2012). A lower level of literacy is also substantially associated with mortgage defaults and delinquency. Also, it appears that numerical ability is a strong predictor of mortgage defaults even after controlling for cognitive ability and general knowledge (Gerardi, Goette and Meier 2013). Those unable to compute the interest rate out of a stream of payments often borrow more and accumulate less wealth (Stango and Zinman 2009).

Endogeneity and measurement problems

Based on the previous discussion, financial and economic literacy seems to be an effective mechanism to improve existing outcomes. However, if policy makers want to target economic and financial literacy, it is necessary to account for the potential endogeneity problem. Does economic and financial literacy improve economic outcomes or does a certain type of economic behavior enhance financial literacy? Or is there another factor such as numerical ability, education or general intelligence, which increases financial literacy and also improves existing outcomes? We may illustrate it by an example of individuals with higher levels of financial literacy, who are more likely to participate in a retirement plan sponsored by an employer, since they find it advantageous. However, if an employer automatically enrolls employees in company's retirement plan, they may acquire financial literacy automatically by their participation in this plan. This personal experience might then account for reverse causality, as noted by Hilgert et al. (2003). Hastings et al. (2013) noted that this endogeneity does not rule out the possibility that financial literacy affects economic outcomes, but the magnitude of the effect might be biased upwards and therefore be difficult to interpret.

One approach on how to evaluate the impact of financial literacy on subsequent behavior is the adoption of instrumental variables technique. Fernandes, Lynch and Netemeyer (2013) point out that using instrumental variables approach substantially alleviates the effect of financial literacy. Lusardi and Mitchell (2009) used high school financial education mandates adopted at different points in time as an instrument for financial literacy and interacted them with state expenditures on education. At the same time, education might represent not that strong a proxy for financial literacy, since both are significant in regressions on retirement planning, as noted by Lusardi and Mitchell (2011a).

Christiansen, Joensen, and Rangvid (2008) used the opening of a new university in a local area as instrumental variable for knowledge, and suggested economic education as an important determinant of stock investments.

Klapper, Lusardi, and Panos (2012) instrumented financial literacy by the number of public and private universities available in Russia and by the total number of newspapers. Their findings suggested that financial literacy affects various areas like having a bank account, using bank and informal credit, or having spending capacity. We have already mentioned the study of Behrman et al. (2012), who investigated the effect of financial literacy and years of schooling on wealth by adopting a set of instrumental variables such as age-dependent variables, family background factors, and respondent personality traits.

Other confounding or unobservable factors might be present, which could bias financial literacy impact and many studies attempt to account for them. For instance, more future-oriented individuals are also more likely to participate voluntarily in educational courses (Meier and Sprenger 2010). Also, patience might induce individuals to invest more in health and save up more for retirement as proved by Hastings and Mitchell (2011). Many other factors might bias results, such as family background (Cunha and Heckman 2007), personality (Borghans et al. 2008), discount rates (Meier and Sprenger 2013) or intelligence (Grinblatt, Keloharju, and Linnainmaa 2011). We have already tackled poor numeracy, which was accounted for by Christelis, Jappelli, and Padula (2010), and cognitive ability incorporated for instance by Lusardi, Mitchell, and Curto (2010) and Gerardi, Goette and Meier (2013). Nevertheless, numeracy has the effect far beyond the cognitive ability as suggested by Gerardi et al. (2013).

Another way to identify the effect of economic and financial literacy is to conduct a field experiment in which one treatment group is exposed to an educational effect and the control group is not exposed. Sometimes this approach is known as the "golden rule" of evaluation (Collins and O'Rourke 2010). As an example, the research of Skimmyhorn (2012), who created a variation in financial education exposure in the US army, concluded that financial education course plays substantial role in consequent participation rate of soldiers in the Federal Thrift Savings Plan, with more than double average monthly contributions. The author also considered the effect of education on other financial choices (credit card balances, unpaid debts, etc.), for which he found limited evidence.

Sometimes the exposure to educational effect in terms of the treatment and control group is not strictly confined, which might lead to inconclusive results. As previously mentioned JumpStart (2006) cited by Mandell (2008), who documented a substantially low evidence of any difference in the financial knowledge of high school students who participated or who did not participate in a financial education class. The problem lies in the fact that in some districts financial courses are voluntary and in some mandatory for all students. This naturally creates a difference in the character of the sample examined (Hastings et al. 2013). As a result, causal inference is highly problematic. Walstad, Rebeck, and MacDonald (2010) point out that empirical research did not consider the role of specific factors like course content, test measurement, teacher preparation or amount of instruction.

This suggests that there is a scope for financial education programs to assess the effects of financial literacy, however, careful evaluations of its impact are necessary.

Financial/economic education programs and financial/economic literacy

What is the evidence that financial and economic education increases financial and economic literacy? In the literature, substantial disagreement remains about the efficacy of financial/economic education. This might be because only a few authors conducted careful evaluations of the impact of educational programs as suggested by Lussardi and Mitchell (2014), who address a few key concerns about the research in this area.

First, incentives for investment in financial literacy significantly differ and the program might produce different behavioral responses of individuals. For instance, the financial educational course addressed in study of Skimmyhorn (2012) might boost saving for retirement, but at the same time might induce others to reduce their debt instead. Still, the author has addressed the broader financial behavior of individuals, including credit card balances, unpaid debts, and so on, which eliminates distortion.

Second, the length of exposure to the educational effect might significantly affect the success of the program. If a large portion of population is illiterate even about basic concepts such as inflation or interest rate compounding, it is unlikely that short educational course will substantially improve their decision-making process. Instead, it is advisable to target specific groups due to the prevailing heterogeneity in financial literacy and different preferences of individuals.

Additionally, confounding factors might be present and lead to erroneous estimation unless the evaluation is carefully structured. An example can be found in Mandell (2008), who did not account for different incentives of students induced by mandatory versus voluntary financial education courses. Also, the quality of teaching at schools and in the workplace, seems to be an important indicator to account for.

Selected studies assessing the effects of educational programs

The existing literature on financial and economic education programs and its effect on literacy is rather extensive, but few studies deserve attention. Innovative strategies have been applied quite recently to assess the effects of educational programs. For instance, Walstad, Rebeck and MacDonald (2010) use quasi-experimental design, in which an experimental group of students was exposed to a designed video course, mapping several basic concepts such as saving, money management, banking, credit and debt, followed by six hours of instructions. The experimental group exhibited a significant gain in knowledge compared to students in a matched control group.

Carlin and Robinson (2010) adopted a quasi-experimental design, where economic training involved role-playing fictitious budget situations. Students involved in this game exhibited much better performance in consequent financial decision-making.

Financial programs effective in increasing savings or retirement savings are of particular interest too. Bernheim and Garrett (2003) found a positive effect of education programs on savings. Also, Lusardi (2003) concluded that retirement courses play a substantial role in savings behavior among the elderly.

Financial education programs might also be prospective in terms of reduction of risky borrowing or mortgage delinquency. Agarwal et al. (2011) showed, with the help of a natural experiment in the Illinois area, that the external review of high risk loans demanded by mortgage applicants resulted in the effect of reducing defaults, a decline in the supply of lenders and low-profile borrowers. Also, less risky loans were preferred by borrowers in order to avoid mandatory external review. He also claimed that even voluntary counselling helped to reduce mortgage delinquency rates, which is in line with the study of Hartarska and Gonzales-Vega (2006).

Furthermore, quite profound effects of economic and financial literacy might be investigated by focusing on developing countries. Several studies tried to verify the impact of economic and financial education on individual and household behavior, generally leading to the conclusion that the provision of education improves the basic decision-making of consumers. For instance, Berg and Zia (2013) examined the impact of financial education delivered through mass media on debt management in South Africa. Individuals exposed to financial education were more likely to borrow from standard sources and less likely to gamble. Cole et al. (2014) found the positive effect of financial education on financial decision-making of South African participants. Not only were individuals' awareness and confidence, in terms of saving and use of credit, improved, but a positive effect was also visible in terms of actual saving and borrowing behavior. The effect of education on financial planning was not proved. Carpena et al. (2011) conducted randomized experiments on low-income households in India, that were exposed to a five-week video-based financial education program. Findings showed that the effect of financial education program did not increase the respondents' numeracy, but rather their awareness and attitudes toward financial product and financial planning. Berry, Karlan and Pradhan (2015) found out that financial education had a substantial impact on the savings behavior of youth in Ghana, but not on other economic outcomes. Cai et al. (2015) found out that financial education of farmers in rural China seemed to affect the demand for crop insurance. Also, the network effect, which diffuses the knowledge about insurance, increased take up of insurance for farmers who did not receive financial education.

A few studies were conducted with respect to the effect of economic education on a firm's decision-making and outcomes. Karlan and Valdivia (2011) studied the impact of teaching basic economic knowledge on female micro-entrepreneurs in Peru and found that an education program improves record keeping, but not profits or employment. However, a generalization might not be made too quickly due to focus on poor rural women. Bruhn and Zia (2011) analyzed both female and male entrepreneurs in Bosnia and Herzegovina and found a significant effect of a business training program on business investment and production processes. Drexler, Fischer, and Schoar (2014) studied the impact of economic and financial training on firm-level and individual outcomes for entrepreneurs in the Dominican Republic. They found that the simplified rule-of-thumb training produced more significant improvements in pricing and consequent economic outcomes than standard fundamentals-based training. Martinez, Puentes, and Ruiz-Tagle (2013) assessed the effectiveness of business training for micro-entrepreneurs in Chile, with the help of a randomized controlled experiment. Their findings suggest that business training significantly increased employment and income and improved business practices. Bruhn, Karlan, and Schoar (2012) carried out a randomized evaluation of Mexican small and medium enterprises, where management consulting appears to have a positive effect on firm's productivity and return-on-assets.

The effectiveness of educational steps

However, several doubts remain regarding the effectiveness of educational steps. Although the concept of economic and financial literacy has been conceptualized, the problem is how individuals acquire economic knowledge and how effectively they use it. The first question is, according to Stigler (1970): Why should people be economically literate? An individual considers the potential benefits and costs regarding an economic education. Since the economic disciplines are considered universal, the knowledge used in numerous and highly diverse situations it is definitely worth the cost. However, the condition regarding the cost is not fulfilled in the following sense. It is hard to learn economic logic and apply it in different fields after completing a basic one-semester economics course. Participation in the basic course has little impact on economic knowledge and understanding, according to Salemi (2005), and although individuals recognize basic concepts, they are unable to apply them in real situations. There is the danger that this economic knowledge is rather formal. This suggests that the effect of education on economic outcomes might not be significant as suggested and therefore the education itself not worth it. However, Walstad, and Rebeck (2002) found in their research that a small but significant difference (6 to 11 percent) exists between the economic knowledge of the public and those who have taken a first-year college economics course. A variety of reasons, as already mentioned, might be responsible for the potential weak effect of economic education, for instance, how the education is provided, since, frequently, basic courses are subject to the criticism of artificiality (Salemi 2005). In this sense, it appears that economics might not be a universal knowledge.

Although economic education is not a guarantee that individuals will make decisions based on economic rationality (Wilson and Zhang 1997), it might at least somehow reduce the possibility of the behavior that leads to suboptimal outcomes. Well-educated individuals have a better prerequisite to deal with a significant amount of information, to effectively use it, which also further supports making and communicating the meaning and understanding of issues. If a decision has to be made, this informational advantage gained enables them to achieve their desired outcomes on the basis of enhanced economic literacy (Wilson and Mason 2000). Thus, regardless of the deficiencies mentioned, a sufficient level of economic and financial literacy might be supportive in a way that individuals and firms will better understand relevant information, sort it, and eliminate what is redundant, thus contributing to better decision-making and a reduction of suboptimal outcomes. This is in line with Mishkin (2008), who points out that a call for economic and financial education is based on the idea of better informed individuals, which might lead to better answers and, therefore, a higher probability of the attainment of optimum outcomes.

Therefore, measuring the effects of economic and financial literacy is critical for understanding the potential impact of educatory programs. Besides, in research related to economic efficacy, it is important is to determine the potential effect of economic education on final outcomes. As summarized by this quote from H. G. Stern, (1998, p. 1), President of the Federal Reserve Bank of Minneapolis:

> Economic literacy is crucial because it is a measure of whether people understand the forces that significantly affect the quality of their lives.

Reduction of money illusion in light of economic education

This chapter has addressed the importance of economic and financial literacy, which might improve existing economic outcomes. The preceding chapters dealt with individual and aggregate-level effects of money illusion and their implication for the economy in various areas. Generally, economists assume that money illusion is an error which will disappear through learning or education. However, as we have documented, money illusion seems to be a ubiquitous phenomenon, which leads to suboptimal outcomes in various areas like financial markets, labor markets or consumption-saving decisions itself. In this sense, it appears that a sufficient level of economic literacy, acquired by proper economic training, might contribute to more efficient decisions.

In the context of the preceding discussion, the potential effects of economic literacy acquired through education might be questioned, where our interest is restricted to the narrow field of the money illusion phenomenon, discussed in preceding chapters, which has gained significant attention recently in the studies of Fehr and Tyran (2001), Erber (2010), Shafir et al. (1997), Akerlof and Shiller (2009) and others. Fehr and Tyran (2001) proved on the basis of laboratory experimentation that money illusion, through its direct and indirect effects, largely contributes to prolonged nominal inertia after the fully anticipated negative nominal shock. This is based on the sticky nature of the subject's expectations, where subjects take nominal payoffs as a proxy for real payoffs during the experiment, consequently leading to a multiplication of money illusion through strategic complementarity. Notwithstanding, subjects of heterogeneous educational background participated during their experiment. However, in light of the educational efforts of central banks, the hypothesis is posed as to whether solid economic training might not provide guidance for subjects regarding their decision-making and therefore alleviate not only individual money illusion, but also its resulting indirect effects.

If we assume the effects of education will hold, then agents with their rational behavior might see through the veil of nominal values, which will make their expectations less sticky, since they are supposed to base their decision-making on real values instead of nominal ones. This leads to the elimination of money illusion at the individual level. Moreover, when forming their expectations within a well-educated group, rational agents have no reason to doubt that other agents will behave in a rational way, since they are well-educated. In other words, not only don't these agents expect others to suffer from money illusion, they don't have any reason to assume other agents expect others to suffer from money illusion. This leads to the fact that strategic complementarity, as the main channel of indirect money illusion, might be significantly weakened.

Thus, acquired economic education leading to higher levels of literacy, might significantly alleviate money illusion at the individual level. This might consequently weaken the indirect effects of money illusion, responsible for nominal rigidities. Dissemination of knowledge might ensure that subjects can understand better the signals of the central bank, even ones which would otherwise remain hidden because of an educational constraint.

According to our hypothesis, this might hold true not only for individuals but also for firms. When firms are able (through economic literacy) to use information more effectively, followed by decision-making about their prices, this might significantly reduce the choice of suboptimal outcomes, since they will be less prone to price and wage rigidities.

At the aggregate level, this should contribute to a faster convergence to the economy's equilibrium, when firms immediately adjust their prices with respect to the situation. With the contribution of economic literacy, the effectiveness of monetary policy might be significantly enhanced, since well-informed subjects in the economy will react flexibly to the goal, which is followed by the central bank. In the case of disinflation policy, it might contribute to significantly lower sacrifice ratio, since the understanding of the public and firms in particular is crucial for a smooth adjustment of the economy. In addition, economic knowledge is also beneficial with regards to a central bank´s transparency.

As already suggested, several studies tried to verify the impact of economic and financial education on individual and household behavior, or the effect of this education on a firm's decision-making and outcomes. However, few studies focus on whether the effects of economic education might be beneficial with regards to the elimination of money illusion at the individual level and are based rather on a questionnaire.

Wong (2007) uses a survey questionnaire to analyze whether introductory economic training can generate better outcomes in the form of illusion-free decisions than non-economic education. Results show that the transfer of learning is limited and even with economic education some individuals continue to exhibit money illusion. Thus, little evidence is present for money illusion varying with the economic backgrounds of participants.

Mees and Franses (2011) follow this investigation and through a survey questionnaire analyze whether Chinese individuals are more likely to base their decisions on the real value of monetary transactions. After collecting responses from working individuals, as well as undergraduate students, their conclusion suggests that Chinese individuals are less prone to money illusion and more frequently base decisions on the real monetary value of economic transactions as opposed to the results of Shafir et al. (1997).

Bakshi (2009), through a laboratory experiment, evaluates the performance of economically educated subjects with respect to their coordination in the economy with multiple Pareto-ranked equilibria. However, the evidence is not strong enough that individuals with economic training have better foresight and are not as money illusion free in the long run as expected. A more frequent convergence of subjects toward inefficient equilibrium over time is observed.

Cipriani, Lubian, and Zago (2008), based on survey conducted at the University of Verona, investigated whether economic education might play role in people's proneness to money illusion. The results revealed that undergraduate students of economics and mathematics are less likely to be subject to money illusion compared to students of humanities. In other words, they are less prone to framing effects given the fact that their behavior does not vary with the framing of the question. However, authors don't find support for the learning effect for economics students across different years, which should alleviate money illusion.

We may find respective ties of money illusion toward economic literacy also in study of Tyran and Stephens (2016), who examine the presence of money illusion in households' financial decision making. As already mentioned in Chapter 4, they suggest that money illusion substantially affects the allocation of households toward nominal assets rather than real assets. In addition, their outcomes have implications in terms of economic and financial literacy. Findings suggest that students are less prone to money illusion than other subjects and act more as the rational agents consistently with experimental results of Haigh and List (2005). As a result, there exists a strong case for financial literacy tests and associated effects of economic education, which may substantially improve economic outcomes and possibly weaken the effects of money illusion.

The educational hypothesis outlined may provide enrichment as opposed to the aforementioned studies based on experimental investigation, since it tries to verify the effect of economic education not only on individual money illusion, but also tests the educational effect with respect to the indirect effects of money illusion with the consequent implications derived.

Notes

1 This statement is supported by Hilgert et al. (2003), who found a significant correlation between the level of financial knowledge and good financial management practices, such as cash-flow management, savings and investing. Therefore, economic literacy might be beneficial in order to ensure efficient distribution of resources, by improving ability regarding financial decisions.
2 The International Association for the Evaluation of Educational Achievement (IEA) focuses on how economic education can be evaluated across countries.
3 Institute for Management Development (IMD).
4 For other studies regarding financial sophistication, knowledge of credit, mortgages or risk literacy please refer to studies of Hilgert et al. (2003), Lusardi and Tufano (2009a, 2009b), Moore (2003), Lusardi, Schneider and Tufano (2011).
5 Due to the lack of direct comparability, other surveys are not presented here like Fessler et al. (2007) in Austria, Worthington (2004) in Australia, Keeney and O'Donnel (2009) in Ireland, Atkinson et al. (2007) in UK and others.
6 Measures included three performance tests with three subtests based on 13, 23 or 70 questions and one behavioral task in hypothetical financial decision-making.

References

Abreu, M. and Mendes, V., 2010. Financial Literacy and Portfolio Diversification. *Quantitative Finance*, 10 (5), pp. 515–528.

Agarwal, S., Gene, A., Itzhak B., Souphala Ch., and Evanoff, D. E., 2011. Financial Counseling, Financial Literacy, and Household Decision–Making. In: Olivia S. Mitchell and Annamaria Lusardi (eds.), *Financial Literacy: Implications for Retirement Security and the Financial Marketplace*. Oxford and New York: Oxford University Press.

Agnew J. and Szykman L., 2005. Asset Allocation and Information Overload: The Influence of Information Display, Asset Choice and Investor Experience. *Journal of Behavioral Finance*, 6 (2), pp. 57–70.

Akerlof, G. A. and Shiller, R. J., 2009. *Animal Spirits, How Human Psychology Drives the Economy and why it Matters for Global Capitalism*. Princeton, NJ: Princeton University Press.

Alessie, R., van Rooij, M., and Lusardi, A., 2011. Financial Literacy and Retirement Preparation in the Netherlands. *Journal of Pension Economics and Finance*, 10 (4), pp. 527–545.

Ali, P., Anderson, M., McRae, C., and Ramsay, I., 2014. The Financial Literacy of Young Australians: An Empirical Study and Implications for Consumer Protection and ASIC's National Financial Literacy Strategy. *Company and Securities Law Journal*, 32 (5), pp. 334–352.

Allgood, S. and Walstad, W., 2013. Financial Literacy and Credit Card Behaviors: A Cross–Sectional Analysis by Age. *Numeracy* 6 (2), Article 3.

Almenberg, J. and Säve–Söderbergh, J., 2011. Financial Literacy and Retirement Planning in Sweden. *Journal of Pension Economics and Finance*, 10 (4), pp. 585–598.

An, N., Bostic, R. W., and Yao, V. W., 2015. Financial Literacy and Mortgage Credit: Evidence from the Recent Mortgage Market Crisis. Available at: http://ssrn.com/abstract=2631948> [Accessed 19 September 2016].

Apostoaie, M. C., 2010. Central Banks' Involvement in Encouraging, Economic Education and Literacy. Annals of Dunarea de Jos, University of Galati Fascicle I-2010. *Economics and Applied Informatics*, 16 (2), pp. 147–154.

Arrondel, L., Debbich, M., and Savignac, F., 2013. Financial Literacy and Financial Planning in France. *Numeracy*, 6 (2), Article 8.

Ashok T. and Spataro, L., 2015. Financial Literacy, Human Capital and Stock Market Participation in Europe: An Empirical Exercise under Endogenous Framework. *Discussion Papers* 2015/194, Dipartimento di Economia e Management (DEM), University of Pisa, Italy. Available at: www.ec.unipi.it/documents/Ricerca/papers/2015–194.pdf [Accessed 19 September 2016].

Atkinson, A. and Messy, F. A., 2011. Assessing Financial Literacy in 12 Countries: An OECD/ INFE International Pilot Exercise. *Journal of Pension Economics and Finance*, 10 (4), pp. 657–665.

Atkinson, A. and Messy, F. A., 2012. Measuring Financial Literacy: Results of the OECD / International Network on Financial Education (INFE) Pilot Study. *OECD Working Papers on Finance, Insurance and Private Pensions*, No. 15, OECD Publishing. Available at: http://dx.doi.org/10.1787/5k9csfs90fr4–en> [Accessed 19 September 2016].

Atkinson, A., McKay, S., Collard, S., and Kempson, E., 2007. Levels of Financial Capability in the UK. *Public Money & Management*, 27 (1), pp. 29–36.

Bakshi, R. K., 2009. Rational Agents and Economic Training: The Case of Money Illusion in Experimental Study. *Journal of Economic Theory*, pp. 27–32.

Beal, D. J., and Delpachitra, S. B., 2003. Financial Literacy among Australian University Students. *Economic Papers*, 22 (1), pp. 65–78.

Beck, K. and Krumm, V., 1990. Test zur wirtschaftskundlichen Bildung von W. B. Walstad & J. C. Soper. Manual. Zweite Ausgabe. Auszugsweise ins Deutsche übertragen, ergänzt und kommentiert. Vervielfältigtes Manuskript. Nürnberg/Salzburg.

Beck, K. and Krumm, V., 1991. Economic Literacy in German Speaking Countries and the United States. First Steps to a Comparative Study. *Economia*, 1 (1), pp. 17–23.

Beckmann, E., 2013. Financial Literacy and Household Savings in Romania. *Numeracy* 6 (2), pp. 1–22.

Behrman, J. R., Mitchell, O. S., Soo, C. K., and Bravo, D., 2012. How Financial Literacy Affects Household Wealth Accumulation. *American Economic Review*, 102 (3), pp. 300–304.

Berg, G. and Zia, B., 2013. Harnessing Emotional Connections to Improve Financial Decisions: Evaluating the Impact of Financial Education in Mainstream Media. *World Bank Policy Research Working Paper* No. 6407.

Bernanke, B. S., 2006a. Financial Literacy. Testimony before the Comittee of Banking, Housing and Urban Affairs of the United States Senate, May 23, 2006. Available at:

www.federalreserve.gov/newsevents/testimony/bernanke20060523a.htm [Accessed 19 September 2016].

Bernanke, B. S., 2006b. A Message from Chairman Bernanke. Federal Reserve Bank of Dallas, July 2006. Available at: https://frbatlanta.org/–/media/Documents/filelegacy-docs/BernankeEconEdLetter0706.pdf [Accessed 19 September 2016].

Bernheim, B. D. and Garrett, D. M., 2003. The Effects of Financial Education in the Workplace: Evidence from a Survey of Households. *Journal of Public Economics*, 87 (7–8), pp. 1487–1519.

Bernheim, B. D., Garrett, D. M., and Maki, D. M., 2001. Education and Saving: The Long-Term Effects of High School Financial Curriculum Mandates. *Journal of Public Economics*, 80 (3), pp. 435–65.

Berry, J., Karlan, D., and Pradhan M., 2015. The Impact of Financial Education for Youth in Ghana, *NBER Working Paper* No. 21068.

Blinder, A. S., 1994. Interview with Alan S. Blinder, The Region, Federal Reserve Bank of Minneapolis, December. Available at: www.minneapolisfed.org/publications/the–region/interview–with–alan–s–blinder [Accessed 19 September 2016].

Boisclair, D., Lusardi, A., and Michaud, P., 2014. Financial Literacy and Retirement Planning in Canada, *NBER Working Paper* No. 20297.

Borghans, L., Duckwort, A. L., Heckman J. J., and Weel, B., 2008. The Economic and Psychology of Personal Traits. *Journal of Human Resources*, 43 (4), pp. 972–1059.

Bruhn, M. and Zia B., 2011. Stimulating Managerial Capital in Emerging Markets: The Impact of Business and Financial Literacy for Young Entrepreneurs, *Policy Research Working Paper Series 5642*, The World Bank.

Bruhn, M., Karlan, D. S., and Schoar, A. S., 2012. The Impact of Consulting Services on Small and Medium Enterprises: Evidence from a Randomized Trial in Mexico. *CEPR Discussion Paper*s No. 8887.

Bruine de Bruin, W., Vanderklaauw, W., Downs, S. J., Fischhoff, B., Topa, G., and Armantier, O., 2010. Expectations of Inflation: The Role of Demographic Variables, Expectation Formation, and Financial Literacy. *Journal of Consumer Affairs*, 44 (2), pp. 381–402.

Bucher-Koenen, T. and Lusardi, A., 2011. Financial Literacy and Retirement Planning in Germany. *Journal of Pension Economics and Finance*, 10 (4), pp. 565–584.

Bucher-Koenen, T. and Ziegelmeyer, M., 2011. Who Lost the Most? Financial Literacy, Cognitive Abilities, and the Financial Crisis. *Mannheim Research Institute for the Economics of Aging Working Paper* No. 234.

Bucher-Koenen, T., Lusardi, A., Alessie, R., and van Rooij, M., 2012. How Financially Literate Are Women? Some New Perspectives on the Gender Gap. *Network for Studies on Pensions, Aging and Retirement Panel Paper* 31.

Bumcrot, Ch., Lin, J., and Lusardi, A., 2013. The Geography of Financial Literacy. *Numeracy* 6 (2), Article 2.

Butters, R. B., and Asarta, C. J., 2011. A Survey of Economic Understanding in US High Schools. *Journal of Economic Education*, 42 (2), pp. 200–205.

Cai, J., de Janvry, A., and Sadoulet, E., 2015. Social Networks and the Decision to Insure. *American Economic Journal Applied Economics*, 7 (2), pp. 81–108.

Carlin, B. I. and Robinson, D. T., 2010. What Does Financial Literacy Training Teach Us? *NBER Working Paper* No. 16271.

Carpena, F., Cole, S., Shapiro, J., and Zia, B., 2011. Unpacking the Causal Chain of Financial Literacy. *World Bank Policy Research Working Paper* No. 5798.

Chen, H. C. and Volpe, R. P., 1998. An Analysis of Personal Financial Literacy among College Students. *Financial Services Review*, 7 (2), pp. 107–28.

Chen, H. C. and Volpe, R. P., 2002. Gender Differences in Personal Financial Literacy among College Students. *Financial Services Review*, 11 (3), pp. 289–307.

Christelis, D., Jappelli, T., and Padula, M., 2010. Cognitive Abilities and Portfolio Choice. *European Economic Review*, 54 (1), pp. 18–38.

Christiansen, Ch., Joensen, S. J., and Rangvid, J., 2008. Are Economists More Likely to Hold Stocks? *Review of Finance*, 12 (3), pp. 465–496.

Cipriani, G. P., Lubian, D., and Zago, A., 2008. Money Illusion: Are Economists Different? *Economics Bulletin*, 1 (3), pp. 1–9.

Cole, S., Sampson, T., and Zia, B., 2011. Prices or Knowledge? What Drives Demand for Financial Services in Emerging Markets? *Journal of Finance*, 66 (6), pp. 1933–1967.

Cole, S., Zia, B., Abel, M., Crowley, L., Pauliac, C. S., and Postal, V., 2014. Evaluation of Old Mutual's on The Money Program: Financial Literacy in South Africa. In: Mattias Lundberg And Florentina Mulaj (eds.), *Enhancing Financial Capability and Behavior in Low- And Middle-Income Countries*. Washington DC: The World Bank.

Collins J. M., Gorey R. N., Schmeiser M. D., Baker C. A., and Ziegler D., 2009. *Building Indicators Measures: Analysis and Recommendations*. Baltimore, MD: Anne E. Casey Foundation.

Collins, J. M. and O'Rourke, C. M., 2010. Financial Education and Counseling-Still Holding Promise. *Journal of Consumer Affairs*, 44 (3), pp. 483–98.

Courchane, M., Gailey, A., and Zorn, O., 2008. Consumer Credit Literacy: What Price Perception? *Journal of Economics and Business*, 60 (1–2), pp. 125–138.

Crossan, D., Feslier, D., and Hurnard, R., 2011. Financial Literacy and Retirement Planning in New Zealand. *CeRP Working Papers* No. 01/2011-015, Center for Research on Pensions and Welfare Policies, Turin, Italy.

Cunha, F. and Heckman, J., 2007. The Technology of Skill Information. *American Economic Review*, 97 (2), pp. 31–47.

Deevy, M., Lucich, S., and Beals, M., 2012. Scams, Schemes and Swindles: A Review of Consumer Financial Fraud Research. Financial Fraud Research Center, Stanford Center on Longevity. Available at: http://longevity3.stanford.edu/ blog/2012/11/19/scams–schemes–and–swindles–a–review– of–consumer–financial–fraud–research/ [Accessed 19 September 2016].

Drexler, A., Fischer, G., and Schoar A., 2014. Keeping it Simple: Financial Literacy and Rules of Thumb. *American Economic Journal: Applied Economics*, 6 (2), pp. 1–31.

Duca, J. V. and Kumar, A., 2014. Financial Literacy and Mortgage Equity Withdrawals. *Journal of Urban Economics*, 80 (C), pp. 62–75.

Erber, G., 2010. The Problem of Money Illusion in Economics. *Journal of Applied Economic Sciences*, 5 (3), pp. 196–216.

Federal Reserve Bank of Minneapolis, 1999. The Symposium on Economic Literacy, May 13–14, 1999. Available at: www.minneapolisfed.org/publications/special–studies/economic–literacy [Accessed 19 September 2016].

Federal Reserve Bank of San Francisco, 2005. Spend Thrift Nation. *Economic Letter* No. 2005-30.

Fehr, E. and Tyran, J., 2001. Does Money Illusion Matter? *American Economic Review*, 91 (5), pp. 1239–1262.

Fernandes, D., Lynch, G. J., and Netemeyer, R. G., 2013. The Effect of Financial Literacy and Financial Education on Downstream Financial Behaviors. *Management Science*, 60 (8), pp. 1861–1883.

Fessler, P., Schurz, M., Wagner, K., and Weber, B., 2007. Financial Capability of Austrian Households. Monetary Policy and the Economy. *Quarterly Review of Economic Policy* 3, pp. 50–67.

Fettig, D., 1998. The Minneapolis Fed's National Economic Literacy Survey. In: Fettig, D. (ed.), *The Region*. Minneapolis: Federal Reserve Bank of Minneapolis.

Fetting, D., 1999. Seeking a Blueprint for Economic Literacy. A Report on the Economic Literacy Symposium held at the Federal Reserve Bank of Minneapolis on May 13–14, 1999, Available at: www.minneapolisfed.org/publications/the–region/a–report–on–the–economic–literacy–symposium [Accessed 19 September 2016].

Finke, M. S., Howe, J. S., and Huston, S. J., 2011. Old Age and the Decline in Financial Literacy Forthcoming in *Management Science*. Available at: http://ssrn.com/abstract=1948627 [Accessed 19 September 2016].

Fluch, M., 2007. Selected Central Bank's Economic and Financial Literacy Programs, Oesterreichische Nationalbank, *Monetary Policy and the Economy*, 02/2007, pp. 85–104.

Fonseca, R., Mullen, K. J., Zamarro, G., and Zissimopoulos, J., 2012. What Explains the Gender Gap in Financial Literacy? The Role of Household Decision Making. *Journal of Consumer Affairs*, 46 (1), pp. 90–106.

Fornero, E. and Monticone, Ch., 2011. Financial Literacy and Pension Plan Participation in Italy. *Journal of Pension Economics and Finance*, 10 (4), pp. 547–564.

Gathergood, J., 2012. Self-control, Financial Literacy and Consumer Over-Indebtedness. *Journal of Economic Psychology*, 33 (3), pp. 590–602.

Gathergood, J. and Weber, J., 2015. Financial Literacy, Present Bias and Alternative Mortgage Products. *Discussion Paper* No. 2015–13, Available at: www.nottingham.ac.uk/cedex/documents/papers/cedex–discussion–paper–2015–13.pdf [Accessed 19 September 2016].

Gerardi, K., Goette, L., and Meier, S., 2013. Numerical Ability Predicts Mortgage Default. *Proceedings of the National Academy of Sciences*, 110 (28), pp. 11267–11271.

Grinblatt, M., Keloharju, M., and Linnainmaa, J., 2011. IQ and Stock Market Participation. *Journal of Finance*, 66 (6), pp. 2121–2164.

Guidolin, M. and La Jeunesse, E. A., 2007. The Decline in the US Personal Saving Rate: Is it Real and is it a Puzzle? *Federal Reserve Bank St. Louis Review*, 89 (6), pp. 491–514.

Haigh, M. S. and List, J. A., 2005. Do Professional Traders Exhibit Myopic Loss Aversion? An Experimental Analysis. Journal of Finance 60 (1), pp. 523–534.

Hartarska, V. and Gonzalez–Vega, C., 2006. Evidence on the Effect of Credit Counseling on Mortgage Loan Default by Low-Income Households. *Journal of Housing Economics*, 15 (1), pp. 63–79.

Hastings, J. S. and Mitchell, O. S, 2011. How Financial Literacy and Impatience Shape Retirement Wealth and Investment Behaviors. *NBER Working Paper* No. 16740.

Hastings, J. S., Madrian, B. C., and Skimmyhorn, W. L., 2013. Financial Literacy, Financial Education, and Economic Outcomes, *Annual Review of Economics*, 5, pp. 347–373.

Hilgert, M. A., Hogarth, M. J., and Beverly, S. G., 2003. Household Financial Management: The Connection between Knowledge and Behavior. *Federal Reserve Bulletin*, 89 (7), pp. 309–322.

Hodges, L. H., 1962. EconEd Online. *Wallstreet Journal*, March 14, 1962, IMF Center, A Public Center for Economics Education. Available at: www.imf.org/external/np/exr/center/econed/ [Accessed 19 September 2016].

HRS, 2004. Health and Retirement Study. Available at: http://hrsonline.isr.umich.edu/index.php?p=start [Accessed 19 September 2016].

Hsu, J. W., 2011. Aging and Strategic Learning: The Impact of Spousal Incentives on Financial Literacy. *Indiana State University Networks Financial Institute Working Paper* 2011-WP-06.

Huddlestone-Casas, C. A., Danes, S. M., and Boyce, L. M., 1999. Impact Evaluation of a Financial Literacy Program: Evidence for Needed Educational Policy Changes. *Consumer Interests Annual*, 45, pp. 109–114.

Hung, A., Parker, A. M., and Yoong, J., 2009. Defining and Measuring Financial Literacy. *RAND Working Paper Series* WR-708. Available at: http://ssrn.com/abstract=1498674 [Accessed 19 September 2016].

Hung, A. A., Meijer, E., Mihaly, K., and Yoong, K., 2009. Building Up, Spending Down: Financial Literacy, Retirement Savings Management, and Decumulation. *RAND Corporation Publications Department Working Paper* No.712.

Huston, S. J., 2010. Measuring Financial Literacy. *Journal of Consumer Affairs*, 44 (2), pp. 296–316.

Jacob, D. R., 1995. *Economic Literacy: What Everyone Needs to Know about Money and Markets*. New York: Three Rivers Press.

Jappelli, T., 2010, Economic Literacy: An International Comparison. *Economic Journal*, 120 (548), pp. 429–451.

Jappelli, T. and Guiso, L., 2009. Financial Literacy and Portfolio Diversification. Centre for Studies in Economics and Finance (CSEF), University of Naples, Italy, *CSEF Working Paper* No. 212.

Jappelli, T. and Padula, M., 2013. Investment in Financial Literacy and Saving Decisions. *Journal of Banking and Finance*, 37 (8), pp. 2779–2792.

Joint Council on Economic Education, 1989. *National News Report*, Spring 1989.

Karlan, D. and Valdivia, M., 2011. Teaching Entrepreneurship: Impact of Business Training on Microfinance Clients and Institutions. *Review of Economics and Statistics*, 93 (2), pp. 510–527.

Keeney, M. J. and O'Donnell, N., 2009. Financial Capability: New Evidence for Ireland. *Research Technical Papers* No.1, Central Bank and Financial Services Authority of Ireland.

Klapper, L. and Panos, G. A., 2011. Financial Literacy and Retirement Planning: The Russian Case. *Journal of Pension Economics and Finance*, 10 (4), pp. 599–618.

Klapper, L. F., Lusardi, A., and Panos, A. G., 2012. Financial Literacy and the Financial Crisis. *NBER Working Paper* No. 17930.

Lusardi, A., 2003. Saving and the Effectiveness of Financial Education. *Pension Research Council Working Paper* No. 2003–14.

Lusardi, A., 2005. Financial Education and the Saving Behavior of African American and Hispanic Households. Available at: www.dartmouth.edu/~alusardi/Papers/Education_African%26Hispanic.pdf [Accessed 19 September 2016].

Lusardi, A., 2011. Americans' Financial Capability. *NBER Working Paper* No. 17103.

Lusardi, A. and de Bassa Scheresberg, C., 2013. Financial Literacy and High–Cost Borrowing in the United States. *NBER Working Paper* No. 18969.

Lusardi, A. and Mitchell, O. S., 2007a. Baby Boomer Retirement Security: The Roles of Planning, Financial Literacy, and Housing Wealth. *Journal of Monetary Economics*, 54 (1), pp. 205–224.

Lusardi, A. and Mitchell, O. S., 2007b. Financial Literacy and Retirement Preparedness: Evidence and Implications for Financial Education. *Business Economics*, 42 (1), pp. 35–44.

Lusardi, A. and Mitchell, O. S., 2008. Planning and Financial Literacy: How Do Women Fare? *American Economic Review*, 98 (2), pp. 413–417.

Lusardi, A. and Mitchell, O. S., 2009. How Ordinary Consumers Make Complex Economic Decisions: Financial Literacy and Retirement Readiness. *NBER Working Paper* No. 15350.

Lusardi, M. and Mitchell O. S., 2011a. Financial Literacy and Planning: Implications for Retirement Well–Being. In O. S. Mitchell and A. Lusardi (eds.), *Financial Literacy: Implications for Retirement Security and the Financial Marketplace*. Oxford and New York: Oxford University Press.

Lusardi, M. and Mitchell, O. S., 2011b. Financial Literacy and Retirement Planning in the United States. *Journal of Pension Economics and Finance*, 10 (4), pp. 509–525.

Lusardi, M. and Mitchell, O. S., 2011c. Financial Literacy around the World: An Overview. *Journal of Pension Economics and Finance*, 10 (4), pp. 497–508.

Lusardi, M. and Mitchell, O. S., 2011d. The Outlook for Financial Literacy. In: O. S. Mitchell and A. Lusardi (eds.), *Financial Literacy: Implications for Retirement Security and the Financial Marketplace*, pp. 1–15. Oxford and New York: Oxford University Press.

Lusardi, M. and Mitchell, O. S., 2013. The Economic Importance of Financial Literacy: Theory and evidence. *NBER Working Paper* No. 18952.

Lusardi, M. and Mitchell, O. S., 2014. The Economic Importance of Financial Literacy: Theory and Evidence. *Journal of Economic Literature*, 52 (1), pp. 5–44.

Lusardi, A., Mitchell, O. S., and Curto, V., 2010. Financial Literacy Among the Young. The *Journal of Consumer Affairs*, 44 (2), pp. 358–380.

Lusardi, A. and Tufano, P., 2009a. Debt Literacy, Financial Experiences, and Over–indebtedness. *NBER Working Paper* No. 14808.

Lusardi, A. and Tufano, P., 2009b. Teach Workers about the Perils of Debt. *Harvard Business Review*, 87 (11), pp. 22–24.

Lusardi, A., Schneider, D., and Tufano, P., 2011. Financially Fragile Households: Evidence and Implications. *Brookings Papers on Economic Activity*, pp. 83–134.

McArdle, J., Smith, J. and Willis, R., 2009. Cognition and Economic Outcomes in the Health and Retirement Survey. *NBER Working Paper* No. 15266, pp. 209–233.

Mahdavi, M. and Horton, N., 2014. Financial Literacy among Educated Women: Room for Improvement. *Journal of Consumer Affairs*, 48 (2), pp. 403–417.

Mandell, L., 2008. The Study of Young American Adults, Results of the 2008 National Jump$tart Coalition Survey of High School Seniors and College Students, *the JumpStart Coalition for Personal Financial Literacy*, Available at: www.jumpstart.org/assets/files/2008SurveyBook.pdf [Accessed 19 September 2016].

Mandell, L. and Klein, L. S., 2009. The Impact of Financial Literacy Education on Subsequent Financial Behavior. *Journal of Financial Counselling and Planning*, 20 (1), pp. 15–24.

Martinez A. C., Puentes E., and Ruiz-Tagle, J., 2013. Micro-Entrepreneurship Training and Asset Transfers: Short Term Impacts on the Poor. *Documentos de Trabajo, Departamento de Economa, Universidad de Chile*, 380, pp. 1–54.

MasterCard Worldwide, 2011. How Well Do Women Know Their Money: Financial Literacy Across Asia/ Pacific, Middle East, and Africa. Available at: www1.mastercard.com/content/intelligence/en/research/press–release/2011/australian–women–top–three–in–money–matters–in–asia–pacific.html [Accessed 19 September 2016].

Mees, H. and Franses, H. P., 2011. Are Chinese Individuals Prone to Money Illusion? Tinbergen Institute *Discussion Paper*, 2011–149/4.

Meier, S. and Sprenger, C. D., 2010. Present-Biased Preferences and Credit Card Borrowing. *American Economic Journal: Applied Economics*, 2 (1), pp. 193–210.

Meier, S. and Sprenger, C. D., 2013. Discounting Financial Literacy: Time Preferences and Participation in Financial Education Programs. *Journal of Economic Behavior and Organization*, 95, pp. 159–174.

Minehan, C. E., 2006. The Role of Central Banks in Economic and Personal Finance Education, Speech held in Warsaw, Poland, at the Conference of Narodowy Bank Polski, 28 September 2006. Available at: www.bos.frb.org/news/speeches/cem/2006/092806.htm [Accessed 19 September 2016].

Mishkin, F., 2008. The Importance of Economic Education and Financial Literacy, Speech at the Third National Summit on Economic and Financial Literacy, Washington DC, February 27, 2008. Available at: www.federalreserve.gov/newsevents/speech/mishkin20080227a.htm [Accessed 19 September 2016].

Monticone, C., 2010. How Much Does Wealth Matter in the Acquisition of Financial Literacy? *Journal of Consumer Affairs*, 44 (2), pp. 403–422.

Moore, D., 2003. Survey of Financial Literacy in Washington State: Knowledge, Behavior, Attitudes, and Experiences. *Washington State University Social and Economic Sciences Research Center Technical Report* 03–39.

Mottola, G. R., 2013. In Our Best Interest: Women, Financial Literacy, and Credit Card Behavior. *Numeracy*, 6 (2), Article 4.

Oanea, D. and Dornean, A., 2012. Defining and Measuring Financial Literacy: New Evidence from Romanian Students of the Master in Finance, Scientific Annals of the Alexandru Ioan Cuza. *University of Iasi Economic Sciences*, 59 (2), pp. 113–129.

OECD, 2005. Improving Financial Literacy: Analysis of Issues and Policies. Paris and Washington, DC: Organization for Economic Cooperation and Development. Available at: www.oecd.org/finance/financial–education/improvingfinancialliteracyanalysisofissuesandpolicies.htm [Accessed 19 September 2016].

OECD, 2014a. PISA 2012 Results: Students and Money: Financial Literacy Skills for the 21st Century (Volume VI), PISA, OECD Publishing. Available at: www.oecd.org/pisa/keyfindings/PISA–2012–results–volume–vi.pdf [Accessed 19 September 2016].

OECD, 2014b. Launch of PISA Financial Literacy Assessment, Angel Hurria, OECD Secretary–General. Available at: www.oecd.org/about/secretary–general/launch–of–pisa–financial–literacy–assessment.htm [Accessed 19 September 2016].

Pahnke, H. and Honekamp, I., 2010. Different Effects of Financial Literacy and Financial Education in Germany, *MPRA Working Paper* 10. Available at: https://mpra.ub.uni–muenchen.de/22900/1/Financial_Literacy_and_Retirement_Savings_20100509.pdf [Accessed 19 September 2016].

Parker, A. M., Yoong, J., Bruine de Bruin, W., and Willis, R., 2012. Inappropriate Confidence and Retirement Planning: Four Studies with a National Sample. *Journal of Behavioral Decision Making*, 25 (4), pp. 382–389.

Roberts, R. and Polley, W., 2005. Knowledge Deficit, Econoblog. *The Wall Street Journal*, [online] 21 September. Available at: http://online.wsj.com/public/resources/documents/econoblog0921.htm [Accessed 19 September 2016].

Salemi, M. K., 2005. Teaching Economic Literacy: Why, What and How. *International Review of Economics Education*, 4 (2), pp. 46–57

Sekita, S., 2011. Financial Literacy and Retirement Planning in Japan. *CeRP Working Paper* No. 01/2011–016, Center for Research on Pensions and Welfare Policies, Turin (Italy).

Shafir, E., Diamond, P., and Tversky, A., 1997. Money Illusion. *Quarterly Journal of Economics*, 112 (2), pp. 341–374.

Shen, R., 1993. Economic Thinking in China. Economic Knowledge and Attitudes of High School Students. *Journal of Economic Education*, 24 (1), pp. 79–84.

Shim, S., Barber, B. L., Card, N. A., Xiao, J. J., and Serido, J., 2010. Financial Socialization of First-Year College Students: The Roles of Parents, Work, and Education. *Journal of Youth and Adolescence*, 39 (12), pp. 1457–1470.

Skimmyhorn, W., 2012. Essays in Behavioral Household Finance. Doctoral dissertation, Harvard University. Available at: https://dash.harvard.edu/handle/1/9369052 [Accessed 19 September 2016].

Stango, V. and Zinman, J., 2009. Exponential Growth Bias and Household Finance. *Journal of Finance*, 64 (6), pp. 2807–2849.

Stark, J., 2006. The Role of Central Banks in Economic and Personal Finance Education, The International Conference of Central Bankers and Economic Educators, Warsaw, 29 September 2006. Available at: www.ecb.int/press/key/date/2006/html/sp060929.en.html [Accessed 19 September 2016].

Stern, G. H., 1998. Do We Know Enough About Economics? *Region*, 12 (1998).

Stigler G. J., 1970. The Case, If Any, for Economic Literacy. *Journal of Economic Education*, 1 (2), pp. 77–84.

Tyran, J. and Stephens, T. A., 2016. Money Illusion and Household Finance. *University of Copenhagen, Dept. of Economics Discussion Paper* No.16-14. Available at: www.economics.ku.dk/research/publications/wp/dp_2016/1614.pdf/ [Accessed 6 January 2017].

Valentine, G. P. and Khayum, M., 2005. Financial Literacy Skills of Students in Urban and Rural High Schools. *Delta Pi Epsilon Journal*, 47 (1), pp. 1–10.

Walstad, W. B. and Rebeck, K., 2001. Assessing the Economic Understanding of US High School Students. *American Economic Review*, 91 (2), pp. 452–457.

Walstad, W. B. and Rebeck, K., 2002. Assessing the Economic Knowledge and Economic Opinions of Adults. *Quarterly Review of Economics and Finance*, 42 (5), pp. 921–935.

Walstad, W. B. and Soper, J. C., 1989. What is High School Economics? Factors Contributing to Student Achievement and Attitudes. *Journal of Economic Education*, 20 (1), pp. 23–39.

Walstad, W. B., Rebeck, K., and Butters, R. B., 2013. The Test of Economic Literacy, Development and Results. *Journal of Economic Education*, 44 (3), pp. 298–309.

Walstad, W. B., Rebeck, K., and MacDonald, R., 2010. The Effects of Financial Education on the Financial Knowledge of High School Students. *Journal of Consumer Affairs*, 44 (2), pp. 336–357.

Williams-Harold, B., 1999. Saving is Fundamental. *Black Enterprise*, vol. 29, p. 30.

Wilson, R. M. S. and Mason, C., 2000. Conceptualizing Financial Literacy, Loughborough University. *Business School Research Series Paper* 2000 (7).

Wilson, R. M. S. and Zhang, Q., 1997. Entrapment and Escalating Commitment in Investment Decision Making: A Review. *British Accounting Review*, 29 (3), pp. 277–305.

Winick, D. M., 2006. Economics Framework for the 2006 National Assessment of Educational Progress. Washington: National Assessment of Governing Board U.S. Department of Education. Available at: http://wvde.state.wv.us/NAEP/frameworks/economics2006.pdf [Accessed 19 September 2016].

Witt, R. and Kotte, D., 1995. Chance and Challenge: Assessing Economic Literacy. In W. Bos and R. H. Lehmann (eds.), *Reflections on Educational Achievement: Papers in honor of* T. Neville Postlethwaite, *Munster, Waxmann*. Available at: www.leselounge.de/postleth.html [Accessed 19 September 2016].

Wong, Wei-Kang, 2007. Nominal Increases and the Perception of Likelihood. *Economics Letters*, 95 (3), pp. 433–437.

Worthington, A. C., 2004. The Distribution of Financial Literacy in Australia. Discussion Papers in Economics, Finance, and International Competitiveness. *Queensland University of Technology Working Paper* No. 184, November.

Xia, T., Wang, Z., and Li, K., 2014. Financial Literacy Overconfidence and Stock Market Participation. *Social Indicators Research*, 119 (3), pp. 1233–1245.

Xu, L. and Zia, B., 2012. Financial Literacy Around the World: An Overview of the Evidence with Practical Suggestions for the Way Forward. *World Bank Policy Research Working Paper* No. 6107.

6 Economic literacy and money illusion

An experimental approach

The previous chapter outlined the educational hypothesis, where the question is addressed as to whether economic education might not eventually suppress the indirect effects of money illusion and, therefore, weaken nominal inertia based on successful coordination in the strategic environment. The laboratory experiment represents in this sense a unique opportunity to verify whether a particular level of economic literacy, acquired through economic education, may account for the improved decision-making of subjects. This chapter will, first, provide the reader with a brief description of the experimental approach selected for an examination of our educational hypothesis. Second, the methodological considerations of a macroeconomic experiment related to our investigation are discussed. Finally, the educational hypothesis will be outlined more thoroughly with regards to the examination of the effects of economic education on the potential reduction of money illusion.

Effect of economic education under money illusion, an experimental approach

To examine our educational hypothesis, the way the laboratory experiment is conducted is inspired by a study of Fehr and Tyran (2001). Individuals are placed in the role of firms, setting the price for production in an artificial experimental economy. The returns of these firms are affected by their selling price and by the price level, which is determined by prices set by other firms in the artificial economy. Players in the role of firms, with strong incentives supported by financial reward, try to maximize their profit, defined as a function of their particular price and the average price level. During the process of learning, subjects are assumed to select the profit-maximizing price, which should be consistent with the total general equilibrium of the economy, if other subjects choose the correct price, maximizing their profits as well. Contrary to the original experiment of Fehr and Tyran (2001), where nominal and real framings were employed to investigate the presence of money illusion, we make an additional distinction between subjects taking their master's degree study with solid economic backgrounds, whose course of knowledge is related to the highly demanding theoretical character of the game, and subjects taking their bachelor's degree with a weak background in economic relationships. This distinction related to economic education will enable the obtainment of two treatments where the well-educated group is the experimental group, whereas the less-educated one is the control group. Through this mechanism, the effect of economic education under the nominal frame might be verified. The first treatment is composed of the well-educated experimental group of subjects taking their master's degree who have advanced knowledge of microeconomics, macroeconomics, game theory and other related economic courses. This gives them solid economic training, enabling them to apply basic economic concepts to various situations. This implies that the effect of economic education within this group should, according to our assumption, lead to better economic outcomes. The second treatment is in the role of the control group, which consists of students in the first year of their bachelor's degree who have only a minimum knowledge of basic economics. According to Salemi (2005), this leads only to formal knowledge, which implies a significantly lower ability to reach optimum outcomes. Therefore, the effect of economic education should be the least possible.

There are several reasons why these subjects tend to be the best choice for our experimentation. First, by the inclusion of an experimental and control group with the aforementioned characteristics we are able to distinguish between a literate and illiterate person. The well-educated experimental group had the prerequisite to fulfill the requirements of an economically literate person, because through participation in various economic courses it should acquire particular analytical skills and the ability to think in economic terms. Second, whether well-educated individuals see through the veil of nominal values may easily be identified because of the inclusion of a control group with a significantly lower level of economic education. Still, a minimum amount of knowledge is guaranteed, where we opted for a narrow target group which has a common interest. This should reduce common problems, where two groups do not exhibit reasonably similar characteristics due to the fact of significantly different educational attainment, income status, and so on. The choice of this narrow group of students (i.e., non-probability sample) from the same university also ensures that the sample will be more homogenous, which contributes to a lower variability in experimental outcomes. Additionally, the students chosen are appropriate subjects, since they are interested in the subject of their study, having opted for this specialization. The decision to study the economic field initially assumes that individuals should have a higher level of economic efficacy and, therefore, interest, in learning economics than the wider population. For these students, the utility gained from economic knowledge is higher than the costs of learning. Additionally, proper incentives are ensured in experimental design by adequate financial rewards, where the subjects know that they can significantly affect their outcomes through adequate pricing behavior. With the help of experimental design, the functional definition of an economically educated individual has been specified for our purpose.

Methodological considerations of macroeconomic experiment

Since our experiment aims to verify an educational hypothesis connected with potential implications at the aggregate level, it naturally raises methodological questions regarding the validity of the experimental results gained. In other words, the link between results gained at the experimental level and implications at the aggregate level is of great interest.

According to Duffy (2008), macroeconomic theories have traditionally been tested by using non-experimental field data, where controlled manipulation of the economy with consequential insight regarding the effects of alternative institutions and policies was considered as relatively impossible. Generally, it was argued that macroeconomic questions are not to be derived with the help of experimental methods (among others, Sims 1996).

Despite that, there has been a growing body of literature in the past twenty years, as indicated by Duffy (2008), that encompasses macroeconomic theories and models examined through controlled experimental framework. It has been a while since Lucas (1986) invited macroeconomists to conduct controlled laboratory experiments to cope with coordination problems, which remained unsolved by macroeconomic theory. The origin of the macroeconomic experiment might possibly be dated to that time. Notwithstanding, his invitation was followed up on by many influential economists, among them Lim, Prescott and Sunder (1994), Marimon and Sunder (1993, 1994, 1995), with a consequent expansion of macroeconomic theories tested in the laboratory, among others by Duffy and Fisher (2005), Van Huyck et al. (1990, 1991, 1994), Arifovic and Sargent (2003), Bernasconi and Kirchkamp (2000), Deck (2004), Duffy and Ochs, (1999, 2012), Fehr and Tyran (2007, 2008), Heinemann, Nagel, and Ockenfels (2004), Hey (1994), Noussair, Plott, and Riezman (2007), Lei and Noussair (2007), and others.

One might ask what major impulse is causing the use of controlled laboratory experiments (with implications derived for macroeconomic theory) to be on the increase nowadays? So far, macroeconomic issues have been perceived to be too great to be examined via controlled laboratory experiments with a small number of subjects, according to Duffy (1998). However, the situation has changed tremendously, with a particular reason being the widespread application of macroeconomic models with explicit micro-foundations. The focus of these models is how institutional changes or policies may affect the decision making of households and firms. However, the representative agent's characteristic, where artificial restrictions are imposed on his or her behavior, is not embraced in any available field data. As a result, the aggregate predictions that emerge from these micro-founded models are often not empirically testable. Additionally, if the possibility to test the aggregate predictions of models is the case with available field data, often these data are unsuitable to test whether the behavior adjusts to the prediction or assumptions of macroeconomic models. In this context, controlled laboratory experiments might be understood as a complement to standard econometric techniques, where both the aggregate and individual predictions of micro-foundation models might be tested. Although economists need to be careful in making generalizations based on the results of an experiment that involves a small number of subjects, less objection should be made against using experiments to test predictions of macroeconomic models based on explicit micro-foundations. Because these models are based on individual behavior, experiments might provide guidance on how the subjects perceive examined phenomenon. For instance, in the economy with multiple equilibriums, it might indicate what equilibrium subjects consider as more relevant (Duffy 1998, 2008).

Experimental literature, according to Riciutti (2008), distinguishes among two types of macroeconomic experiments:

- Experiment centered on single market, which is in line with the current trend of macroeconomic modelling based on micro-foundations.
- Macroeconomic experiment of Walrasian nature, which centers on inter-relations between several markets and the spill-over between them.

Our experiment falls within the latter category, which is in line with current macroeconomic modelling based on micro-foundations. Thus, the size of the sample $z = 194$ is sufficient to derive appropriate implications at the aggregate level. This is also documented by an array of studies, which use a similar size of sample for this type of experiment. See, for instance, Fehr and Tyran (2008), with number of subjects $z = 76$; Fehr and Tyran (2001), $z = 130$; Fehr, Kirchsteiger and Riedl (1998), $z = 52$; Adam (2007) $z = 30$; Duffy and Fisher (2005), $z = 10$; Arifovic and Sargent, (2003), $z = 12$; Van Huyck et al. (1994), $z = 40$; and others. This argument is further supported by Vernon Smith (1962), who proves that the convergence to competitive equilibrium is sufficient with only a few subjects (three to five) on the side of supply and demand. Additionally, he confirms that the big sample size is necessary neither in a strategic environment, nor a non-strategic environment. Considerations about the sample size may be summarized in the vein of Duffy (2011, p. 6): "In practice, experimental macroeconomics is not distinct from microeconomic laboratory experiments, there is just a different focus or interpretation. A macroeconomic experiment is one that tests the predictions of a macroeconomic model or its assumptions or is framed in the language of macroeconomics."

With regard to the methodological discussion of Duffy (2008), the following comments are worth mentioning with regards to laboratory experiment applied in our study:

One dimension concerns the number of subjects under scrutiny due to the belief that it is difficult to approximate a macroeconomic world through a laboratory experiment with a small number of subjects. However, our macroeconomic experiment rests on experimental design in the vein of Fehr and Tyran (2001), which is based on micro-foundations, where the number of participating subjects need not be the relevant issue. Moreover, as emphasized by Duffy (2008), evidence from many auction experiments since Smith (1962) suggests that equilibration to competitive equilibrium occurs reliably with just a few individuals on the supply or demand side market, so a large number of subjects is not a necessary condition.

Second, our experiment enables the collecting of a type of data less directly observed in the field. For instance, the examination of expectation formation after the shock is valuable output. Further, it is extremely difficult to collect individual information sets regarding the actual price in the pre-shock and the post-shock phase needed for comparison with ideal equilibrium prices to identify nominal inertia. Also identifying whether the shock is anticipated or not is a serious constraint. The experimental method (as opposed to field data) possesses an immense advantage in its control over the environment and information conditions. This is closely associated with causal relations, which are directly under experimental control, where the frame can be easily set by specification of treatment conditions as emphasized by Fehr and Tyran (2000, 2005a, 2005b). In our case, not only are nominal versus real treatment conditions specified, but there are also different educational treatment conditions set, as already mentioned, which enable the identification of our educational hypothesis. As a result, the effects of monetary policy on a subject's behavior with respect to different educational background might be examined.

Additionally, objections might be raised regarding the external validity of experimental results.[1] However, in the case of the more theoretical character of the experiment examined, there are fewer objections against lower external validity, which is supported also by the study of Schram (2005). The same holds for the critique of students as experimental subjects, where it is claimed that participation of graduate students instead of professionals is rather an advantage in this case. Abbink and Rockenback (2006) compare the behavior of students and professionals in an option pricing experiment. It was shown that the behavior of professionals is surprisingly far from the theoretical price compared to the behavior of students and, therefore, it does not follow that experienced participants always reach better outcomes. Students are able to get quickly into the structure of highly theoretical experiment and face abstract tasks with ease, based on a background course of knowledge related to academic training.

General description of the experimental design

Experimental design partially inspired by Fehr and Tyran (2000, 2001) is based on n-player pricing game with strategic complementarity and unique equilibrium.[2] All n subjects in the role of firms must simultaneously set their nominal prices in each period of the game, but at no cost in any period. The experimental game is divided into a pre-shock and post-shock phase, with 2T length periods each, depending on the type of treatment.[3] The pre-shock phase, which lasts T periods serves the purpose of equilibrating the system and is given by M_0. Afterwards, a fully anticipated negative monetary shock is implemented, where money supply is reduced to M_1. The post-shock phase then lasts an additional T periods. We need to emphasize that the shock was fully anticipated and was therefore common knowledge to participants, together with the length of the post-shock phase. The post-shock phase enables us to observe how nominal prices adjust in response to the shock in various treatment conditions. Distinction between the pre-shock and post-shock phase is crucial, since it will allow us to identify not only whether money illusion might be a disequilibrating force if equilibrium was reached before the shock, but also to identify the potential educational effects according to the hypothesis already outlined.[4]

The subject's pricing behavior is governed by the size of payoffs and might be described in line with study of Akerlof and Yellen (1985), Blanchard and Kiyotaki (1987), and Fehr and Tyran (2001) as follows:

The *real payoff* of subject i, π_i, is given by

$$\pi_i = \pi_i \; (P_i, \bar{P}_i, \mathrm{M}) \quad \mathrm{i} = 1, ..., \mathrm{n} \tag{1}$$

Where P_i stands for i's nominal price, $\bar{P}_{-i}$ is the average price of the other n-1 group members and M denotes a nominal shock variable (money supply). The *nominal payoff* is expressed as $\bar{P}_{-i}\pi_i$.

We use the aforementioned payoff function in our experimental setting, which has four treatment conditions, which differ along two dimensions:

The *first dimension* relates to the form in which payoffs are expressed, which can be either real or nominal. The real treatment marks the situation, where subjects receive the payoff information for their decision making in real terms. RC (real computers) and RH (real humans) are included under this treatment. In the nominal treatment, subjects receive the payoff information for their decision-making in nominal terms. This treatment consists of NH (nominal humans) and NC (nominal computers). To compute their real payoffs, subjects in the nominal treatment have to divide their nominal payoffs by the average price of the other n-1 group members, that is $\bar{P}_{-i}\pi_i/\bar{P}_{-i}$.

The *second dimension* concerns the fact, whether experimental subjects are in a group with other n-1 human subjects, or whether they play against n-1 pre-programmed computerized opponents. The distinction between computerized and human opponents is significant, since in the computerized session the human subject has the advantage regarding the aggregate response rule of n-1 computerized opponents. This response rule of computers, which he knows in advance, is given by the best replies of the computers, based on their payoff functions. In other words, other n-1 computerized opponents are simulated agents with perfect foresight. This implies that computerized session possesses zero strategic uncertainty. The decision making of our human subject is easier, since he or she does not have to form expectations about the behavior of the other n-1 computerized players. The subject's task is reduced to an individual optimization problem, where he or she has no incentive for not arriving at unique equilibrium, if he or she knows where it is. Thus, a computerized session based on the best reply given the payoff function, eliminates the behavior related to money illusion or any other form of irrationality. If we compare it with a human session, the aggregate response rule is not known in advance and the subject has to form expectations about price choices of the other n-1 human opponents in his group. This also includes an estimation regarding money illusion of other n-1 players.

As opposed to the initial adopted experimental design composed of two dimensions, a *third dimension* is added as a new element with regards to our educational hypothesis. It concerns the question of whether our subjects are endowed with advanced economic skills or whether they have only a basic knowledge of economic literacy. We distinguish subjects in the nominal treatments with advanced economic skills (NH Mgr) and basic economic knowledge (NH Bc) and subjects in the real treatment with advanced economic skills (RH Mgr) and basic economic knowledge (RH Bc).

The effect of economic literacy is secured by setting two types of groups in the experiment, which can then be compared. The first treatment is composed of a well-educated experimental group of subjects taking their master's degree, who have advanced knowledge of microeconomics, macroeconomics, game theory and other related economic courses. This gives them a solid background in economic and analytical skills, which enables them to apply basic economic concepts to various situations. The second treatment is in the role of control group, where students are in their first year of a bachelor's degree, therefore having only minimum formal knowledge of basic economics. There are several reasons why these subjects tend to be the best choice for our experimentation, which has been specified previously. It is important to note that the educational dimension does not comprise NC and RC, since it makes no sense to test behavior, where no uncertainty is induced.

Hypotheses based on experimental design

Based on experimental design with the payoff function applied and dimensions as stated, we are able to examine determinants of nominal inertia and potential effects of economic education.

Hypothesis regarding the impact of money illusion

The nominal versus real representation of payoffs together with distinction among agents with imperfect/perfect foresight enables us to investigate various factors related to nominal inertia. We may outline four possible treatments according to the two dimensions in line with Fehr and Tyran (2001).

First, in the real treatments with computerized opponents (RC), payoffs are expressed in real terms and human subjects play against pre-programmed computerized opponents with perfect foresight.[5] This implies that any deviation from equilibrium prices must be due to individual optimization mistakes connected with individual-level irrationality not associated with money illusion. Rather inattention or confusion induced by monetary shock might be responsible for the fact that prices will not adjust to the nominal shock instantaneously. Therefore, the post-shock deviation of prices from the equilibrium serves as a measure for the individual level of irrationality. To sum up, this treatment measures nominal inertia caused by individual optimization errors that are not due to money illusion.

Second, in the nominal treatments with computerized opponents (NC), payoffs are expressed in nominal terms and human subjects play against pre-programmed computerized opponents with perfect foresight. Due to these agents, the subjects again do not have to form expectations about pricing decisions of the other subjects. Still the individual optimization problem is more demanding due to the presence of nominal payoffs, because subjects have to deflate them correctly at the various (P_i, P_{-i})

combinations. The distinction between NC and RC is made on the basis of real versus nominal representation of payoffs. Since the pricing decision regarding NC involves a more complicated decision related to the nominal payoff, we may observe a different speed of adjustment to the equilibrium compared to RC. As subjects do not have to form expectations in either case (RC or NC), the difference in the convergence between these two groups enables us to identify whether the effect of individual-level money illusion, that is, the direct effect of money illusion is present. This would be the case if prices in NC would be much inertial than in RC. To sum up, this treatment measures nominal inertia caused by individual-level money illusion once compared with RC.

Third, in the real treatments with human opponents (RH), payoffs are expressed in real terms and human subjects play against human opponents.[6] Through the presence of human subjects instead of computerized opponents, uncertainty is induced. Subjects have to not only manage the individual optimization problem, but also have to form expectations about the prices of the other opponents. In other words, coordination of the expectations of all human subjects is required to converge to the equilibrium. Although before the shock, unique equilibrium may be achieved by coordination in relatively successful way, this may not be true after the shock is imposed. Even though the monetary shock is announced in advance, uncertainty is induced regarding the expectations of subjects about the behavior of the other subjects. As a result, some subjects may not head toward new post-shock equilibrium, but get stuck at the old equilibrium. This is even strengthened by the presence of subjects that have no reason to believe that other subjects will adjust to the new equilibrium, but believe that others are anchored at the old equilibrium. Thus, a coordination problem among human subjects may lead to prolonged adjustment to the new post-shock equilibrium. Delineation of the relationship between RH and RC may bring additional findings, because a coordination problem in RC is absent. If individual irrationality will also be absent in RC, we can compare the level of adjustment to the new equilibrium in RC and RH. The difference in findings and observed nominal inertia in RH then may be fully attributed to the coordination problem in RH. To sum up, this treatment measures nominal inertia caused by discoordinated expectations and actions once compared with RC.

Last, in the nominal treatments with human opponents (NH), payoffs are expressed in nominal terms and human subjects play against human opponents. These subjects have to solve individual optimization problems, which also include the correct deflation of nominal payoffs. In addition, these subjects need to form expectations as in RH, but the formation of expectations is more difficult in the environment of the nominal payoffs; therefore, the coordination problem is strengthened here. If we compare the adjustment speed of RH versus NH, the total effect of money illusion might be measured. The total effect of money illusion not only consists of the direct effect but also of the indirect effect. The direct effect is associated with the individual optimization problem, where the ability to recognize the nominal frame is required as exhibited in NC. In addition, the indirect effect is present, owing to the presence of the coordination problem induced by the presence of human players, where individual effects of money illusion are multiplied. This is given by the fact that subjects with money illusion may significantly affect the behavior of subjects without money illusion in the nominal treatment because of the channel of strategic complementarity. Moreover, subjects without money illusion may suppose that all other subjects suffer from money illusion, although it may not be necessarily so. This may induce additional inertia. To sum up this treatment measures the total effect of money illusion (direct and indirect).

Hypothesis regarding educational effects

In addition to the abovementioned hypotheses, a third "educational dimension" is implemented in the nominal and the real treatment conditions. This educational dimension could be considered as an additional treatment, because well-educated treatments versus low-educated treatments are present. This framework will enable the verification of whether well-educated subjects are capable of breaking through the veil of nominal values as opposed to low-educated subjects, and are therefore expected to be mostly free of money illusion not only at the individual (direct) level, but also at a multiplied (indirect) level as already outlined in Chapter 3. For our purpose, it is mainly the post-shock adjustment to the equilibrium that is crucial. Table 6.1 illustrates in more detail two educational treatments (with basic and advanced economic knowledge), exposed to nominal versus real environment.

NH Mgr and RH Mgr differ in the framing of payoffs, but both are endowed by advanced economic knowledge. If we compare the behavior of well-educated subjects in the nominal and the real treatment, the difference in the speed of the adjustment after the shock should be almost negligible. We assume that subjects endowed by economic knowledge will be able to overcome the nominal barrier quickly, which will lead to relatively fast price adjustment, comparable with the adjustment of subjects with real payoffs. Thus, appropriate economic education should be the factor which weakens the effects of money illusion and presence of nominal inertia. Not only does it imply significant reduction or almost absence of an individual level of money illusion, but also the multiplier

Table 6.1 Educational treatment conditions

	Real payoffs	*Nominal payoffs*
Master students opponents (Mgr)	The real treatments with economically well-educated opponents (RH Mgr)	The nominal treatments with economically well-educated opponents (NH Mgr)
Bachelor students opponents (Bc)	The real treatments with basically-educated opponents (RH Bc)	The nominal treatments with basically-educated opponents (NH Bc)

Source: Own elaboration.

effects of individual money illusion will be weaker or almost absent, since the subjects have no reason to consider other players being prone to money illusion. Nevertheless, the subjects still have to form expectations. Development is therefore expected to closely follow the trend of RH Mgr group, where only the coordination problem is solved. Thus, the effect of economic education might be reflected in the amount of nominal inertia present, which is expected to be significantly reduced and also comparable to the occurrence of inertia present under the real treatment.

NH Bc and RH Bc subjects are endowed only with basic economic knowledge, but differ in the expression of payoffs. A low level of economic education should significantly affect the ability of NH Bc to cope with the nominal framing. Therefore, the occurrence of individual money illusion should be more frequent, which in turn implies that the indirect effects of money illusion might be multiplied. This is explained by the fact that although there might be individuals who are rational, they have no reason to consider others not to be prone to money illusion and, therefore, have no incentive to adjust prices after the shock more than what is needed in the vein of strategic complementarity. As a result, we expect substantial nominal inertia to be present after the shock, where the speed of convergence to unique equilibrium should be slower and far away from the speed of convergence of RH Bc.

Crucial within our educational hypothesis is the comparison of the behavior of NH Mgr versus NH Bc, where the former is well-educated compared to the latter. Both of these treatments have to deal with an environment of nominal values that differ, however, by educational background. If the effect of economic education holds we should observe a substantial difference in pricing adjustment of these treatments after the shock. Well-educated subjects are expected to cope comfortably with the nominal frame and even their expectations about other players being prone to money illusion should be approaching zero. As a consequence, the channel of strategic complementarity, through which indirect effects of money illusion are addressed, should be weakened. The total effects of money illusion (direct and indirect), which generate inertial adjustment are expected to be negligible under well-educated treatment. Thus, the speed of adjustment of NH Mgr will be significantly faster due to the infrequent presence of nominal inertia as opposed to NH Bc.

By making a comparison between RH Mgr versus RH Bc, one might ask if economic education might be used for the assessment of a coordination problem among agents in the real treatment. Since coordination is a complex task, which puts pressure on the cognitive abilities of individuals, one may believe that well-educated individuals may significantly reduce uncertainty after the shock, which might contribute to a lower variability of prices and also faster adjustment to equilibrium values.[7]

A distinction among RC and NC with respect to educational level was not performed, since the behavior of subjects in these treatments is not cognitively demanding, because subjects face agents with perfect foresight. Thus, value added with respect to the analysis of educational effects is rather weak.

Properties of the payoff functions

The payoff function[8] used during the experiment, in line with Fehr and Tyran (2001), has the following important properties:

1 Is homogenous of degree zero in P_i, P_{-i} and M
2 The best reply is increasing in $\bar{P}_{-i}$

Functional specification of payoff function ensures that:

4 The equilibrium is unique for every M
5 Equilibrium is the only Pareto-efficient point in payoff space
6 Equilibrium can be found by iterated elimination of weakly dominated strategies.

The same payoff functions were used in all treatment conditions, with the difference only in the framing of payoffs, where for RC and RH payoffs are expressed in real terms and for NC and NH, payoffs are expressed in nominal terms.

We also need to distinguish between the average price $\bar{P}$ and the average price of the other n-1 subjects in the group $\bar{P}_{-i}$. Real payoff of subject was made dependent on $\bar{P}_{-i}$ and not $\bar{P}$, since it is easier to set a best price for a given expectation about the average price of the other subjects. If the real payoff of subject would be made dependent on $\bar{P}$, it would be much more difficult for the subject to play the best reply, because he would have to also include his own price choice. In addition, the nominal payoff for subject *i* is also computed as $\bar{P}_{-i}\pi_i$ instead of $\bar{P}\pi_i$. Thus, the correct deflation of the nominal payoff to the real payoff is simplified, because it is not contingent on the individual's own price choice. Conditions 1 and 3, which reflect the neutrality condition, were implemented to examine the effects of money illusion on the adjustment process in the economy with a unique money-neutral equilibrium P_i^*, $i = 1, ..., n$. If M changes from M_0 to λM_0 and if prices change to λP_i and $\lambda \bar{P}_{-i}$, the real payment remains unaffected in order to ensure neutrality. In addition, if λP_i, $i = 1, ..., n$, is a best reply to $\bar{P}_{-i}$ at M_0, then $\lambda P_i'$, is a best reply to $\lambda \bar{P}_{-i}$ at λM_0. The post-shock equilibrium is then for all *i* equal to λP_i^*. Also, strategic complementarity was imposed in the experimental setting, which is reflected by condition 2.[9]

Property 4 ensures that the equilibrium is the unique Pareto-efficient point in the whole economy. Unique equilibrium was selected due to complications induced by the initial implementation of the price-setting game with monopolistic competition. To maximize their real payoff gains, subjects proved to behave in out-of-equilibrium way in the real and also in the nominal frame. The adjustment toward equilibrium in pre-shock and the post-shock phase was distorted by attempts to cooperate. Specification of the payoff function with respect to unique equilibrium eliminated these other sources of nominal inertia.

Property 5 ensures that the framing of payoffs has no effect on whether a particular strategy is dominated. A method for finding the equilibrium remains the same regardless of the character of payoffs. In the real frame a (weakly) dominated strategy P_i is set such as it has smaller real payoffs values at any level of $\overline{P}_{-i}$. Also in the nominal frame a (weakly) dominated strategy P_i has smaller nominal payoff values at any level of $\overline{P}_{-i}$. Subjects, therefore, only face a task of elimination of (weakly) dominated strategies with smaller payoff values at any given level of $\overline{P}_{-i}$. Since the best reply function is the same regardless of the nominal or the real frame and this holds also for the number of dominated strategies, the adjustment between RH and NH should not differ in the case of the absence of money illusion.

Additionally, the number of dominated strategies before and after the shock is not the same, but is identical across all the treatments in a given phase. It means that if after the shock the money supply will be lowered by two thirds, there will be a lower number of dominated strategies in the post-shock phase too. In other words, if money supply in the post-shock phase is given by $M_0/3$ and the nominal price will be changed by one unit, it has the same real effect as if the nominal price would be changed in the pre-shock phase (i.e., at M_0) by three units. This is given by the fact that the nominal strategy space and nominal accounting unit remains constant in the post-shock phase, although the money supply has decreased. As a consequence, if the number of dominated strategies differs in the pre-shock and post-shock phase, the speed of adjustment might differ in these two phases too. In the pre-shock phase, a higher number of dominated strategies leads to the fact that the multiplier (indirect) effects of money illusion have less impact. This is explained by the fact that if a strategy is dominated, it is not optimal to play it for subjects, irrespective of the expectations of the other n-1 players in the group. This leads to the situation that expectations about other players' money illusion are significantly reduced and, therefore, nominal inertia is less frequent. Thus, there is quicker adjustment to the equilibrium in the pre-shock phase compared to the post-shock phase. For experimental subjects the pre-shock phase should serve to test whether they are able to come to equilibrium. After they gain some knowledge, the post-shock phase with uncertainty induced by nominal shock will come, which will test whether they are also able to overcome more difficult conditions. The number of dominated strategies is identical across all treatments, which will enable us to compare the performance in the adjustment speed across these treatments. The only difference across the treatments is framing of payoffs.

Experimental procedures and parameters

In our experiment, a group size of n=4 is set and remains constant for the whole period before and after the shock. Each group has two types of subjects, subject of type x and subject of type y, equally distributed within the group. The payoff function differs among the players, where x types have to select a relatively low price in equilibrium, whereas y types have to choose a relatively high price. First, the size of the group was selected as in the original design, since no significant net effects are associated with a different size of the group. With more members in the group, the probability of subjects who suffer money illusion increases, but also the capability of an individual to affect average prices is smaller. Second, with regards to the heterogeneity of the players, the case of four different players with four different payoff functions would be the most realistic one. However, the more different payoff functions are present in the design, the more complicated the case. As a result, only two types of players x and y, with two different payoff functions, are present in our experimental design.

Major experimental parameters, inspired by Fehr and Tyran (2001), are as follows: The money supply before the shock in each treatment was given by M_0= 42, while in the post-shock phase it was given by M_1=M_0/3=14. The average equilibrium price over all n group members in the pre-shock phase is given by $\overline{P}_0^* = 18$, whereas in the post-shock equilibrium $\overline{P}_1^* = 6$. The length of the pre-shock and the post-shock phase differs among treatments with human and computerized opponents. In the treatments with human opponents, both the pre-shock and the post-shock phase length is T=20, whereas in the treatments with computerized opponents, the length of the pre-shock and the post-shock phase is only T=10. The reason for different number of periods T between the treatments is that subjects in human treatments have to cope with a coordination problem related to expectations formation and as a consequence the adjustment to the equilibrium takes longer. Therefore, human players were given more time to ensure comparable adjustment across human and computerized treatments.

Experimental subjects interact via computer terminals and have to select in each period an integer price, P_i, in interval from 1 to 30. They also have to form an expectation $\overline{P}_{-i}^e$ about $\overline{P}_{-i}$. Moreover, they have to indicate their confidence about their expectation $\overline{P}_{-i}^e$, which was measured by choosing an integer on scale from 1 to 6, where 1 indicates that the subject is not at all confident, and 6 indicates that the subject is absolutely confident. In the treatments with human opponents, subjects have to face a coordination problem, which is closely associated with uncertainty. Confidence, therefore, serves as an indicator of subjects' perceived uncertainty about the other subjects' choices. At the end of each period (after the choice is made) subjects are informed about their performance on an outcome screen. The size of their actual real payoff together with the actual realization of $\overline{P}_{-i}$ is depicted for the current round. Additional information regarding the subject's past real payoffs and past choices of $\overline{P}_{-i}$ is also available there.

To make the appropriate decisions, the subjects receive instructions and information about their payoffs in a matrix form.[10] The payoff matrices are designed for x and y types for all treatment conditions. Either the real or the nominal payoff is present in the matrix for each feasible combination of $(P_i, \overline{P}_{-i})$. The best reply for any given $\overline{P}_{-i}$ is easily found owing to setting of payoffs given by properties of the payoff function. Subjects have to select the highest real or nominal payoff associated with a given $\overline{P}_{-i}$ given their expectations $\overline{P}_{-i}^e$. It is important to note that not only do subjects receive their own payoff tables, but also payoff tables of the other type.

Subjects in the treatments with computerized opponents receive the same tables and instructions as in the treatments with human opponents. Half of the human subjects receive the payoff tables of an x-player and the other half the payoff tables of a y-player. However, they also receive additional tables (with respect to the type of player they represent), which inform them about the $\overline{P}_{-i}$ response of the other n-1 computerized players in the group to particular price choice $P_i \in \{1, 2, \ldots, 30\}$. Uncertainty is therefore reduced by the inclusion of aggregate response rule and coordination problem removed. These additional tables also differ with respect to the type of player x and y.

Publicly announced negative monetary shock is implemented in the last period of the pre-shock phase. Based on that, subjects of x and y-types receive the new payoff tables, adjusted for the new level of money supply $M_1=M_0/3$. Except for the shock, nothing changes, which is common knowledge together with the length of the post-shock phase, which is another T period. Subjects also receive payoff tables of the other type. In addition, they are still equipped by the pre-shock tables and are allowed to compare it with the post-shock ones. To fully understand the change and ensure that the nominal shock was anticipated, subjects have sufficient time to study the new and old payoffs.

General information regarding the experiment

In total, 194 subjects participated in the experiment. Table 6.2 summarizes the composition of various treatments, which will be analyzed with respect to the previously discussed hypotheses. Eighteen subjects participated in the nominal treatment with computerized opponents (NC) and twenty subjects participated in the real treatment with computerized opponents. These two treatments were tested regardless of their educational achievement. In the nominal and the real treatment with human opponents, the educational status is distinguished. In the nominal treatment NH, forty subjects participated as master students and forty subjects as bachelor students. In the real treatment RH, forty subjects participated as master students and thirty-six subjects as bachelor students.

Subjects were selected from the University of Economics, Prague. The common interest should reduce frequent experimentation problems, where two groups

Table 6.2 Composition of treatments with respect to groups.

	Nominal payoffs	*Real payoffs*
Educational effect	NH Mgr (10 groups with n human players) Bc (10 groups with n human players in each group)	RH Mgr (10 groups with n human players in each group) Bc (9 groups with n human players in each group)
No educational effect	NC (18 groups with 1 human and n-1 computerized players in each group)	RC (20 groups with 1 human and n-1 computerized players in each group)

Source: Own elaboration.

do not exhibit reasonably similar characteristics due to the fact of significantly different educational attainment, income status, and so on. Basically educated individuals in economics were chosen from the first year of bachelor studies, with only backgrounds of basic economics.[11] Well-educated subjects were master students of the Faculty of Economics in their last year, with advanced knowledge of microeconomics, macroeconomics, game theory and other related advanced economic courses.

Subjects were paid a show-up fee of 150 CZK. This was also the minimum amount, which they could win during the game. The total earnings of the subjects in the experiment were approximately 450 CZK on average. The experimental session lasted ninety minutes on average. The experiment was conducted in the Laboratory of Experimental Economics, Prague, in June 2011. To experimentally test the subjects' behavior through computers, the Java program was used to set up the experiment. The experiment consisted of eight sessions due to the highly demanding requirements regarding the number of participants. Still, the capacity constraint of the laboratory, which disposes with thirty-six available places for experimental subjects, is a significant number. These sessions were conducted over four different days.[12] Students were invited to participate in the experiment with the help of special web pages, where they could register for a particular session depending on the level of education attained. This selection of participants was chosen instead of standard registration within the database of the Laboratory of Experimental Economics, since the laboratory database during the process of registration did not enable us to sort out students with regards to our purpose. After registration finished, the appropriate educational attainment was checked in order to eliminate participation of students unsuitable for particular educational treatment. Additionally, multiple participation was not allowed either and this was also checked.

Notes

1 For more details regarding the problematic of internal and external validity and subject samples in experimental economics, see Guala (2005) and Chytilova (2012a, 2012b).
2 Strategic complementarity included in design causes the following behavior among competitors: if an individual expects his competitors to increase prices, it is optimal for him to increase his price as well. This theoretical framework of Haltiwanger and Waldmann (1989) was already outlined in Chapters 2 and 3.
3 Computerized versus human opponents differ with respect to the length of the post-shock period, which will be explained in more detail later in the chapter.
4 One-time shock investigated within the experiment is considered to be representative for our purpose insofar as it can be compared to the one-time shock crisis, which might hit the economy.
5 More precisely, a subject in each group plays against n-1 pre-programmed computerized opponents.
6 Human subject in each group plays against n-1 human opponents.
7 However, as will be shown further, this hypothesis is not only irrelevant with respect to the main hypothesis outlined at the beginning, but is also shown to be indemonstrable in this type of experiment.
8 For full mathematical specification of the payoff function please refer to Fehr and Tyran (2001).

9 Strategic complementarity and its implications have been outlined already in Chapter 2 and 3.

10 Payoffs were presented to subjects in form of payoff tables in vein of Fehr and Tyran (2001) from the already mentioned payoff function. Readers who are interested in the full set of payoff tables utilized in this experiment and experimental instructions, should refer to the Appendix E and C respectively in Chytilova (2013), which is available at: https://theses.cz/id/1s2nq5/ISIS_32032_chyh01.pdf?lang=en.

11 These students came from Faculty of Economics (43%) and the Faculty of Informatics and Statistics (57%).

12 Experimental sessions were held in the Laboratory of Experimental Economics, Prague, during these days: Pilot experiment: 6.6. 2011; Regular experiment: 9.6.2011, 10.6., 2011, 11.6.2011, 13.6.2011, 14.6.2011.

References

Abbink, K. and Rockenbach, B., 2006. Option Pricing by Students and Professional Traders: A Behavioral Investigation. *Managerial and Decision Economics*, 27 (6), pp. 497–510.

Adam, K., 2007. Experimental Evidence on the Persistence of Output and Inflation. *Economic Journal*, 117 (520), pp. 603–636.

Akerlof, G. A. and Yellen, J. L., 1985. A Near–rational Model of the Business Cycle, with Wage and Price Intertia. *The Quarterly Journal of Economics*, 100 (5), pp. 823–838.

Arifovic, J. and Sargent, T. J., 2003. Laboratory Experiments with an Expectational Phillips Curve. In Altig D. E. and Smith B. D. (eds.), *Evolution and Procedures in Central Banking*. Cambridge, UK: Cambridge University Press, pp. 23–55.

Bernasconi, M. and Kirchkamp, O., 2000. Why Do Monetary Policies Matter? An Experimental Study of Saving and Inflation in an Overlapping Generations Model. *Journal of Monetary Economics*, 46 (2), pp. 315–343.

Blanchard, O. J. and Kiyotaki, N., 1987. Monopolistic Competition and the Effects of Aggregate Demand. *American Economic Review*, September, 77 (4), pp. 647–666.

Chytilova, H., 2012a. Experimental Economics. Trade-off Between External and Internal Validity Justified? Conference Proceedings, 12th International Conference IMEA 2012.

Chytilova, H., 2012b. Subject Samples in Experimental Economics, Professionals versus Students, Conference Proceedings, 8th International Bata Conference.

Chytilova, H., 2013. Money Illusion and Economic Education, an Experimental Approach. Doctoral dissertation, University of Economics, Prague. Available at: https://theses.cz/id/1s2nq5/ISIS_32032_chyh01.pdf?lang=en [Accessed 19 September 2016]

Deck, C. A., 2004. Avoiding Hyperinflation: Evidence from a Laboratory Economy. *Journal of Macroeconomics*, 26, pp. 147–170.

Duffy, J., 1998. Monetary Theory in the Laboratory. *Federal Reserve Bank of St. Louis Review*, 80, pp. 9–26.

Duffy, J., 2008. Experimental Macroeconomics. In Durlauf, S. and Blume, L. (eds.), *New Palgrave Dictionary of Economics*, 2nd edition. New York: Palgrave Macmillan.

Duffy, J., 2011. Macroeconomics: A Survey of Laboratory Research. *Working Papers* 334, University of Pittsburgh, Department of Economics.

Duffy, J. and Fisher, E. O'N., 2005. Sunspots in the Laboratory. *American Economic Review*, 95 (3), pp. 510–529.

Duffy, J. and Ochs, J., 1999. Emergence of Money as a Medium of Exchange: An Experimental Study. *American Economic Review*, 89 (4), pp. 847–877.

Duffy, J. and Ochs, J., 2012. Equilibrium Selection in Static and Dynamic Entry Games. *Games and Economic Behavior*, 76, pp. 97–116.

Fehr, E. and Tyran, J., 2000. Does Money Illusion Matter? *IEW – Working Paper* No. 045, Institute for Empirical Research in Economics, University of Zurich.

Fehr, E. and Tyran, J., 2001. Does Money Illusion Matter? *American Economic Review*, 91 (5), pp. 1239–1262.

Fehr, E. and Tyran, J., 2005a. Expectations and the Effects of Money Illusion. In B. Agarwal and A. Vercelli (eds.), *Psychology, Rationality and Economic Behavior: Challenging Standard Assumptions*. London: Palgrave Macmillan and the International Economic Association.

Fehr, E. and Tyran, J., 2005b. Individual Irrationality and Aggregate Outcomes. *Journal of Economic Perspectives*, 4 (19), pp. 43–66.

Fehr, E. and Tyran, J., 2007. Money Illusion and Coordination Failure. *Games and Economic Behavior*, 58 (2), pp. 246–268.

Fehr, E. and Tyran, J., 2008. Limited Rationality and Strategic Interaction: The Impact of the Strategic Environment on Nominal Inertia. *Econometrica*, 76 (2), pp. 353–394.

Fehr, E., Kirchsteiger, G., and Riedl, A., 1998. Gift Exchange and Reciprocity in Competitive Experimental Markets. *European Economic Review*, 42 (1), pp. 1–34.

Guala, F. (ed.), 2005. *The Methodology of Experimental Economics*. New York: University of Cambridge Press.

Haltiwanger, J. and Waldman, M., 1989. Limited Rationality and Strategic Complements: Implications for Macroeconomics. *Quarterly Journal of Economics*, 104 (3), pp. 463–483.

Heinemann, F., Nagel, R., and Ockenfels, P., 2004. The Theory of Global Games on Test: Experimental Analysis of Coordination Games with Public and Private Information. *Econometrica*, 72 (5), pp. 1583–1599.

Hey, J. D., 1994. Expectations Formation: Rational or Adaptive or ...? *Journal of Economic Behavior and Organization*, 25 (3), pp. 329–344.

Lei, V. and Noussair, C. N., 2007. Equilibrium Selection in an Experimental Macroeconomy. *Southern Economic Journal*, 74 (2), pp. 448–482.

Lim, S. Prescott, E. C., and Sunder, S., 1994. Stationary Solution to the Overlapping Generations Model of Fiat Money: Experimental Evidence. *Empirical Economics*, 19 (2), pp. 255–277.

Lucas, R. E. Jr., 1986. Adaptive Behavior and Economic Theory. *Journal of Business*, 59 (4), pp. 401–426.

Marimon, R. and Sunder, S., 1993. Indeterminacy of Equilibria in a Hyperinflationary World: Experimental Evidence. *Econometrica*, 61 (5), pp. 1073–1107.

Marimon, R. and Sunder, S., 1994. Expectations and Learning under Alternative Monetary Regimes: An Experimental Approach. *Economic Theory*, 4, pp. 131–162.

Marimon, R. and Sunder, S., 1995. Does a Constant Money Growth Rule Help Stabilize Inflation? *Carnegie-Rochester Conference Series on Public Policy*, 43, pp. 111–156.

Noussair, C. N., Plott, C. R., and Riezman, R. G., 1997. The Principles of Exchange Rate De–termination in an International Financial Experiment. *Journal of Political Economy*, 105 (4), pp. 822–861.

Riciutti, R., 2008. Bringing Macroeconomics into the Lab. *Journal of Macroeconomics*, 30 (1), pp. 216–237.

Salemi, M. K., 2005. Teaching Economic Literacy: Why, What and How. *International Review of Economics Education*, 4 (2), pp. 46–57.

Schram, A., 2005. Artificiality: The Tension between Internal and External Validity in Economic Experiments. *Journal of Economic Methodology*, 12 (2), pp. 225–237.

Smith, V. L., 1962. An Experimental Study of Competitive Market Behavior. *Journal of Political Economy*, 70 (2), pp. 111–137.

Van Huyck, J. B., Battalio R. C., and Beil R. O., 1990. Tacit Coordination Games, Strategic Uncertainty, and Coordination Failure. *American Economic Review*, 80 (1), pp. 234–248.

Van Huyck, J. B., Battalio, R. C., and Beil R. O., 1991. Strategic Uncertainty, Equilibrium Selection, and Coordination Failure in Average Opinion Games. *The Quarterly Journal of Economics*, 106 (3), pp. 885–910.

Van Huyck, J. B., Cook J. P., and Battalio R. C., 1994. Selection Dynamics, Asymptotic Stability, and Adaptive Behavior. *Journal of Political Economy*, 102 (5), pp. 975–1005.

7 Experimental results

In this chapter, the results of the experiment will be analyzed to verify our hypotheses relating to nominal inertia, the educational effects and potential implications at the aggregate level.

First, we neglect the educational effects and focus solely on the investigation of a possible presence of nominal inertia, induced by individual effects of money illusion and compare it with individual optimization errors that are not due to money illusion. Also, we analyze the nominal adjustment of subjects in the real environment, where the source of nominal inertia is not money illusion but coordination problems. A comparison of individual and indirect money illusion occurrence follows. Second, we switch to an analysis of well-educated subjects and compare their performance under nominal versus real frame. Finally, we focus on the comparison of the well-educated and low-educated treatment under the nominal frame and their ability to cope with multiplied effects of money illusion.

Nominal price adjustment as an individual optimization problem

The relationship between RC (real computers) versus NC (nominal computers) enables us to investigate individual irrationality and individual money illusion.[1] Subjects play against computerized agents with perfect foresight, where zero uncertainty is induced and the decision-making process is, therefore, reduced to individual optimization problems.[2] This puts minimum educational requirements on subjects and, therefore, no potential is hidden in the comparison of the performance between well-educated and low-educated individuals. This will also be confirmed by the results, which show that deviation from an optimal pricing path is negligible for less-educated subjects.

The performance of subjects in RC proved to be perfect, since subjects adjust immediately to the post-shock equilibrium price $P_1^* = 6$, with only small insignificant deviations in two post-shock periods, which indicates that inertial behavior is almost absent. This can be compared with the performance of NC, which depicts the development of the average price of RC and NC for the pre-shock and the post-shock phase. Subjects in NC appear to be less flexible in price adjustment and the average price for the whole post-shock phase is slightly above the

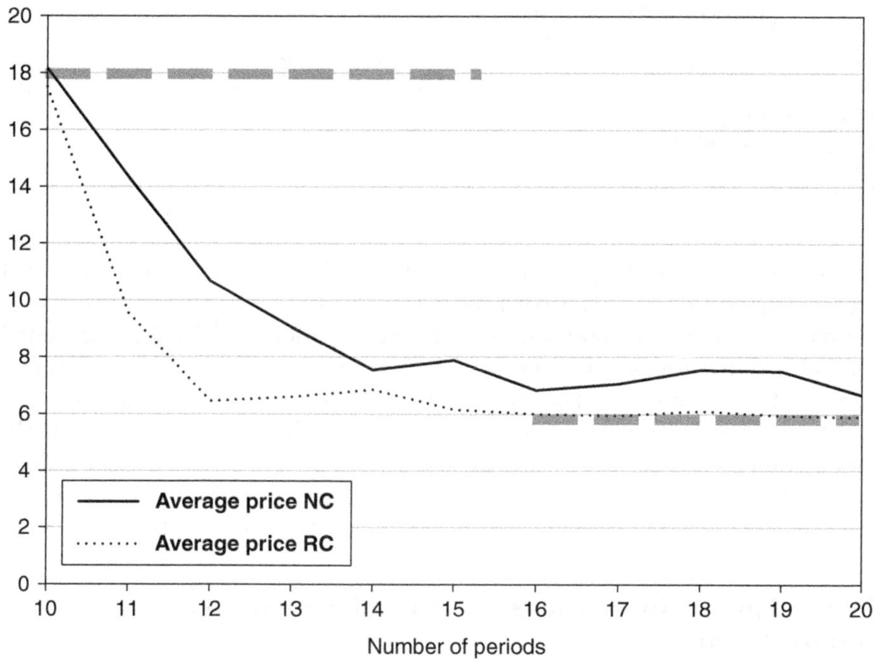

Figure 7.1 Difference of RC and NC from optimum price in the economy in the post-shock phase.

Source: Own computation.

equilibrium price. More can be seen from Figure 7.1, which depicts the difference from the optimum price for NC versus RC in the post-shock phase. RC subjects show clear equilibrium incidence almost for the whole phase, whereas NC subjects still deviate from the equilibrium price, although relatively close to RC. This indicates that some nominal inertia is present in the case of NC. On the other hand, the individual level of irrationality in the case of RC cannot be taken into consideration due to the behavior associated with minimum deviations from the equilibrium almost for the whole post-shock phase.

The comparison of the total sum of average income losses[3] among RC and NC in Table 7.1 is associated with respective pricing behavior of RC and NC. The average welfare loss for RC is very low and there is almost no difference in income losses between the pre-shock and post-shock phase. This suggests that the nominal shock imposed has no effect in the case of RC.[4]

In contrast, income loss in the case of NC has increased compared to the pre-shock phase, which indicates that despite the absence of uncertainty, nominal environment contributes to the slightly distorted decision-making of the subjects. Increase in income loss in the post-shock phase, together with continuing deviation of the average price from equilibrium price after the shock, indicates that small non-negligible nominal inertia is present in NC. However, the average efficiency

Table 7.1 The sum of average welfare losses for RC, NC (percent), pre-shock and the post-shock phase

Average welfare loss	*RC*	*NC*
The pre-shock phase	–5.8%	–8.5%
The post-shock phase	–5.4%	–15%

Source: Own computation.

loss for NC is still relatively small and, therefore, only a small amount of individual money illusion is present. The experimental results confirm that no individual level of irrationality is present in RC due to post-shock equilibrium behavior, and a small level of individual money illusion is present in NC. Additionally, it suggests that individual money illusion in conditions of zero uncertainty plays a negligible role at the aggregate level with unimportant nominal inertia. In other words, multiplication of direct effects of money illusion is not the case in an environment where agents know the aggregate response rule in advance, which is reflected in relatively fast convergence to the economy's equilibrium in the case of both treatments.

Nominal price adjustment as a coordination problem in the real treatment

In the case of RH Bc (real humans with basic economic knowledge), the source of inertia is not money illusion itself (as is the case of the nominal treatments), but a coordination problem induced by the factor of uncertainty, where subjects need to form expectations about the behavior of others.[5] Thus, the deviation problem is caused by the fact that the subjects do not face perfectly foresighted agents, like in the case of RC. Development of the average price in Figure 7.2 shows that RC is much closer to the equilibrium, especially in the post-shock phase, directly after the nominal shock is announced. In contrast, RH Bc exhibit inertial behavior after the shock, where the economy's equilibrium price $\overline{P}_1^* = 6$ is not attained.[6]

The subjects stopped to converge mainly during the second half of the post-shock phase, where the price stayed for a longer time at nine. This is also reflected in the size of average welfare losses (the first period after the shock, real income loss is –53 percent). It decreases over time, where in the period 33 it is already at level –11 percent, but did not reach lower values. In contrast RC's losses in the post-shock phase are mostly negligible.

Induced uncertainty (through necessity to form expectations about the average price of the other n – 1 players), is also reflected in the level of confidence, which is the indicator of how serious the coordination problem is among the players. RC treatment faces zero uncertainty due to known aggregate response rule as opposed to RH Bc. Uncertainty of RH Bc in the pre-shock phase improved over time and mostly reached level 5 (very confident). In contrast, the implementation of the negative monetary shock significantly decreased subject's confidence in post-shock phase with most responses at level 3 or 4 on average until the end of the experiment.[7]

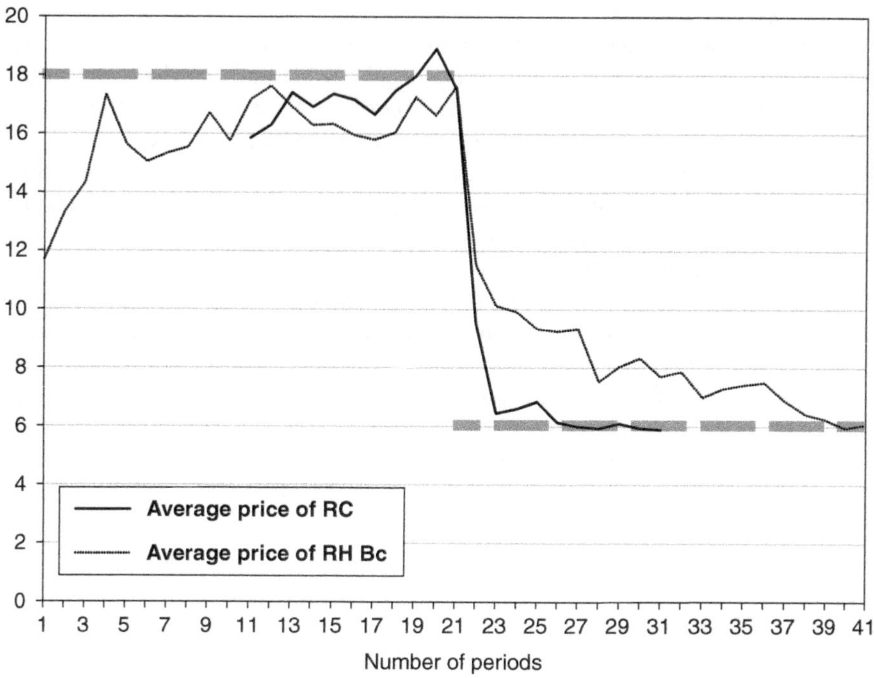

Figure 7.2 Development of the economy's average price in RC versus RH Bc.

As was already stated, RC results are a good indicator of the coordination problem faced by subjects in RH Bc treatment, since treatments differ in known versus unknown aggregate response rule. Since in RC all individual irrationality is eliminated, subjects in RH Bc surely face coordination problem. In particular, RH Bc subjects may still believe that other n–1 players remained stuck in the old equilibrium and, therefore, form expectations about the average price of the other n–1 players still based slightly on pre-shock average price. Therefore, nominal inertia is non-negligible, which in turn leads to slower convergence at the aggregate level.

The comparison of individual and indirect money illusion occurrence

This section will compare an environment with individual (direct) money illusion (given by the NC with zero uncertainty) with one where money illusion can have indirect effects (given by NH Bc with uncertainty).[8] In particular, NH Bc subjects not only have to form expectations because of the unknown aggregate response rule, but uncertainty is also strengthened because they have to deal with nominal payoff environment. In light of this evaluation, the link between the nominal treatments to the real treatments will be taken into consideration for the analysis of the speed of the adjustment in the economy with computerized or human opponents.[9]

Directly after the shock is imposed, the highest incidence to equilibrium play is visible for RC treatment, since these individuals face neither the coordination problem, nor the nominal frame given by experimental design, and are, therefore, prone only to individual irrationalities, which are almost absent (See Figure 7.3).[10] NC treatment exhibits slower convergence, despite zero uncertainty, because subjects have to cope with individual money illusion, but the length of the period is sufficient to converge to equilibrium.

In RH Bc treatment, the coordination problem, free of money illusion, has a much stronger effect on the adjustment speed than individual money illusion (NC). As a result, the presence of the human factor slows down the convergence process. The most severe nominal inertia is present in the case of NH Bc treatment, where individual effects of money illusion are multiplied into indirect effects through coordination problem. The price in this case was reduced only by one unit on average, which is the lowest value from all the treatments and documents significantly inertial backward-looking behavior directly after the shock.

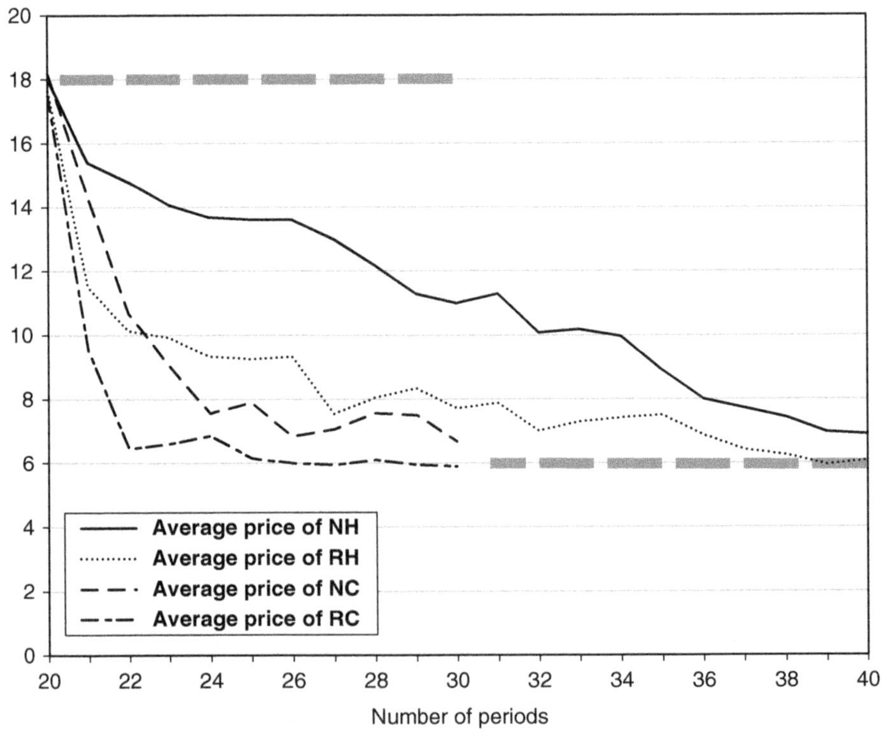

Figure 7.3 Development of the average price of human and computerized opponents (the post-shock phase).

Table 7.2 The total difference in the average price adjustment among human versus computerized treatments for all rounds

	NH Bc-RH Bc	*NC-RC*
Total difference in the average price adjustment for all rounds	67.7	20.8

Source: Own computation.

This inertial behavior was also reflected in the size of welfare loss right after the nominal shock, which was 63 percent for NH Bc and 48 percent for NC. NH Bc welfare loss in the post-shock period was falling only slowly, which was reflected in the total average welfare loss in the post-shock phase (33 percent for NH Bc whereas only 15 percent for NC).

Also, the adjustment difference in the average price of NH Bc and RH Bc is larger than the difference of NC and RC. Table 7.2 compares the total difference in the average price adjustment among human versus computerized treatments for all rounds. From these values, we can derive that the nominal frame causes stickier prices in the treatment with human opponents by 30 percent more compared to the treatment with computerized opponents.

From the comparison among treatments, we may derive that the indirect effects of money illusion in the setting with low-educated human players are much stronger at the aggregate level as opposed to individual money illusion effect in the case of computerized low-educated players when strategic uncertainty is not present. Individual effects of money illusion in NC cause only slight price deviation after the shock in contrast to NH Bc, which is consequently reflected in the higher income loss of the latter treatment.

The nominal and the real treatment, well-educated subjects

In this section, the impact of the nominal frame will be evaluated at the same educational level but different frames. This means that only real versus nominal treatments and different ability to adjust in these environments will be analyzed regardless of education. In the next section, the impact of the nominal frame will be evaluated across educational levels, but in nominal frames only. In other words, the ability of individuals to break through the money illusion will be analyzed according to the level of their economic education.

In the case of well-educated individuals, individual money illusion should be present in a negligible form, thereby leading to elimination of indirect effects of money illusion. In other words, expectations of rational agents are not affected in the vein of strategic complementarity, which should be seriously weakened in the nominal treatment. According to our expectations, we should observe a fairly low occurrence of nominal inertia since rational well-educated subjects have no reason to think that others are prone to money illusion. In addition, comparison with RH, treatments should also yield a smaller difference, since in the absence of direct and indirect money illusion in the nominal treatment (i.e., zero effect of the nominal frame), nominal inertia is induced solely by a coordination problem. However, as opposed to initial assumptions, the average price of the nominal treatment (NH Mgr – nominal treatments with advanced economic skills) is significantly more inertial than in the real treatment (RH Mgr – real treatment with advanced economic skills). The difference is visible directly after the shock, when strategic uncertainty is induced. This is given by the fact that NH Mgr subjects have to also deal with nominal payoffs apart from coordination (see Figure 7.4).

In the pre-shock period, both treatments converge to the equilibrium price $\bar{P}_0^* = 18$ on average over the last few periods. After the monetary shock is implemented, the difference between the two treatments is striking in terms of the convergence toward $\bar{P}_0^* = 6$. The indirect effects of money illusion despite economic education, are also reflected in the different size of incomes achieved. Figure 7.5 suggests that not in any period did NH Mgr performed better than RH Mgr, since the difference in the average size of the income between RH and NH gained by all players in each period is positive for the whole pre-shock and the post-shock phase, ranging from two to eight on average.

The size of the welfare loss of NH Mgr economy reached –69 percent in the first post-shock period compared to RH Mgr economy, where it increased to –59 percent. However, the welfare loss of NH Mgr fell only slowly compared to RH Mgr. This is reflected in the size of the average welfare loss as a percent of the

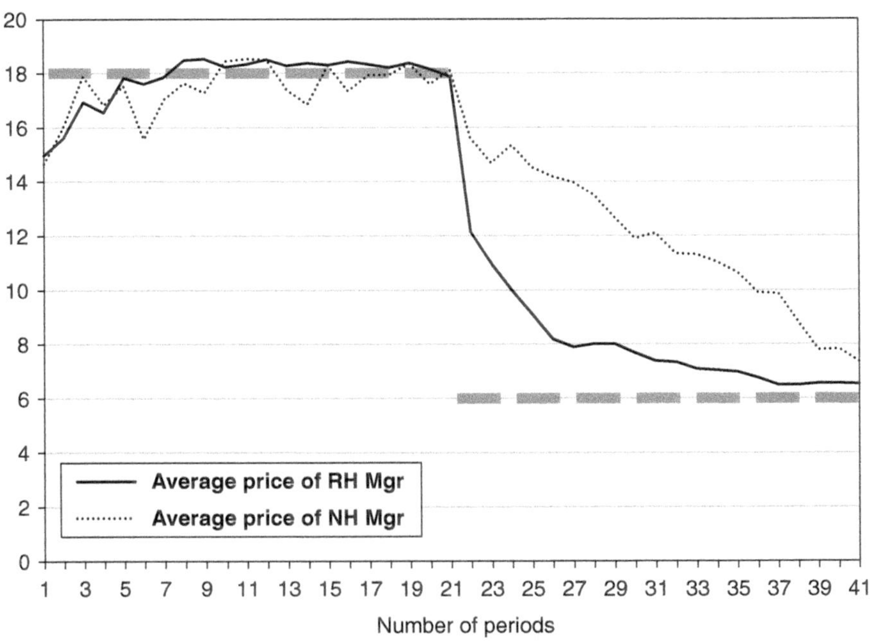

Figure 7.4 Development of the economy's average price in NH Mgr versus RH Mgr.

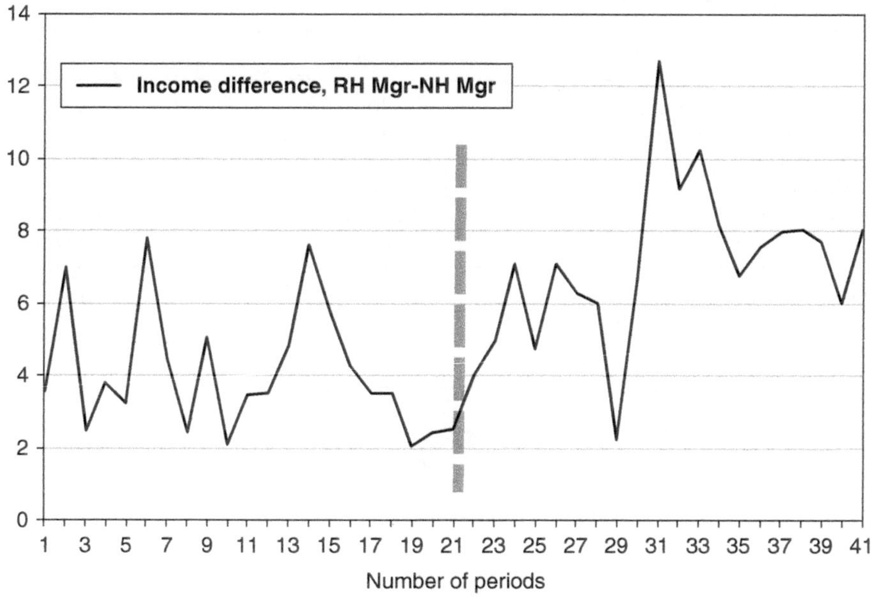

Figure 7.5 Difference in income (RH Mgr–NH Mgr).

whole pre-shock and the post-shock phase in Table 7.3. The welfare loss of NH Mgr economy was –23 percent of the total income, whereas the welfare loss of RH Mgr was only –9 percent of the total income. For the whole post-shock phase, the average welfare loss had risen to –30 percent for NH Mgr as a result of the monetary shock introduction. For RH Mgr, the average welfare loss had increased by –12.4 percent. Values related to the total income achieved in the pre-shock and the post-shock phase suggest that higher income reduction after the shock occurred in case of NH Mgr.

Also, the total size of income is lower for NH Mgr. Predominantly the post-shock phase appeared to be crucial for the performance of both economies, because of uncertainty induced. According to the results, the occurrence of nominal inertia is much less frequent at the aggregate level for RH Mgr economy since subjects do not have to face the environment of nominal values and therefore no multiplication of individual money illusion is the case. Thus, the economy of RH Mgr does not stay below the potential product for the whole post-shock phase. In other words, the coordination problem encountered in the RH Mgr treatment is not as serious an issue as the indirect effects of money illusion in NH Mgr intensified by the coordination problem itself. This suggests that even well-educated subjects might experience problems with the environment of nominal values.

The comparison of post-shock price convergence of the nominal and the real treatment with regards to the simulated case of a backward-looking economy might bring additional findings (see Figure 7.6).

Table 7.3 Income development and average welfare losses (WL) for NH Mgr, RH Mgr (percent), pre-shock and the post-shock phase

	NH Mgr	*RH Mgr*
Pre-shock total income	700,4091	785,875
Post-shock total income	559,25	700,8
Total income	1259,659	1486,675
Total WL	–23,19%	–9,35%
Pre-shock WL	–16,62%	–6,44%
Post-shock WL	–30,09%	–12,40%

Source: Own computation.

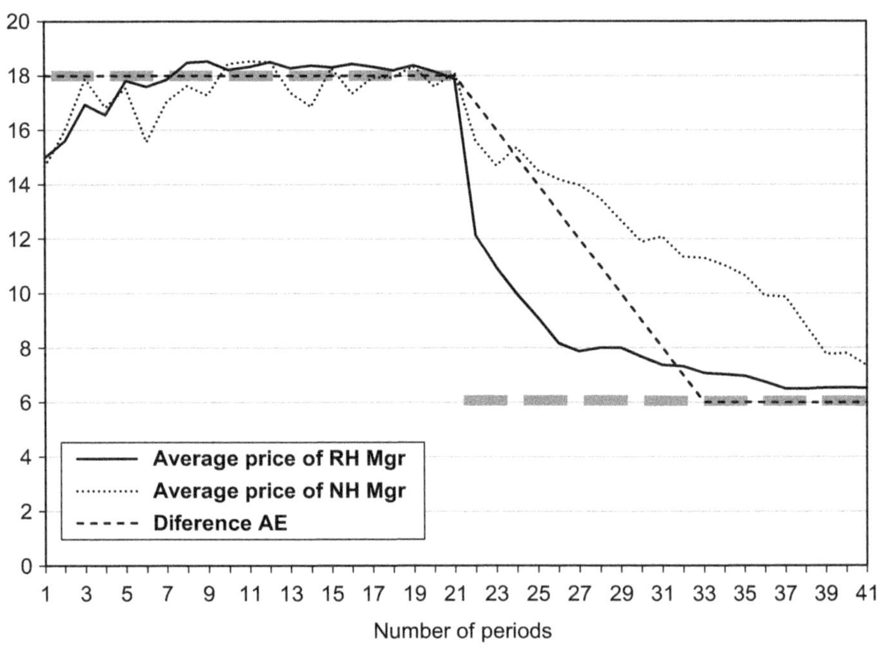

Figure 7.6 Development of the average price in the economy of NH Mgr, RH Mgr and AE.

In a purely backward-looking economy, which was simulated for our purpose, players behave according to the past and their expectations are simply guided by the pre-shock development. We may understand the behavior of these players as rule of thumb simplifying decision in conditions of uncertainty (Kahneman 2003). In other words, players are not subject to coordination problems. However, this heuristic feature leads to cognitive biases in terms of slower adjustment. Still, nominal inertia in this economy is lower than in the nominal treatment, where players face coordination problems and therefore indirect effects of money illusion. This explains why the pricing path of NH Mgr is above the adaptive line.

The performance of the real treatment is below the backward-looking one because no nominal frame (followed by indirect effects of money illusion) is present and subjects only have to deal with the coordination problem, which is much easier under the real frame and exceeds the performance of rule of thumb behavior.

If expectations are to be evaluated, the nominal treatment exhibits more inertial expectations compared to the real treatment for the whole post-shock period. In period 22 directly after the shock, the nominal treatment expects price $\bar{P}^e = 18$, whereas the real treatment expects $\bar{P}^e = 12$. This again confirms greater stickiness of actual prices, where considerations arise as to whether well-educated individuals are able to break through the nominal barrier.[11]

In addition, there is another interesting feature that is present. In the first post-shock period expected price $\bar{P}^e = 18$ is equal to the actual average price for the nominal treatment. One might suppose that if expectations are in line with the actual price in the economy in this period, subjects should receive adequate rewards, thus high income on average in the economy. However, this is not the case, as we will see later in the income analysis, since the nominal treatment is far from equilibrium with its expectations and price. Although the expected and actual price of the real treatment differs in the period directly after the shock, this economy will gain a higher income than NH Mgr, since the actual price is closer to equilibrium. Still, the size of income achieved by RH Mgr is not high. The reason is that although closer to equilibrium, expectations were not fulfilled for the whole post-shock phase, where delay is present. Thus, the income achieved depends on how far the economy is from the equilibrium price and if expectations are delayed or not. Still, the economy (in this case RH Mgr), which is closer to the equilibrium, will achieve sufficient income compared to the economy, which is far from equilibrium (NH Mgr), but the income would be even higher if expectations were not delayed.

Effect of economic education on money illusion occurrence, investigation across educational levels, NH Mgr versus NH Bc

So far, the indirect effects of money illusion have been examined at the same educational level.[12] Although in case of NH Mgr, nominal inertia proved to be the case as opposed to RH Mgr, we cannot conclude for sure that education has no effect. Therefore, the impact of the nominal frame and its indirect effects will be evaluated across educational levels. The comparison between NH Mgr and NH Bc, which serves as a control group, will enable us to isolate the difference in the performance for which the economic education might be responsible (see Table 6.2 in Chapter 6). In other words, it enables us to identify whether the economic education has a substantial effect or not. We assume that well-educated nominal treatment (NH Mgr) contributes to a significant reduction in variability of prices, a significant reduction in individual money illusion, and resulting indirect effects. This might then have a non-negligible impact on the speed of the convergence and elimination of nominal inertia in the economy of well-educated

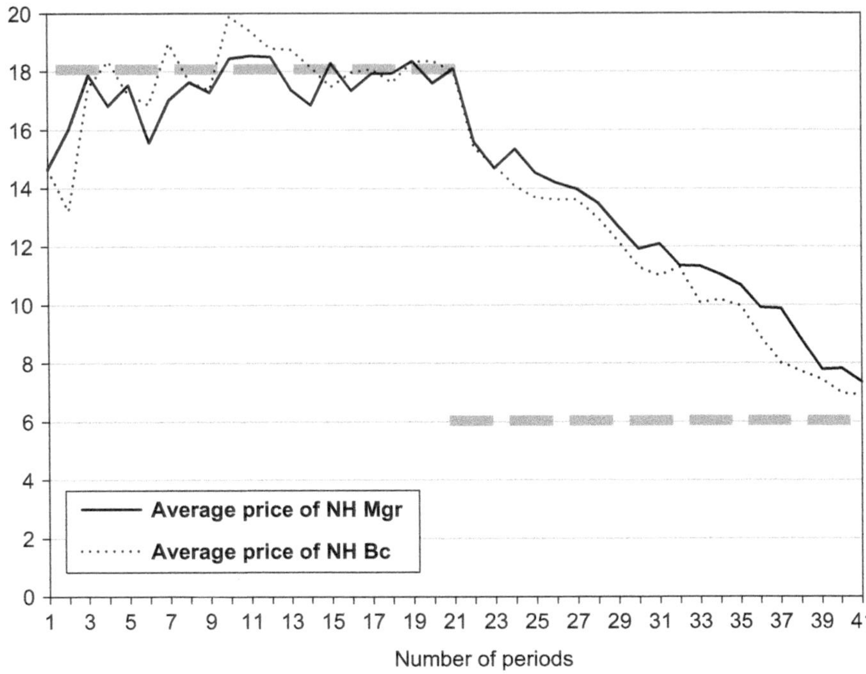

Figure 7.7 Development of the economy's average price in NH Mgr versus NH Bc.

individuals at the aggregate level. Figure 7.7 compares the development of the average price across educational treatments. In the pre-shock phase, development of both treatments is very similar with comparable price variability.

Crucial for our investigation of the performance of both economies, is the first period after the shock, in which both treatments reduce the price only slightly (NH Mgr by 2 units, NH Bc only by 0.5 units) and the price is governed by the pre-shock equilibrium price. In following periods of the post-shock phase, the pricing path is inertial and almost indistinguishable. This suggests that severe and comparable nominal inertia are present at the aggregate level, not depending on the level of economic education. In addition, neither of the treatments converged to the equilibrium. The price of NH Mgr in the last period of the post-shock phase is $\overline{P}_1 \doteq 9$, and for NH Bc is $\overline{P}_1 = 11$, which differs significantly from the equilibrium price $\overline{P}_1^* = 6$.

A possible explanation for the incomplete adjustment of both treatments lies in the fact that the only presence of one irrational in the group significantly affects other players in the group, which in turn affects the whole treatment. Before the shock, prices are relatively stable, but after the shock the impact of an irrational becomes higher due to induced uncertainty. As a result, subjects won't coordinate at all and instead do not change their prices in the unstable environment because they achieve at least satisfactory rewards with this strategy. Thus, there are no incentives to adjust to the equilibrium, which is even intensified by the possibility that expectations are in line with the actual price, which creates false conjectures about the economy being stable and working on its potential.[13] Taken together, the presence of an irrational individual might affect the convergence of the economy to the equilibrium by an unwillingness to coordinate at the individual level within the group because other rational subjects do not want to adjust their prices, since their expectations are line with the average price (although out of equilibrium) and the size of income earned is satisfactory at the individual level.[14]

Both economies are persecuted for inertial behavior in terms of income, where the product stays below the potential for the whole post-shock phase. Inadequate adjustment in the first post-shock period leads to huge income decrease for both treatments. The performance regarding the pricing behavior is comparable and educational effect in no way privileges NH Mgr treatment over NH Bc (see Figure 7.8).

This development is also supported by Figure 7.9, which speaks neither in favor of NH Bc nor in favor of NH Mgr.

The product being below the potential in the case of both economies is also reflected in the size of the average welfare loss directly after the shock in Figure 7.10 (–69 percent for NH Mgr and –63 percent for NH Bc). These high values of losses in the first post-shock period, which decline only slowly for the whole post-shock phase, suggest the presence of nominal inertia. At the end of the post-shock phase, the average welfare loss for NH Mgr is still –23 percent and for

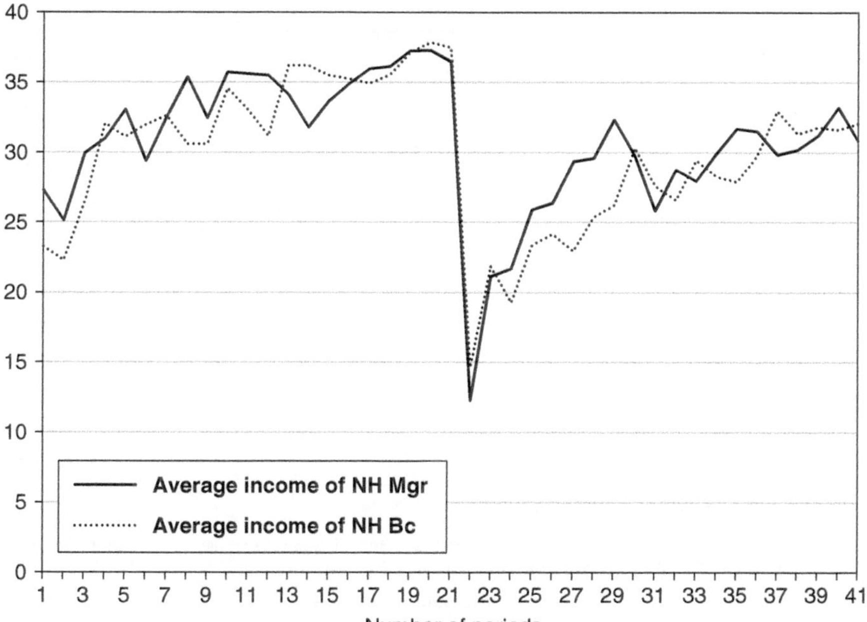

Figure 7.8 Development of average income in the economy of NH Mgr and NH Bc.

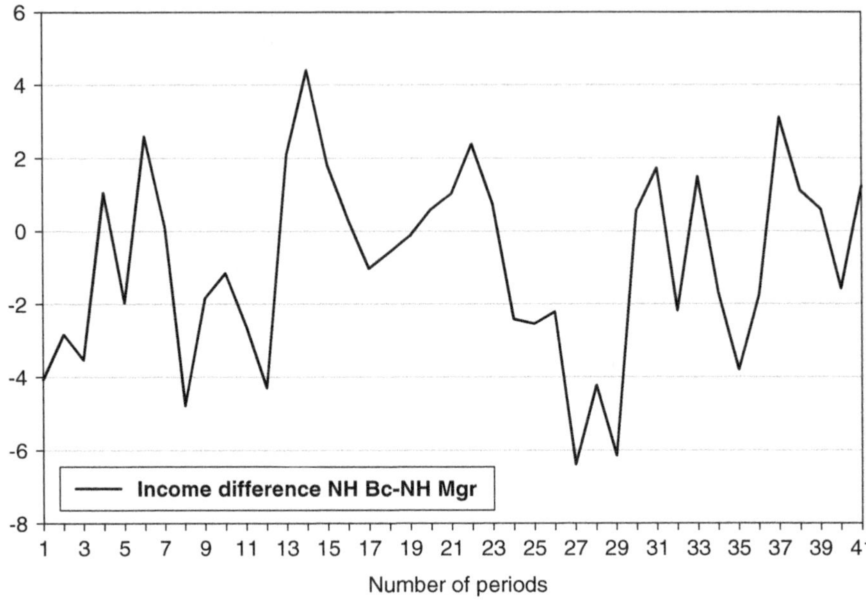

Figure 7.9 Difference in incomes (NH Bc–NH Mgr).

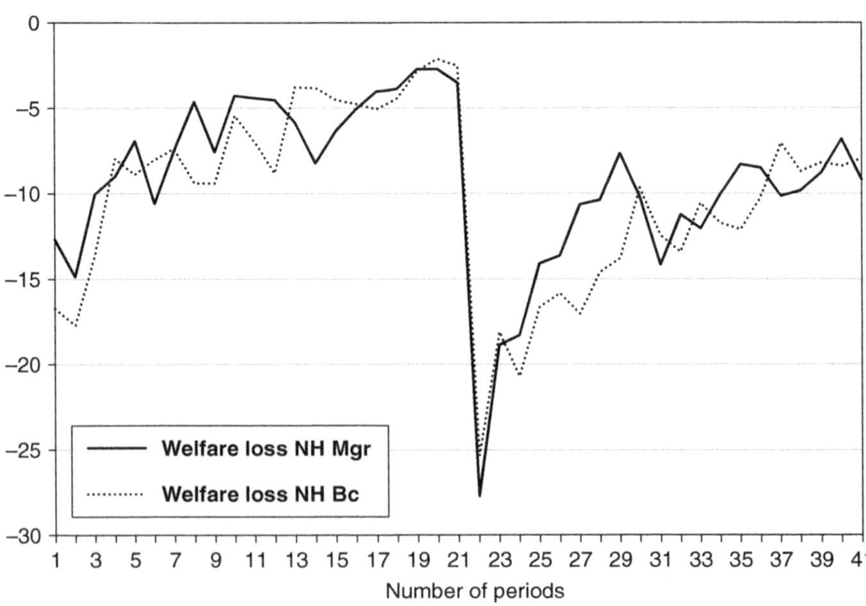

Figure 7.10 Development of average welfare losses of NH Mgr versus NH Bc.

NH Bc 19 percent. Thus, significant inertial behavior did not vanish even at the end of the phase. In contrast, the size of welfare loss for RH Mgr treatment at the end is equal to –2.9 percent, since subjects only have to cope with the coordination problem and not with nominal environment.

More can be seen from Table 7.4. If we would expect that a well-educated economy performs well, this should have been reflected in the lower income loss after the shock. Actually, the average welfare loss has risen by almost half for both treatments, compared to the pre-shock period, with negligible difference in the size of welfare loss, (–32 percent for NH Bc and –30 percent for NH Mgr). Total welfare loss for the pre-shock and the post-shock period is also comparable across treatments. After the monetary shock is announced, a significant reduction in income takes place for both treatments. In the case of NH Bc, the income was reduced by 148 units and in the case of NH Mgr it has decreased by 141 units, which suggests that the impact of monetary shock is almost of the same intensity for both treatments, regardless of economic education achieved. Also, the total value of income earned by both treatments is very similar.

It is important to emphasize that the size of the post-shock welfare loss of the real treatment (–12.4 percent for RH Mgr) is less than half of the average welfare loss of both the nominal treatments (NH Bc and NH Mgr—compare Tables 7.3 and 7.4). This suggests that coordination does not represent a serious problem in the real environment, where indirect effects of money illusion are absent. However, the coordination problem becomes a mediator in the nominal environment, through which individual effects of money illusion are multiplied, creating much more severe nominal inertia. In addition, the effect of the nominal frame is so intensive, that even well-educated subjects (NH Mgr) were not able to get over this cognitive constraint and experienced serious problems to coordinate under indirect effect of money illusion. This slows down the convergence even further.

Figure 7.11 provides the summarization regarding the performance of not only the nominal but also the real treatments in the post-shock phase. Firstly, if the nominal treatments are compared across educational levels, both NH Mgr and NH Bc have flatter development, without any distinct peak, which would speak

Table 7.4 Income development and average welfare losses for NH Mgr, NH Bc (percent), pre-shock and the post-shock phase

	NH Bc	**NH Mgr**
pre-shock income	685,55	700,409
Post-shock income	537,275	559,25
Total income	1222,83	1259,66
Total WL	–25,44%	–23,19%
Pre-shock WL	–18,39%	–16,62%
Post-shock WL	–32,84%	–30,09%
Difference in income loss between treatments	–2,92%	

Source: Own computation.

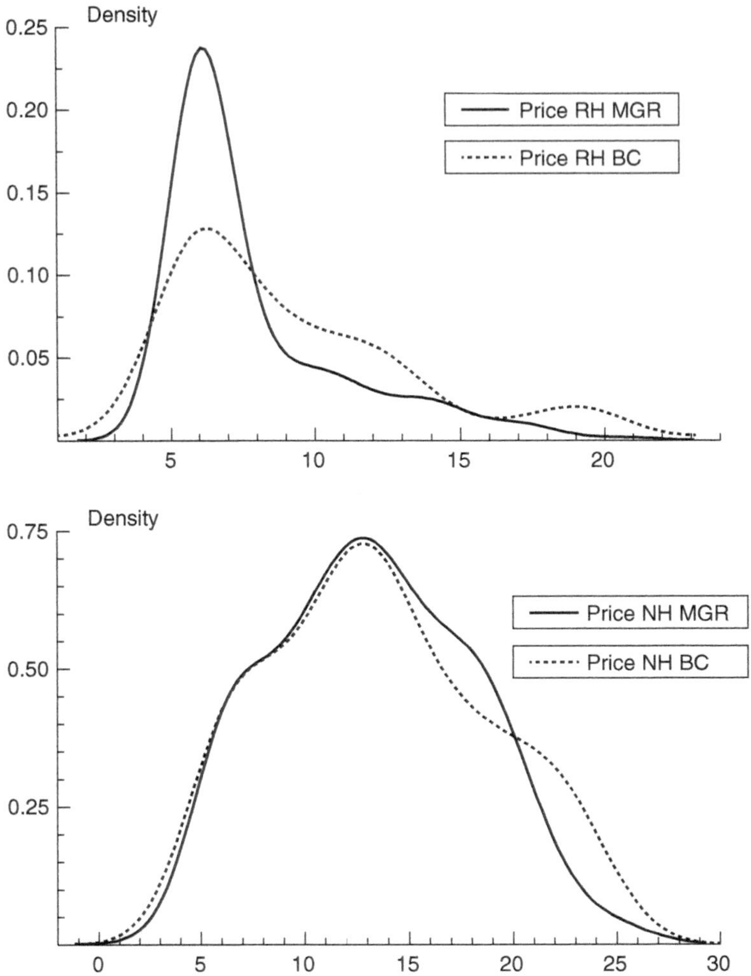

Figure 7.11 Relative frequency density of prices in the post-shock phase, comparing nominal treatment of master versus bachelor students (NH Mgr versus NH Bc) and real treatment of master versus bachelor students (RH Mgr versus RH Bc).

in favor of the equilibrium play. In an ideal case, when subjects would be able to cope with the effects of the nominal frame and suppress the money illusion effect, we would expect that mostly equilibrium post-shock price $\overline{P}_1^* = 6$ would be selected. This would be illustrated by the curve, with a tall thin peak directly at the level of equilibrium post-shock price. This is the case neither for low-educated treatment (NH Bc), nor for the well-educated treatment. Both treatments opt for out of equilibrium prices.

As no distinct difference is present between the treatments, both being out of the center of gravity, this is additional confirmation that indirect effects of money illusion might be pervasive even in case of well-educated subjects. Still, the channel of strategic complementarity seems to play a substantial role, since well-educated subjects are not capable of eliminating conjectures about other players being prone to money illusion.

Additionally, if we would suppose the effect of economic education to hold within the nominal treatment economy (NH Mgr), its performance regarding equilibrium selection should be close to the real treatment economy (RH Mgr) in the post-shock phase. This assumes that indirect effects of money illusion should be approaching zero if the effect of economic education holds. However, dispersion of prices is much higher for well-educated nominal treatment (NH Mgr) in contrast to the real one (RH Mgr). This is given by the nominal frame with which subjects have to cope. As a result, it is much more difficult for subjects to form expectations and set a correct optimum price, thereby leading to discoordination at the aggregate level. This higher dispersion of prices is also reflected by the lower income earned in the well-educated nominal treatment.

It is directly visible that the incidence to the equilibrium is substantially higher for the real treatments. Development of the RH Mgr treatment shows that the thin narrow peak speaks in favor of the post-shock equilibrium price $\overline{P}_1^* = 6$, which was selected by more subjects and thus their behavior is directed toward the center of gravity. Exactly 25 percent of subjects selected the price $\overline{P}_1^* = 6$. A similar development is visible for the RH Bc treatment, although some small nuances are visible.

Based on the this discussion, the hypothesis about the effect of economic education on money illusion doesn't seem to be proven. The performance of the well-educated economy of NH Mgr after the shock is almost indistinguishable from the performance of the low-educated economy NH Bc at the aggregate level. As opposed to initial assumptions, pricing behavior in well-educated economy exhibits substantial nominal inertia in the vein of strategic complementarity, comparable with the development of the low-educated economy. Thus, the indirect effects of money illusion are so strong that even economic education is not able to break through the nominal barrier and ensure proper adjustment toward equilibrium. This results in a situation where the product in a well-educated economy is below the potential for the whole post-shock phase, which is consequently reflected in the size of welfare loss comparable to a low-educated economy.

Investigation of deviations from the post-shock equilibrium across educational treatments under nominal frame

To summarize the aggregate level analysis, the formal statistical test was conducted (Fehr and Tyran 2001), which will evaluate for how long subjects significantly deviate from equilibrium, depending on the nominal treatment and educational level. Since the ability of subjects to set prices in the nominal environment is tested via anticipated monetary shock, the investigation is concentrated on the post-shock phase. It is important to mention, that our test is part of more complex experiment. As a result, the effect of economic education in nominal environment is tested with the real treatment taken as a benchmark.

To check how long the average price in the nominal treatment deviates from equilibrium, the following regression is conducted:

$$\bar{P}_{it} - \bar{P}_1^* = \sum_{t=1}^{19} \alpha_t d_t + \sum_{t=1}^{20} \beta_t (1 - d_t) \tag{1}$$

Where $\bar{P}_{it}$ is the average price of group i in period t, $\bar{P}_1^*$ is the average equilibrium post-shock price, $d_t = 1$ is a dummy variable, which denotes if price observation in period t comes from RH, the coefficients α_t measure the deviation from equilibrium in RH, while the coefficients β_t measure the deviation in NH.[15] Results of regression are presented in Table 7.5.

If we compare the performance of NH Mgr and NH Bc, results for both the nominal treatments show that deviation from the equilibrium for all post-shock rounds is significant at the 1 percent level. In addition, coefficients exhibit positive values in both treatments. The high values of coefficients indicate that deviations from the equilibrium are quite severe. In addition, values of coefficients for both treatments exhibit very similar development over time. A very slow decrease in the size of coefficients over time reflects the fact that the behavior of the

Table 7.5 Deviation from the post-shock equilibrium in treatments with well-educated and low-educated human opponents (NH Mgr and NH Bc)

Post-shock period	*The nominal treatment with human opponents (NH Mgr) Coefficient β_t*	*The nominal treatment with human opponents (NH Bc) Coefficient β_t*
1	10.8182***	10.7500***
2	10.3182***	10.1000***
3	10.4318***	9.27500***
4	10.0000***	8.62500***
5	9.38636***	8.10000***
6	9.13636***	7.75000***
7	8.88636***	8.02500***
8	8.04545***	7.77500***
9	7.40909***	7.22500***
10	7.36364***	6.97500***
11	6.84091***	7.22500***
12	6.93182***	6.27500***
13	6.56818***	6.07500***
14	5.97727***	5.52500***
15	5.56818***	4.77500***
16	5.59091***	3.87500***
17	4.40909***	4.27500***
18	3.43182***	4.65000***
19	3.54545***	4.75000***
20	3.29545***	4.82500***

Source: Own computation.

*** Significance at the 1 percent level

** Significance at the 5 percent level

well-educated treatment is quite sticky (and comparable with the low-educated treatment), with the presence of severe nominal inertia, which is documented in Figure 7.7 in the post-shock phase. The speed of adjustment of both treatments is very slow at the aggregate level, without the final convergence to the equilibrium at the end, which is documented in Table 7.5, where all the periods are significant. The inertial behavior of both treatments, with the product being below the potential, is then persecuted by the low level of income earned in both cases (see Figure 7.8). The results support the conclusion that deviations from the equilibrium are significant for all periods of the post-shock phase without any difference between treatments. This is in line with results from previous section of this chapter, again supporting that the educational effect has a negligible impact in terms of the convergence at the aggregate level and is exceeded by the indirect effects of money illusion through the channel of strategic complementarity.

Concluding remarks

For several decades, money illusion has been regarded as largely irrelevant. The preceding chapters demonstrate that money illusion was resurrected not only at the individual level (Shafir et al. 1997) but also at the aggregate level (Fehr and Tyran 2001), with significant implications on economic outcomes in terms of the non-neutrality of money. We also demonstrated that money illusion is an important fact of economic life, affecting areas like financial markets, housing markets, labor markets or consumption-saving decisions.

We discussed the connection between economic literacy and educational programs with respect to money illusion. This is highly topical in the context of the contemporary growing interest of central banks to enhance economic and financial literacy through investment into educational programs, which is understood as a prerequisite for wise economic choices of consumers and business, with positive implications for monetary policy. With continuity related to money illusion occurrence, which is generally assumed by economists to be easily wiped out through learning, the question was asked whether economic education might not eventually suppress the indirect effects of money illusion and therefore weaken nominal inertia. In other words, solid economic training should provide sufficient support for individuals to coordinate successfully in a strategic environment and ensure proper adjustment to equilibrium through the elimination of money illusion.

Whether economic education really matters and enables rational agents to see through the veil of nominal values, is a question elaborated on with help of a laboratory experiment. The subjects in the experimental economy were expected to cope comfortably with the nominal frame, under the assumption that the effect of economic education holds. In light of the educational effect, individuals might cease to be afflicted by nominal confusion. Moreover, the effects of strategic complementarity might be substantially weakened when agents' expectations will cease to be sticky in an ideal case, with an immediate adjustment to the equilibrium in the vein of rational theory expectations. The indirect effects of money illusion, eliminated through weaker strategic complementarity, may no longer suppress the adjustment to equilibrium at the aggregate level. This is given by the fact that rationally well-educated agents have no reason to believe that other economically trained individuals suffer from money illusion. In addition, even the biased belief about other agents expecting the other agents to suffer from money illusion might become non-existent because of the highlighted educational effect.

However, individual money illusion appeared to be a problem in the strategic environment, when subjects need to form expectations about the behavior of other players. When different educational treatments were assessed under the nominal frame, it became apparent that the formation of expectations proved to be difficult task even for well-educated individuals, if the aggregate response rule was not known. As a result, negligible individual confusion regarding the nominal frame under strategic uncertainty was translated into expectations of other players who did not suffer from money illusion yet. The indirect effects of money illusion were intensified. Previous assumptions that well-educated subjects will be able to break through the nominal barrier after the shock were not confirmed. Thus, the results show that money illusion is a rather persistent phenomenon, despite solid economic education. It appears that it is not easy to uncover the veil of nominal values after a fully anticipated monetary shock under strategic uncertainty, where the aggregate response rule is not known and the formation of expectations is highly demanding.

Still, an interesting feature proved to be that the economy, under the real frame, did significantly better in terms of the adjustment after the shock than the simulated economy, where individuals apply rule of thumb behavior. In contrast, the performance of the economy under the nominal frame was the worst among all the treatments. This may suggest that the effect of economic education might be at least beneficial in the case of well-educated individuals in the real environment, but the cognitive barrier is too high in the nominal environment where strategic complementarity is present.

To summarize, the results of our analysis are two-fold. Solid economic training does not eliminate money illusion, which appears to be a rather persistent phenomenofiguren under strategic uncertainty, even in the case of anticipated monetary shock. Even well-educated people do not possess the ability to pierce the veil of money illusion and do not form their expectations properly after a fully anticipated shock. As a consequence, New Keynesian predictions, addressed by Fehr and Tyran (2001) and Vaona (2013), about the short run non-neutrality of money might be reinforced. Even a well-educated individual, not subject to money illusion, is seriously constrained in his or her coordination effort. Coordination issues at the aggregate level intensify the indirect effects of money illusion, which consequently leads to nominal rigidities and the slow speed of convergence, even for the economy consisting of well-educated individuals.

Still, we may not take the conclusion as given, since results of other experimental or survey studies (Bakshi 2009, Mees and Franses 2011, and Wong 2005 among others) are rather inconclusive. Further investigation of the effects of economic education with respect to money illusion is highly desirable with possible application in various areas like the stock markets, housing markets, consumption-saving behavior and others.

Notes

1 This trend is not evaluated from the educational perspective as illustrated in Table 6.2, Chapter 6.

2 Because subjects only have to cope with individual optimization problems, the adjustment will be faster and therefore the length of the post-shock phase is exactly half of the length of the post-shock phase with human opponents.

3 Income loss was computed as $\varepsilon_{it} = (\pi^* - \pi_{it})/\pi^*$ for all players in each period t, where ε_{it} is expressed as the income loss relative to the equilibrium payoff as a percentage of the equilibrium payoff. Consequently, the total sum of average income losses for all periods was computed as the sum of the average income losses for all players in each period and expressed as a percentage of total possible size of payoffs gained in a particular phase.

4 Since the experimental design implies that the equilibrium of the economy is efficient, we may consider the income loss as a measure of the welfare loss. Therefore, income loss and welfare loss, which will be used throughout the analysis, have exactly the same meaning. The total possible size of payoffs is understood as the maximum number of payoffs earned if behavior were to be absent from all kinds of deviations from optimum price.

5 This trend is not evaluated from the educational perspective, as illustrated in Table 6.2, Chapter 6, because both treatments are endowed by basic economic knowledge.

6 It might seem that the comparison between RH Mgr and RH Bc could be beneficial. However, the educational hypothesis regarding coordination among the real treatments proved difficult to manage, since the experiment is not arranged for the analysis of such delicate differences regarding coordination issues. Although nine groups participated in the RH Bc, it proved to be insufficient due to the high sensitivity of the experiment to any small irrational deviation from the optimum, which is partly given by the setting of parameter n, which reflects the group size. Moreover, the quite vulnerable behavior of bachelor students also contributed to this issue, since the more frequent the occurrence of irrational behavior in the groups, the higher the sensitivity of the experiment. Issues mentioned above resulted in a noisy character of data in the case of the RH Bc treatments, as noted above, and the inability to detect any reliable difference in the coordination of bachelor versus master's students in the real treatments. Therefore, the evaluation of coordination issues related to educational effect is less the subject of our research. The educational hypothesis will focus primarily on the ability of individuals to deal with the veil of nominal values, whose effect is prevalent over real coordination issues.

7 The level of confidence was for most of the time in line with the subject's distance from the equilibrium price and was also affected by income loss incurred.

8 Again, comparison is made at the same low educational level.

9 The post-shock phase for computerized opponents ends in the midst of the adjustment of human opponents, given by parameters of experimental design.

10 The pre-shock price converged to the equilibrium price $P_E = 18$ for all the treatments; thus, the reduction in the price of each treatment directly after the shock may be assessed. The reduction in case of RC was eight units, which is more than in case of all other treatments.

11 Whether economic education really matters might, however, be detected finally by the comparison of well-educated group NH Mgr with the low-educated control group NH Bc in the next section.

12 We restricted our analysis to the investigation of NH Mgr and RH Mgr, because comparison of lower educational level NH Bc and RH Bc yields similar outcomes. The development is also characterized by slower speed of the convergence. This is reflected in the product being below the potential for the whole post-shock phase. Although occurrence of nominal inertia is more frequent in case of NH Bc economy at the aggregate level because of indirect effect of money illusion, the performance of the real

treatment economy is not substantially better. We may outline only one important difference. The post-shock welfare loss of RH Bc (–25%) is close to the nominal treatment economy NH Bc (–33%). This is in contrast with development of NH Mgr (–30%) and RH Mgr (–12.4%) economies, where a much bigger difference is visible in the post-shock welfare loss. Although we have to be careful with implications due to the noisy data of RH Bc, these results may suggest that some slight differences might be present in the performance across real educational treatments, however without any sign of differences in the adjustment with regards to money illusion.

13 If the irrational is fixing the price, which proved to be case in our experiment, this means that he stabilizes the price at a particular level, which induces other subjects to have expectations even more in accordance with this average price induced by the irrational, although the economy is out of equilibrium otherwise.

14 In addition, experimental results proved various forms of how irrational might behave, which is beyond our scope of research. The individual may be a random walk player, which may for a short moment decrease the income of other players because of the uncertainty induced. He or she may also fix the price at a particular level, which contributes to the stable environment, where expectations are in line with average price and this will also affect the income of the others, which will be slightly lower, but still satisfactory. He or she may also start with the price at a very low level and then increase it, which induces rigidity.

15 No dummy variable was included for period 20 of RH Mgr (see regression) in order to prevent linear dependence among the set of regressors. Moreover, both of the treatments are included in one regression and not given in separate regressions to ensure the comparable variability of treatments.

References

Bakshi, R. K., 2009. Rational Agents and Economic Training, The Case of Money Illusion in Experimental Study. *Journal of Economic Theory*, 3 (2), pp. 27–32.

Fehr, E. and Tyran, J., 2001. Does Money Illusion Matter? *American Economic Review*, 91 (5), pp. 1239–1262.

Kahneman, D., 2003. Maps of Bounded Rationality: Psychology for Behavioral Economics. *American Economic Review*, 93 (5), pp. 1449–1475.

Mees, H. and Franses, H. P., 2011. Are Chinese Individuals Prone to Money Illusion? Tinbergen Institute Discussion Paper, 2011–149/4.

Vaona, A., 2013. Money illusion and the Long-run Phillips Curve in Staggered Wage-Setting Models. *Research in Economics*, 67 (1), pp. 88–99.

Wong, Wei-Kang, 2007. Nominal Increases and the Perception of Likelihood. *Economics Letters*, 95 (3), pp. 433–437.

Index